Wok Magic

Wok Magic
Chinese Cooking for Pleasure

YONG YAP COTTERELL

Weidenfeld and Nicolson

London

For my husband

First published in Great Britain in 1987 by
George Weidenfeld & Nicolson Limited
91 Clapham High Street, London SW4 7TA

Copyright © 1987 by Yong Yap Cotterell
Map drawn by Richard Natkiel

ISBN 0 297 79123 0

Photoset by Deltatype, Ellesmere Port
Printed and bound in Great Britain by
Butler & Tanner Ltd
Frome and London

Contents

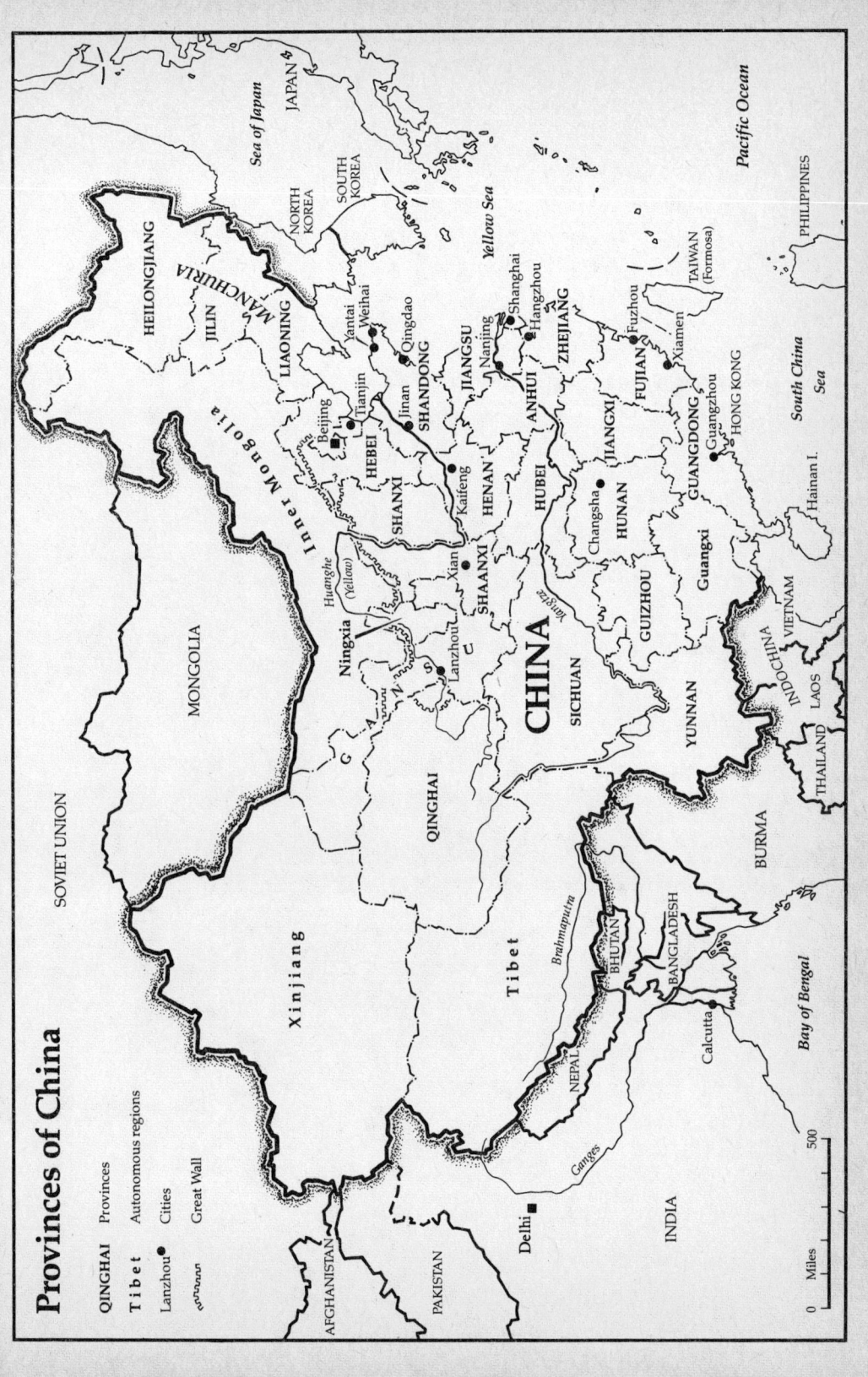

Provinces of China

QINGHAI   Provinces
T i b e t   Autonomous regions
Lanzhou•   Cities
∿∿∿∿   Great Wall

SOVIET UNION

MONGOLIA

Xinjiang

QINGHAI

Tibet

Ningxia

Lanzhou

Huanghe (Yellow)

Xian

SHAANXI

SHANXI

HEBEI

Beijing   Tianjin

Yantai Weihai

Jinan   Qingdao

SHANDONG

Kaifeng

HENAN

CHINA

SICHUAN

HUBEI

Changsha

HUNAN

GUIZHOU

YUNNAN

Guangxi

GUANGDONG

Guangzhou   HONG KONG

Hainan I.

JIANGXI

ANHUI

JIANGSU

Nanjing

ZHEJIANG

Hangzhou

Shanghai

FUJIAN

Fuzhou

Xiamen

TAIWAN (Formosa)

Yangtze

Inner Mongolia

MANCHURIA

HEILONGJIANG

JILIN

LIAONING

NORTH KOREA

SOUTH KOREA

JAPAN

Sea of Japan

Yellow Sea

Pacific Ocean

PHILIPPINES

South China Sea

INDOCHINA

VIETNAM

LAOS

THAILAND

BURMA

Brahmaputra

BHUTAN

BANGLADESH

NEPAL

INDIA

Delhi

Calcutta

Bay of Bengal

Ganges

AFGHANISTAN

PAKISTAN

0   500

Miles

Acknowledgements

I should like to thank Professor Chen Hsinpo of the Beijing Foreign Studies University for the calligraphy used on the cover of the book. Closer to home, I am grateful to my son, Alan, for the technical illustrations which appear in the text.

YYC

Preface

In this book I have tried to present both festive and folk cuisine as well as the dishes found in everyday Chinese meals. The repertoire therefore ranges over breakfasts, lunches, dinners and snacks, and even to the old favourites of the imperial kitchens.

Because there is no obsession with weights and measures in Chinese cooking, as there often is in formal Western cuisine, work in the kitchen is relaxing as well as an opportunity to develop one's creative interests. There is always room for the personal touch, which gives pleasure not only to oneself but more, to family and friends. The Chinese ideal is 'to release flavour where it exists (in an ingredient)' and 'to let in flavour where there is none (in an ingredient)'. When this is achieved, 'the fragrance of sumptuous food even tempts the immortals to desert their caves for the haunts of men'.

Food in China has never been regarded as a belly-filler or a fuel. On the contrary, it is looked upon as something that gives pleasure, so that the sharing of food, even a simple dish, often has deep cultural meaning. Today the Chinese have a food lore rich in legendary anecdote and myth, explaining the 'whys' and 'hows' of eating. A customary greeting remains 'Have you eaten?' Concern for the physical well-being and comfort of relatives, friends, guests and acquaintances is second nature. 'For the people food is paradise': this old Chinese proverb has lost nothing of its original force in our time.

Preliminary Preparation

CUTTING THE INGREDIENTS

In Chinese cooking very often the ingredients are cut into slices, or julienned, diced or minced before cooking. This is done mainly to allow the seasoning and flavouring to penetrate into the ingredients better, and to allow the heat to get through quicker in stir-frying and steaming; it is also sometimes done to tenderize the ingredient. Tough meats are cut into chunks in order to absorb liquid during cooking and so become tender.

Less tough meat is minced to tenderize it further, and also in order that it may be combined with flavourings and other ingredients. Tender cuts are thinly sliced and stir-fried quickly so that they remain delicate and tasty. Uniform cutting makes for even cooking and produces an attractive-looking dish.

Shredded meat is usually stir-fried with shredded vegetables, sliced fish with sliced vegetables, peas with similar sized diced ingredients, minced meat with rice-sized winter mushrooms or ham and so on. With lamb and beef every visible trace of fat or sinew is removed before slicing, as the odour of the fat would otherwise overpower the taste of the finished dish. For stir-frying beef is cut across the grain to tenderize it. For the same reason squid and cuttlefish, fresh or dried, are scored criss-cross before slicing. But tender chicken and fish are sliced with the grain.

The main Chinese cutting techniques

Straight vertical slicing: the knife is held vertically and straight over a soft, tender ingredient such as liver, scallops or mushrooms. (*See illustration.*)

1

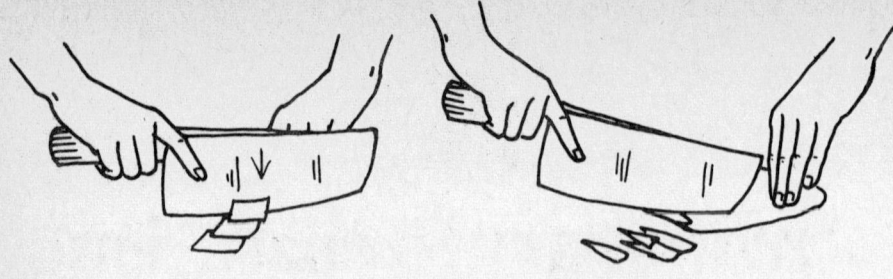

Straight vertical slicing

Roll cutting

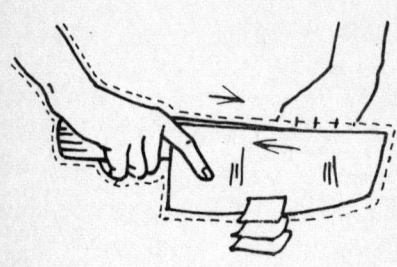

Saw cutting

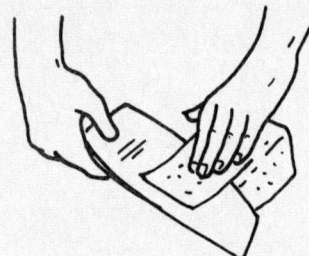

Flat slicing

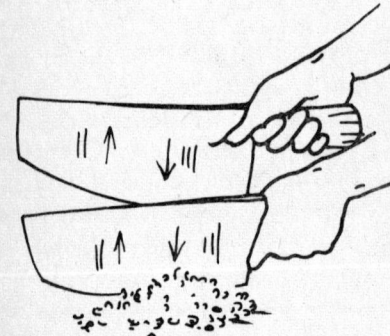

Mincing with two choppers

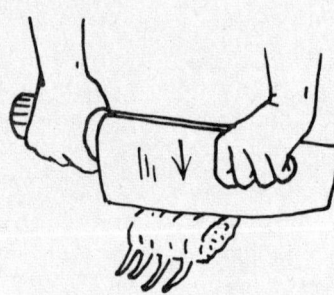

Hay cutting a piece of meat with small bones

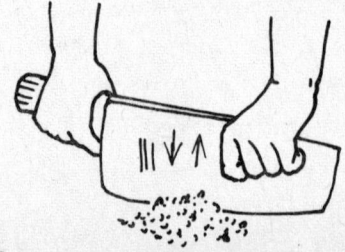

Hay cutting spices

Diagonal slicing: used on tough meat and fibrous vegetables. The knife is held at an angle of 60 degrees to the ingredient (e.g. spring onion, white, young leek, asparagus and French beans) which is cut into 2.5 cm (1 in) pieces.

Roll-cutting: a variation of diagonal cutting, but the ingredients are usually root vegetables such as taros, carrots and radish for slow cooking. Make a diagonal cut about 4 cm (1⅝ in) from one end of the vegetable, roll it a quarter turn, make a second cut the same distance along, and continue rolling and cutting to the end. (*See illustration.*)

Saw-cutting: a method of finely slicing meat with a slow and gentle sawing action. Any fat or bone is removed, and the meat is frozen or chilled until firm. Then it is cut into paper-thin slices. Use the left hand to hold the frozen meat with a clean folded tea towel and slice with the right hand in a sawing motion. (*See illustration.*)

Flat-slicing: done by holding the knife blade horizontally parallel to the ingredient and slicing from right to left. This is usually employed on soft ingredients such as *doufu*, congealed pig's blood and cold jellied meat. (*See illustration.*)

Dicing: the ingredient is cut into cubes. In Chinese cooking there are three sizes: cubes of about 3.5 to 5 cm (1½ to 2 in) for deep-frying and slow cooking; dice from about 0.3 to 1.3 cm (⅛ to ½ in) for stir-frying; and rice-size or mince dice from 0.1 to 0.3 cm (1/16 to ⅛ in) for steaming and filling. The ingredient is cut into appropriate sized strips and then cut crosswise into cubes or dice.

Shredding: similar to juliennes in Western cuisine. The ingredient is cut into strips about 0.3 cm (⅛ in) thick and 5 to 7.5 cm (2 to 3 in) long. Sometimes this is called 'matchstick size'. Cut the meat into 0.3 cm (⅛ in) thick slices, stack them together and cut into strips of the same width. Sometimes a recipe calls for finely shredded ingredients, in which case they are shredded hair-fine.

Sliver cutting: similar to shredding but coarser. The ingredient is sliced to about 5 cm (3/16 in) thick, stacked together and cut into strips of the same width.

Mincing: also called fine chopping, mostly used for meat and fish. Either one or two choppers may be used. The meat is first diced small, then chopped rhythmically from right to left and back. As the meat spreads out, flip it over with the knife and continue chopping. Repeat till it is reduced to an even fine texture. This may be done very quickly in a

3

food processor, but over-processing makes the mince dry. (*See illustration.*)

Crushing: smashing with the back of the chopper, as used for garlic, ginger and the stems of vegetables to release their flavour or for easier penetration of seasonings and heat.

Scoring: usually made on large cuts of meat or whole fish. Some shallow slashes are made on the surface to allow seasonings and heat to penetrate better. Often scoring is done lengthwise and crosswise in a regular criss-cross pattern on smaller ingredients such as pig's kidneys, chicken or duck's gizzards (otherwise well-nigh indestructible), chicken breasts, cuttlefish and squid (which can also be very tough), and also for decorative effect.

Hay-cutting: the right hand holds the handle of the knife while the left hand holds the back of the blade towards the end and the cutting is done with a firm pressure. This gives better control and an accurate cut on foods such as crabs, boiled salted eggs in their shells or meat with small bones. Another way is to cut in a see-saw fashion, with the left and right ends going up and down alternately, as in the chopping of spices. (*See illustrations.*)

Utensils in the Chinese Kitchen

The following is a list of basic equipment, simple to use and efficient.

Brass wire mesh strainer: shallow, fine brass strainers with long bamboo handles in a wide range of sizes. They are excellent for taking food out of hot oil or boiling water so that the liquid may be used again. They also allow better control over smaller pieces of food in hot oil or boiling water. Some are large enough to hold a bird. The smallest are about the size of a Western soup spoon and completely made of fine brass wire, and are used in fire pot cooking (*see also* 'Fire pot' *below*).

Chopper: a large, heavy knife rather like a butcher's cleaver, with a rectangular blade of tempered steel, and sometimes with a wooden handle. It is used in chopping meat with bones, and in mincing. The thick blunt back of the blade serves for pounding and tenderizing meat, crushing garlic, bruising ginger and so on. A lighter version with a thinner and narrower blade is used for slicing cooked or raw meat and vegetables. Choose a chopper with a blade of tempered carbon steel rather than stainless steel which is harder to sharpen.

Chopping block: the traditional chopping block is a sturdy round solid piece of wood from 15 to 20 cm (6 to 8 in) or more thick, but the ones found here are only about 5 to 10 cm (2 to 4 in). Many sizes are available, and large ones have stands. Normally one is kept for cooked food and another one for raw ingredients. To season a new chopping board, rub it with salt and water or soak it in brine.

Earthenware pot: its name, *saguo*, means 'sand pot', referring to its sandy texture on the outside; inside it is dark glazed. Some have wire netting on the outside for strengthening. They come in various shapes and sizes, and are used for slow-cooked dishes, soups, stock, tonic food and rice. Rice is tastier when cooked in the *saguo*, particularly on a charcoal fire. They can only be used on the stove, electric or gas rings.

Fire pot: also known as 'steamboat', this is a metal soup tureen with a built-in charcoal stove at the base. The soup is placed in the moat-shaped top round the chimney or funnel, which leads up from the stove. The cover has a hole to fit over the chimney. This is a special utensil for 'steamboat' dishes, in which the food is cooked by the diners themselves at the table in individual little brass wire mesh strainers. Various sizes and qualities are available, and the pots may be made of iron, brass, stainless steel or aluminium. Electrically heated ones are also available, but are not very efficient and the flex looks ugly and gets in the way.

Fish scaler: this is a piece of metal with a curved end and serrated edges and is very efficient for scaling fish.

Kitchen scissors: Chinese kitchen scissors are smaller and more slender than Western ones, and have very sharp pointed blades. They are excellent for boning birds or snipping pastry and dough.

Long chopsticks: these are special thick, 35 cm (14 in) long chopsticks for the kitchen, very useful in deep-frying and other hot jobs. For beating eggs use five or six ordinary chopsticks at once.

Metal steamers: these are a version of the bamboo steaming baskets (*see below*) with perforated bases, and usually comprise a set of two steamers with a bottom pot. Some are large enough to hold a whole bird. These steamers are more efficient than some Western ones in that the baskets are fitted over the bottom pot rather than inside, and this allows for more water and longer steaming time; also, the food is kept well away from the water.

Pot mat: traditionally a woven latticed bamboo mat (not easily available here) is put in the bottom of the pot to prevent sticking in slow-cooked dishes. A metal version, a round flat disc with perforated holes, is available here. You can improvise with a small plate.

Rice pot: an ordinary metal pot, with a thick, heavy base and a tight-fitting lid is perfect for the cooking of rice. Reliable automatic cookers are available. The *saguo* (*see* 'Earthenware pot') may be used for a very traditional pot of rice.

Steaming baskets: cylindrical woven bamboo baskets with latticework bottoms which allow the steam to go through and cook the food. A lid is provided. Two or three baskets may be stacked together and steamed over a pot of boiling water, provided the air holes are not completely blocked by food. The larger baskets may be used over a wok (*see illustration*). They are completely washable, but should be dried away from heat.

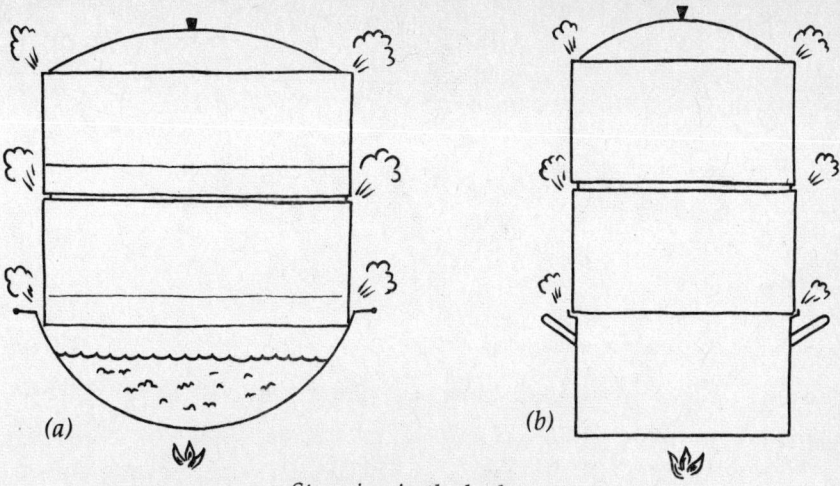

(a) (b)

Steaming in the baskets

Wok: a most versatile utensil – one can stir-fry, sauté, deep-fry, boil, braise or steam in it. It is fat-saving, as the oil is collected at the base and the food being sautéed may be left on the sides, draining off excess oil to be used again. The high, smooth, sloping sides ensure even distribution of heat and prevent spilling when stir-frying. Various qualities are available in iron, stainless steel and aluminium. A traditional heavy iron one, which gives the greatest evenness and retention of heat, is to be preferred. Aluminium is not tough enough and best avoided. Also the Chinese suspect that this metal is liable to produce poisonous substances when in contact with some food, especially if this is highly acidic. Although a metal ring is sometimes provided to hold the wok steady on the stove, this is not really necessary. It may be used to hold the wok on the worktop when taken off the heat, but a woven bamboo or straw basket is better here as it insulates as well. When choosing a wok always make sure that it has a rounded bottom and that the lid has a high, round dome; these are the essentials of an efficient wok, particularly in steaming and stir-frying. For a small family, a wok of about 30 to 35 cm (12 to 14 in) diameter is sufficient; though two woks, a larger one and a small one, for different jobs, are useful. To season a new wok, thoroughly clean it with hot water and a liquid detergent. Rinse thoroughly, dry and heat 2 tablespoons of cooking oil in it until very hot. Swirl the wok round so that the entire inside of the wok is covered. Pour off the oil and wipe the wok with kitchen paper until it is smooth and shiny.

Cooking Methods

The following are some basic Chinese cooking methods.

Boiling (zhu): food, either raw or par-cooked, is put in plenty of water or stock and brought to the boil over a high heat, then skimmed and allowed to cook on a low heat. The method produces a soup for which no thickening is needed. For example, white chopped chicken is cooked this way.

Fast boiling (cuan): this is boiling quickly in water or stock. The ingredients are small: sliced, shredded or made into meat balls. The stock or water is brought to the boil over a high heat; then the ingredients are put in and the seasoning added. They are brought to the boil again and dished up immediately without thickening. Food cooked in this way has plenty of clear soup and tastes fresh.

Plunging and rinsing (shua): the cooking is done at the table with the fire pot or 'steamboat' in the middle surrounded by the raw, thinly-sliced meat, fish, seafood and vegetables, and pre-boiled noodles, along with dips and sauces. A strong, well-flavoured stock is put into the fire pot, which has a built-in charcoal stove underneath. Each diner puts food into a small individual brass wire mesh strainer and lowers it into the stock; when it is done the strainer is lifted out. The food is eaten with dips, sauces and seasoned salts.

Care should be taken not to put in too much food at a time, so that the temperature of the boiling stock is not lowered. Lastly, noodles or vermicelli are added and eaten as a noodle soup. This is mainly a festive method of cooking for the cold months.

Meeting (hui): blending or cooking together several ingredients cut small. One way is to season the oil, add flavourings and stock or water before adding the main ingredients, which have been sliced, shredded or diced; sometimes parboiled or deep-fried. The food is covered and simmered over a low heat, and thickened before dishing up. Sometimes

8

the liquid is thickened before the main ingredients are added. When the cooking liquor is not thickened, the method is called 'clear meeting'.

Simmering (dun): this means simmering the food very slowly in plenty of water, rather as in the French *pot au feu*. The ingredient is scalded in boiling water, refreshed in cold water, drained and placed in an earthenware pot (*saguo*) with plenty of water to cover; the proportion of food to water is one to two. Seasonings are added. The food is brought to the boil, skimmed, covered and left to barely simmer on a low heat for about 2 to 3 hours. Usually the lid is sealed with parchment or greaseproof paper. The soup is crystal clear and not thickened.

Indirect steaming (dun): as in a *bain-marie*, the food is not in direct contact with the source of heat. It is cooked in a closed container surrounded by boiling water so that the liquor with the food is kept barely simmering. A whole piece of meat or poultry is scalded before being put into an earthenware or enamelled casserole or deep bowl with seasonings (spring onion, ginger and rice wine) and stock or water to cover. This is then sealed and placed in a larger pot filled with water to about halfway up the side of the casserole. Too much water would boil over the inner pot or cause it to float. Sometimes the inner pot is raised by means of an upturned bowl or saucer. The outer pot is also covered tightly. The steaming is done over a medium heat throughout and the water in the outer pot is replenished regularly with boiling water; it must not be allowed to boil dry. The time taken is about 2 to 3 hours. (*See illustration.*) Tonic food, such as game with herbs, is often steamed in this way.

 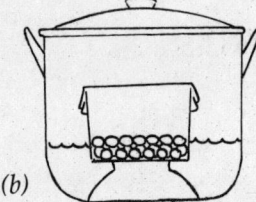

(a) (b)

Indirect steaming, in a pot

Direct steaming (zheng): this is the most commonly used steaming method in Chinese cooking. The food is exposed and in direct contact with the steam. The method is usually used for small ingredients such as pieces of fish, chicken, egg custard, minced meat cakes, meat balls, cakes and puddings, which require a short cooking time, from 5 minutes to 1 hour. This is done mostly in a wok, as the hemispherical domed cover allows free circulation of the steam. The food is put in a bowl or plate which stands on a rack in the wok. The water should not be too high, which would flood the food; nor too low, or it would not generate sufficient steam and would dry out too quickly. Generally about 5 cm (2 in) below the top of the dish is best. A space of about 2.5 cm (1 in) all round between the wok and the plate or bowl should be allowed so that the steam may circulate freely and cook the food. (*See illustration*).

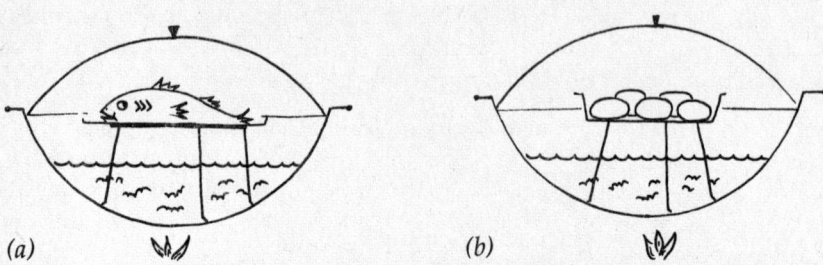

(a)   *(b)*

Steaming in the wok

A large bamboo steaming basket placed in a wok or over a saucepan is another excellent way of steaming food. A 35 cm (14 in) wok takes a 30 cm (12 in) basket nicely. Large and dry ingredients may be placed directly in the basket, which is usually lined with a damp piece of folded muslin to absorb excess moisture or prevent smaller pieces of food (e.g. rice) from falling through. With steaming baskets it is possible to cook several baskets of food at once, stacking them together over a pot of boiling water, provided that the airholes are not completely blocked by food, and that the top-most basket is covered. The pot used should have a rim of suitable width for the basket to sit on. Metal steamers are also very efficient.

Whether steaming in a wok or a basket or steamer, it is important to preheat or pre-steam, i.e. bring the water to a fast boil for several minutes before the food is put in. In steaming, the water in the wok or pot should be replenished regularly so that it does not dry out. Before lifting food out of the wok or steamer always tip a little cold water into the boiling water from the side, which lowers the temperature and prevents the hands from being scalded.

Braising (men): the ingredient is usually left whole and brushed with a colouring such as dark soya sauce or caramel, and then deep-fried or pan-fried till par-cooked before being put in a pot with some stock or water (not necessarily to cover) with the classic seasoning of dark soya sauce, sugar and spices. After bringing to the boil the heat is reduced and the pot covered and left to simmer for about 1½ to 3 hours, when the meat is tender and the juice reduced and thickened.

Fry-stewing (shao):   the food is normally stir-fried, pan-fried, deep-fried, steamed or boiled before seasoning and stock are added. When brought to the boil over a high heat, it is cooked on a low heat till the food is well-flavoured. The heat is then raised and the juice reduced. Sometimes delicate fish or meat is transferred to a warmed dish and the juice is reduced separately.

Deep-frying (zha):   similar to deep-frying in Western cuisine. Plenty of oil is needed in proportion to the amount of food cooked. Generally the oil has to be heated to a very high temperature. But there are some variations in deep-frying such as paper-parcel deep-frying, in which the food is cut fine, seasoned and wrapped up envelope-wise in rice paper or grease-proof paper. The oil is heated to a fairly hot temperature, 110°C (230°F). The parcels are put in a few at a time, and when the temperature of the oil rises again the parcels are cooked and rise to the top.

Quick-thickened gravy method (liu):   the food has a thickened velvety sauce sometimes flavoured with vinegar. The ingredient is precooked by deep-frying, boiling or steaming. A sauce made with seasoned oil and thickened with a starch is poured over. Sometimes the sauce is made by thickening a stock without oil. Sometimes the precooked food is heated through in the gravy. If the ingredient is deep-fried it is cut into slices, shreds or dice. But steamed or boiled ingredients, such as fish, may be left whole. There are several variations of this method, mainly in the preparation of the raw ingredients; for example they may be coated.

Quick-frying (bao):   this is very quick cooking done over a high heat. The ingredient is boned, shredded or diced evenly and sometimes par-cooked in boiling water or oil. It is stir-fried quickly over a high heat in hot oil, seasoned and thickened with a small amount of a mixture of stock or water and starch. There are three variations of this method: *youbao*, quick-frying in oil, where the ingredient is deep-fried before quick-frying; *jiangbao* or quick-frying in salted soya bean paste, where the main seasoning is the salted paste and the food is not thickened with starch; and *congbao*, quick-frying with spring onion, which is used in the same way as, and instead of, bean paste.

Stir-frying (chao):   the wok is preheated over a high heat till really hot and smoking slightly, and the oil is put in, heated and seasoned with garlic, or spring onion, with ginger and salt before the ingredients are added. The food is tossed rapidly to ensure every bit is covered with the oil. If it is too dry, 1 tablespoon of water may be sprinkled on to prevent sticking, charring or burning. If things get too hot, the heat may be reduced or the wok removed from the heat temporarily, but you should continue stir-frying.

With green leafy vegetables a special technique is required. Use only fresh, young and tender vegetables. Separate the stems from the leaves. Peel or bruise and slice the stems. Stir-fry the stems first, quickly, in hot oil and salt for 1 minute. Then add the leaves, sometimes with 1 tablespoon of water if they are delicate and liable to burn, and cover immediately. When the sound of boiling begins and the steam is puffing out (about 1 to 2 minutes), lift the cover, stir to mix well, add 1 or 2 teaspoons of oil, mix well and dish up. The oil gives the vegetables a glistening look. The cooking is done on a high heat throughout.

Beans need slightly longer cooking and more water. One can stir-fry successfully on electric rings provided that the wok is preheated until smoking hot and the temperature is kept up. If necessary, cover it immediately after the food is put in to build up the heat, though only for 1–2 minutes.

Large amounts of food are best stir-fried in batches of about 200 to 350 g (8 oz to 12 oz). Stir-frying is done so quickly that it is necessary to have everything ready beforehand.

Pan-frying (jian): this is normally done in a thick, flat-bottomed pan, but a wok may also be used. The food is first marinated, sometimes coated in batter or flour, lightly flattened and then cooked on a low heat till both sides are golden. Sometimes a seasoning or sauce is added. The low heat and slow frying gently cook the food through and crisp the outside.

Roasting in the oven (kao): there are two ways of roasting. *Anlukao*, or 'closed oven roasting', is similar to the Western roasting except that the ingredient is either hung on a hook or threaded on to a skewer. The other form is *minglukao*, where the ingredient is skewered, placed on an iron grate and cooked over a charcoal fire, as in a Western barbecue.

Salt-roasting (yenji): the marinated ingredient is wrapped in layers of greaseproof paper and roasted in a pot of preheated salt.

Smoking (xun): usually a raw ingredient is smoked with wood shavings (pine or poplar), tea leaves, sugar-cane pulp and brown sugar and then steamed or deep-fried. Or the ingredient is either steamed or deep-fried first before being smoked to give it colour and a smoky flavour.

Steeping (lu): the ingredient, either raw and scalded in boiling water or par-cooked, is left whole and then simmered in a previously prepared mixed-spice liquor. The same liquor is reserved for future cooking, when the spices are renewed and seasoning readjusted.

Cold mixing (ban): cold cooked meat and raw or cooked vegetables are shredded, sliced or diced and tossed in a seasoned dressing of sesame oil, soya sauce, vinegar and various spices.

Hot salading (qiang): meat or vegetables are boiled in water till just cooked and then tossed in a dressing of seasoned oil while still hot. Sometimes the ingredients may be deep-fried rather than boiled.

Pickling with salt (yenyan): the raw ingredient, e.g. vegetable, is rubbed with salt and left to marinate till water runs out. Treated in this way, the ingredient loses its excess moisture but remains fresh and crisp and tastes slightly salty. It is then seasoned with vinegar, sugar and salt. When the main seasoning is wine it is called 'drunken pickling' or *zuiyan*, as in drunken chicken and drunken prawns. And when fermented glutinous rice and salt are added to a pickle of fish or meat, it is called fermented rice pickling or *zaoyan*.

Candy flossing (basi): literally this means 'pulling the threads'. It is a popular way of preparing a dessert from fruits, nuts, and root vegetables such as yams, taros or sweet potatoes. The ingredient is deep-fried, boiled or steamed before being stirred into a sugar caramel that is cooked to the thread stage. Ideally this is done by two people, so that the piping hot ingredient can be immediately mixed with the syrup prepared at the same time.

Frost coating (guashang): the ingredient is cut small or shaped into balls, deep-fried and rolled in or sprinkled with icing sugar while still hot. One other way is to stir the deep-fried ingredient into a sugar syrup which is cooked to just before the thread stage. After it is thoroughly coated it is taken out. When it cools it is covered in a layer of frosting, as in frosted pork spare ribs. Sometimes the food is rolled in icing sugar again while still warm.

Dinners, Lunches and Banquets

A cold hors d'oeuvre, or cold platter, is served as an opening to special meals or banquets to stimulate the appetite. It may be an assortment of cold cooked meats, seafood, fresh or preserved eggs, salad or pickled vegetables. It can be either elaborate or simple: for a banquet it may be arranged to represent a phoenix or a peacock in display; but in a simple one for a family meal may contain one or two items only. These colourful and attractive dishes are a boon to entertaining as they may be prepared well in advance. On the other hand, hot, tasty, deep-fried morsels may sometimes be served instead.

The points to bear in mind when choosing such a starter are that it should be stimulating and that its ingredients, texture, colour and taste should contrast with those of the course immediately following. It should not be so heavy that one is too full up to enjoy the rest of the meal. Rather, it should be an artistic and pleasurable introduction. The assorted cold platter is a convenient ploy when entertaining a large number of guests, as the most interesting items, colours and textures may be introduced and arranged in an attractive manner. Many of the recipes following may be used as part of an assorted cold platter. Choose them for their contrasting colour, texture and taste.

Agar agar salad (Shandong)

60 g (2 oz) dried agar agar (soaked)
140 g (5 oz) cucumber (deseeded and shredded)
110 g (4 oz) cooked skinned chicken (shredded)
60 g (2 oz) cooked ham (shredded)

For the dressing:
1 tbsp light soya sauce
1 tbsp white wine vinegar
1 tbsp sesame oil
1 tsp salt

Garnish:
coriander leaves or parsley

1. Snip the agar agar into 7.5 cm (3 in) lengths with a pair of sharp scissors. Rinse in warm water and soak in cold water till well swollen, about 30 minutes. The soaking may be done well in advance.
2. Mix together the cucumber and the chicken, and place in a dish. Drain the soaked agar agar, and cover the chicken and cucumber mixture with it. Scatter the ham over the agar-agar.
3. Mix together all the ingredients for the dressing, and pour over the prepared salad. Garnish with the coriander leaves.

Assorted cold platter

110 g (4 oz) charsiu (barbecued pork)
110 g (4 oz) white chopped chicken
110 g (4 oz) steeped pig's liver
110 g (4 oz) steeped beef
½ cucumber
2 tomatoes
80 g (3 oz) crispy cashew nuts

1. Slice the first 4 items thinly and neatly. Rinse the cucumber, cut it in half lengthwise, and slit into semicircles. Arrange the 5 items overlapping and in blocks of contrasting colour round the edge of a large plate, i.e. starting with cucumber, then *charsiu*, pig's liver, chicken and ending the circle with beef.
2. Cut the tomatoes in halves and slice into semicircles. Arrange them in a ring on the inner circle, with the straight sides on the inside and curves slightly overlapping the other 5 items. Put the crispy cashew nuts in the middle.

For *charsiu* (barbecued pork) *see page 35.*
For white chopped chicken *see page 46.*
For crispy cashew nuts *see page 17.*
For steeped pig's liver and beef *see below.*

STEEPED PIG'S LIVER AND BEEF

450 g (1 lb) pig's liver
900 g (2 lb) beef (lean braising steak)

Mixed spice bag:
14 whole star anise seeds
5 cm (2 in) piece cassia bark
3 slices liquorice root
10 cloves
5 cm (2 in) piece tangerine peel
1 pod ovoid cardamom
4 slices dried ginger (sajiang)
1 tbsp fennel
1 tbsp Sichuan peppercorns

Seasoning for the oil:
4 slices fresh ginger (bruised)
2 stalks spring onion whites (whole)

Seasoning for the sauce:
550 ml (1 pint) dark soya sauce
140 ml (5 fl oz) light soya sauce
140 ml (5 fl oz) rice wine
230 g (8 oz) granulated sugar
1 tbsp salt

1 tbsp cooking oil

1. Prepare the steeping liquor. First tie the spices in 2 pieces of muslin to make 2 bags. (Ready mixed spices are available.) Heat a thick-based enamel or stainless steel pot over a medium heat, put in the oil and stir-fry the ginger and spring onion whites till fragrant. Pour in the seasoning for the sauce, and add a generous 1 l (2 pt) water and the spice bag. Stir to dissolve the sugar. Bring to a gentle boil. Lower the heat, cover and simmer for about 40 minutes. Discard the onion and ginger. Skim, and adjust the seasoning, which should be rich and salty.
2. Scald the pig's liver in boiling water for a few minutes, till it tightens and puffs up. Drain, rinse in cold water and dry. Put it in the steeping liquor and bring to a gentle boil. Cover and simmer over a gentle heat for about 30 minutes. Fierce boiling would ruin the texture of the liver, which should be firm and moist. Leave it to cool in the liquor. Remove the liver.

3. Boil a piece of lean braising steak in water for about 10 minutes. Drain, rinse in cold water and dry. Put in the steeping liquor, bring to the boil, reduce the heat, cover and simmer till tender, about 1 hour. Leave to cool in the liquor.

Pig's heart, pig's tongue and tripe, chicken and other meats may be cooked in this way. The steeping liquor is never served with the meat. It may be stored and used over and again. But after each cooking it should be boiled up, skimmed, cooled and stored in the refrigerator. It needs to be boiled up once a week. The soya sauce, sugar and wine may be adjusted each time.

Chicken in sesame and pepper sauce (Sichuan)

1 chicken, just over 1 kg (2½ lb)

For the sauce:
1 tsp Sichuan peppercorns
2 tbsp chopped spring onion (green parts only)
1 tsp salt
3 tbsp light soya sauce
3 tbsp sesame oil
2 tbsp granulated sugar
2 tbsp chicken stock

1. Cook the chicken in a steaming basket or steamer over a high heat till just done, about 45 minutes. Take it out, cool and wipe dry. Bone and dice into bite-size pieces. Arrange neatly on a serving plate in one layer.
2. Pound the Sichuan peppercorns, spring onion greens and salt together. Mix them together with the rest of the ingredients for the sauce and pour over the chicken.

This may be served as part of an assorted cold platter. The chicken may be boiled instead; *see* 'White chopped chicken', *page 46.*

Crispy cashew nuts

170 g (6 oz) cashew nuts
2 tbsp granulated sugar

Syrup for boiling the nuts:
110 g (4 oz) granulated sugar
110 ml (4 fl oz) water

30 g (1 oz) maltose
550 ml (1 pt) cooking oil for deep-frying

1. Dissolve the sugar in the water over a low heat, and add the maltose. Bring gently to the boil, stirring well. Rinse the cashew nuts and boil in the syrup for about 10 minutes.
2. Drain off the syrup and deep-fry the cashew nuts in batches in a brass mesh wire strainer in hot oil on a medium heat till nicely golden. Drain well on kitchen paper. When all are done, sprinkle with the sugar. Separate them if they stick. Leave to cool on a baking sheet. Store in an airtight container.

This appetizer may be served on its own or as part of a cold platter for contrasting texture and taste. It is also delicious with drinks or coffee.

Crispy crab rolls (Anhui)

For the crab meat mixture:
170 g (6 oz) white fish (skinned and boned)
170 g (6 oz) dressed crab meat (white only)
1 tbsp chopped cooked ham
1 stalk spring onion (minced)
1 slice ginger (minced)
2 tsp rice wine
1 tsp granulated sugar
1 tsp salt
1 egg (lightly beaten)
pepper to taste

Egg paste:
2 eggs (lightly beaten)
2 tsp cornflour with a little water

For the wrapper:
3 sheets bean curd skins or 230 g (8 oz) caul fat

850 ml (1½ pt) cooking oil

Dips:
Sichuan pepper salt
sweet salted soya bean paste

Garnish:
tomato wedges

1. Mince the fish finely till sticky, or put it through a food processor.

Mix in the rest of the ingredients for the crab meat mixture. Divide into 6 equal portions.

2. Mix the eggs and the cornflour mixture into a paste, and set aside.
3. Dip the bean curd skins, one at a time, into a tray of hot water, handling them gently as they are very brittle. Drain and pat dry with kitchen paper. Cut each across into 2 rectangles. (If using caul fat, simply cut it into rectangles about 13 × 20cm (5 × 8 in).
4. Lay a piece of the softened bean curd skin on a flat surface. Brush it all over with the egg paste. Put a portion of the crab meat mixture in a neat row along one long side, 2.5 cm (1 in) or so from the edge. Fold in the edge and then fold both ends and wrap up envelope-wise, making sure that the opening is sealed. Make 5 more in the same manner.
5. Deep-fry the crab rolls in hot oil till golden. Drain well on kitchen paper. Cut on a slant into bite-size pieces, and arrange in their original shapes on a plate. Garnish with tomato wedges, and serve with the dips.

This is a popular dish in autumn, when the crabs are fat along the Yangzi river and in the lakes.

Deep-fried won ton (Guangdong)

32 won ton *skins*

For the filling mixture:
110 g (4 oz) minced pork
110 g (4 oz) raw prawn meat or peeled, cooked prawns (chopped)
½ tsp salt
1 tsp granulated sugar
2 tsp sesame oil
1 stalk spring onion (minced)
1 slice ginger (minced)
1 egg white
pepper to taste

Garnish:
parsley and sliced tomato

850 ml (1½ pt) cooking oil
1 egg yolk for sticking

1. Make the *won ton* skins in advance if ready-made ones are not available. (*See below.*)
2. Mix together all the ingredients for the filling mixture, and set aside.

3. Place a single *won ton* skin diagonally across your left palm. Put ½ tsp of the filling in the centre of the skin. Lift up the bottom corner of the skin and fold over the filling into a triangle, so that the bottom and top corners match. Fold the base of the triangle upwards so that only part of the top corner shows. Moisten the ends with a drop of the egg yolk, bring them together and press to stick. (*See illustrations.*) Finish the rest in the same manner.
4. Deep-fry the *won tons* in hot oil till golden. Drain well on kitchen paper, and serve garnished with the parsley and tomato slices.

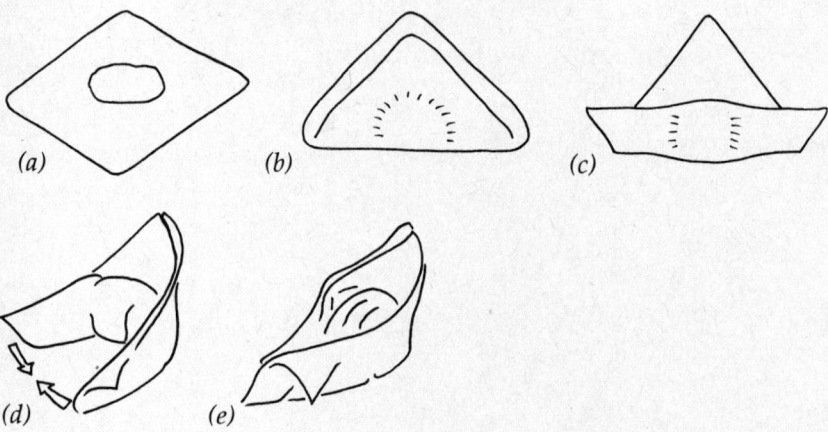

(a)   (b)   (c)

(d)   (e)

Won ton skins (makes 32)
230 g (8 oz) strong plain white flour
1 tsp salt
½ tsp lye water mixed with 3 tbsp cold water
cornflour for dusting

1. Sift the flour and salt on to a flat surface. Make a well and pour in the lye water mixture. Use your hand to work the water and flour into a dough. Knead till smooth and shiny. Cover with an upturned bowl and leave to rest for at least 30 minutes or 1 hour.
2. Cut the rested dough into 2. Roll each out on a board dusted with cornflour into a thin sheet about 1.5 mm (1⁄16 in) thick. Cut into 9 cm (3½ in) squares with a sharp knife. Dust with plenty of cornflour, pile up and store in an airtight container in the refrigerator. They will keep for several days.

Hot and spicy cucumber salad (Sichuan)

1 large cucumber

For the dressing:
3 dried red chillies (chopped into 2.5 cm, 1 in, lengths)
1 tsp Sichuan peppercorns (crushed)
2 tbsp white wine vinegar
2 tbsp granulated sugar
1 tbsp ginger (finely shredded)
1 fresh red chilli (finely shredded)
4 tbsp sesame oil

1. Rinse and quarter the cucumber lengthwise. Deseed and cut into 5 cm (2 in) long pieces. Rub them with some salt and leave for about 1 hour. Drain and put them in a dish.
2. Heat the sesame oil on a low heat and stir-fry the Sichuan peppercorns till fragrant, add the dried chillies and stir-fry till they turn a dark red. Leave the oil and spices to cool, then add together with the sugar, vinegar and ginger to the cucumber, and mix well. Seal with cling film, and leave to marinate for several hours or overnight in the refrigerator.
3. Just before serving, arrange the cucumber pieces, with a pair of chopsticks, neatly in a dish, skin-side-up, pour the spices and marinade over and sprinkle with fresh chilli.

This spicy appetizer may be served as part of a cold platter or a side dish in a family meal. The dried chillies are extremely hot, and the amount may be adjusted to personal taste.

Laver paper prawns (Fujian)

24 uncooked prawns, about 350 g (12 oz) (weight without heads)
3 sheets purple laver paper

For the filling:
80 g (3 oz) white fish (skinned and boned)
60 g (2 oz) parboiled pork fat
2 peeled water chestnuts (finely chopped)
2 caps winter mushrooms (soaked and finely chopped)
1 stalk spring onion (minced)
½ tsp granulated sugar

For the paste:
2 egg whites (lightly beaten)

1 tbsp cornflour with 3 tbsp water

Garnish:
2 tomatoes (in wedges)

Dips:
chilli sauce and prepared mustard

850 ml (1½ pt) cooking oil

1. Mince the fish till sticky. Mince the pork fat finely. Mix the two together with the rest of the ingredients for the filling. Divide into 24 equal portions, and set aside.
2. Cut each laver paper into 8 oblongs with scissors.
3. Mix the egg white, cornflour and water into a thin paste.
4. Shell the prawns but keep the tails on. Rub them with some salt, rinse and dry well on kitchen paper. With the sharp point of a knife, make a slit on the underside of each prawn but do not cut through. Fill each slit with a portion of the fish mixture. Use your fingers to shape the filling over part of the prawn and mould into a cylindrical shape. Dip it in the egg paste and wrap it with a piece of the laver, leaving the tail protruding. Stick the end of the laver down with a drop of the egg paste.
5. Deep-fry the stuffed prawns in batches in hot oil over a medium heat till the tails turn red and begin to curl, about 3 to 4 minutes. Lift them out with a brass wire mesh strainer. Drain on absorbent kitchen paper.
6. Arrange them in a circle on a plate with the tails pointing towards the edge. Arrange the tomato wedges in the centre of the plate, radiating like petals. Serve with the chilli sauce and the mustard.

This highly decorative and delectable dish is often served with drinks in Xiamen (Amoy) where seafood is abundant. It is most suitable for a cocktail party, buffet table or dinner party.

Pickled trotters (Guangdong)

4 pig's trotters

For the pickling liquor:
275 ml (8 fl oz) white wine vinegar
2 tsp salt
110–170 g (4–6 oz) granulated sugar
2 cloves garlic (minced)

½ cucumber
1 small sweet red pepper and 1 fresh chilli pepper

1. Prepare the trotters (*see page* 236).
2. Bring the prepared trotters to the boil in water to cover. Skim, reduce the heat, cover and simmer till tender, about 45 minutes to 1 hour, depending on the trotters.
3. Meanwhile, prepare the pickling liquor. Use a terracotta, enamel or stainless steel pot (vinegar should not be cooked in an aluminium or copper pot). In this, dissolve the sugar in the vinegar. Add the salt and garlic, and bring to the boil. Leave to cool completely.
4. Drain the cooked trotters and rinse under the cold tap to remove any grease. Soak them in cold water for about 3 hours. Bone them and cut into bite-size pieces. Add them to the pickling liquor. Simmer for about 30 minutes. Leave to cool completely.
5. Rinse the vegetables. Quarter the cucumber lengthwise and cut slantwise into 2.5 cm (1 in) long pieces. Deseed the red pepper and chilli, and cut into strips. Rub the vegetables with 1 tbsp salt and marinate for about 30 minutes, till the water begins to run out. Rinse and squeeze out excess water.
6. Arrange the prepared vegetables in the base of a suitable dish, such as an 850 ml (1½ pt) soufflé dish. When the pickling liquor and the trotters begin to solidify, pour them on to the prepared vegetables. Cover with cling film and keep in the refrigerator for at least 6 hours or best overnight, before serving. It keeps well for several days if refrigerated.
7. To serve, unmould the jellied trotters and colourful vegetables onto a plate.

This piquant, crisp, tender and non-greasy appetizer may be served summer or winter. Best of all, it may be prepared well in advance. If preferred it may be reheated and served hot. This famous Cantonese dish was originally called 'White Cloud Trotters', because it was cooked with the spring water from the mountain of that name in Guangdong, which render the meat extremely white and enhances its flavour.

Rainbow tripe (Guangdong)

1 whole raw pig's tripe

For the stuffing mixture:
4 raw salted egg yolks
3 boiled fermented eggs (100-year-old eggs)
170 g (6 oz) minced pork
140 g (5 oz) boiled pig's skin
60 g (2 oz) cooked ham or rindless smoked back bacon

1 tbsp coriander leaves, or parsley
1 tsp salt
1 tbsp sesame oil

1 tbsp rice wine

Garnish:
mixed pickles

2 pints steeping liquor (see page 16)

1. Clean the tripe (*see page 236*).
2. Dice the salted egg yolks (*see page 84*), boiled fermented eggs, boiled pig's skin, and ham into peanut-size pieces. Chop the coriander leaves into 1 cm (½ in) lengths.
3. Mix together all the ingredients for the stuffing. Turn the cleaned pig's tripe inside out and fill it with the mixture. Sew up the openings with thread.
4. Boil the stuffed tripe over a medium heat for 30 minutes. Prick it with a fine skewer in several places to release the air. Lower the heat and continue simmering for about 1 hour or till tender.
5. Drain and put the cooked tripe in a pot with the steeping liquor. Simmer for about 15 minutes, add 1 tbsp rice wine and leave to stand for another 15 minutes.
6. Take out, cool completely, wrap in cling film and chill in the refrigerator for several hours or overnight before serving. Quarter, cut in slices and arrange in a fan shape. Garnish with pickles of your choice.

This is an unusual cold platter dish, colourful and tasty. It keeps well for a couple of days in the refrigerator. Frozen raw pig's tripe is available in Chinese shops.

Salted jellyfish and cabbage salad (Shandong)

1 salted jellyfish
110 g (4 oz) salad cabbage (finely shredded)

For the dressing:
1 tbsp vinegar
1 tbsp granulated sugar
2 tbsp sesame oil
2 cloves garlic (minced)

Garnish:
1 red chilli pepper (finely shredded)

1. Prepare the jellyfish (*see page* 234).
2. Drain the jellyfish, squeeze dry and mix with the shredded cabbage.
3. Mix together all the ingredients for the dressing, and toss the jellyfish and cabbage mixture in it. Place on a serving plate, garnish with the shredded chilli and serve.

This is a favourite seafood delicacy in the coastal villages in Shandong peninsula, where in the early autumn the water is covered with flotillas of huge, pink, semi-transparent, floating discs of jellyfish. They are harvested with a metal hook attached to a bamboo pole. A local speciality is fresh raw jellyfish tossed in a variety of salad dressings. And to deal with the glut, the villagers preserve the jellyfish in salt. The preliminary preparation includes removing the tentacles on the undersides, slitting the bellies open to let out the water and rinsing to remove the slime. They are then covered with plenty of salt, folded in half, twice, packed into an urn, covered with more salt and weighed down with stones. After a day or so when the water begins to run out, they are drained, squeezed dry and hung out on the lines to dry in the sun. The final product looks rather like a piece of brownish leathery rubber sheet. This salad may be served with drinks or as a side dish in a family meal.

Sesame prawn balls (Henan)

For the prawn ball mixture:
230 g (8 oz) peeled, uncooked prawns
1 egg white (lightly beaten)
1 tbsp spring onion and ginger juice
3 tsp salt
2 tsp rice wine
1 tbsp cornflour with a little water
2 tsp lard (melted) or vegetable oil

850 ml (1½ pt) groundnut or other vegetable oil
2 tbsp sesame seeds

Garnish:
3 tomatoes
½ lettuce (Webb's or Iceberg)

1. Remove any debris from the sesame seeds. Rinse, drain and put in a plate.

2. Rub the prawns with 2 tsp salt; this crisps the meat. Rinse and drain. Mince the prawns finely.

3. Mix the egg white with the minced prawns; stirring in one direction till completely blended. Add the spring onion and ginger juice, the remaining salt and the rice wine, stirring in the same direction till absorbed by the prawn mixture. Add the cornflour mixture in the same manner, and finally the melted lard. Make the mixture into walnut-size balls and drop them into the plate of sesame seeds. Roll the balls to cover completely in sesame seeds, pressing them in lightly so that they do not fall off in the cooking.

4. Deep-fry till golden, take out and drain well on kitchen paper. Pile the sesame prawn balls in the middle of a dish.

5. Rinse the vegetables. Shred the lettuce and cut the tomatoes into wedges. Put the shredded lettuce round the prawn balls in a ring and distribute the tomato wedges on the lettuce.

Steamed crab rolls (Shandong)

For the egg skin:
3 eggs (lightly beaten)
½ tsp salt
2 tsp cornflour with a little water

For the filling:
230 g (8 oz) dressed crab meat (white and brown)
1 tsp salt
2 tsp rice wine
2 tsp ginger (minced)
2 stalks spring onion (chopped)
1 egg (lightly beaten)
1 tbsp cornflour

Garnish:
tomato and cucumber slices

1 tbsp cooking oil

1. Make a batter with the eggs, salt and cornflour mixture. Heat the wok and grease it with a little oil. Stir the egg mixture well and pour half of it into the wok. Swirl the wok round so as to spread the egg evenly. Cook till firm and remove. Make another one in the same way.

2. Mix together all the ingredients for the filling.

3. Spread one egg skin on a flat surface. Spread half the crab meat mixture to cover the whole egg skin. Roll up Swiss roll-wise and place it on a plate folded side down. Press lightly to flatten. Make another one in the same way.
4. Steam them (still on the plate) in the wok or a steamer for about 10 minutes over a high heat. Cool completely before slicing into 1 cm (½ in) thick pieces. Arrange them cut side up on a serving plate, and garnish with the tomato and cucumber slices.

These attractive yellow and coral rolls speckled with green are also suitable for the cold table.

Sweet and sour carrot salad (Sichuan)

230 g (8 oz) carrots
2 stalks spring onion (finely shredded)

For the dressing:
1 tsp salt
1 tbsp granulated sugar
1 tbsp white wine vinegar
2 tbsp sesame oil

1. Peel, rinse and cut the carrots into matchstick-size pieces. Rub with 1 tbsp salt and leave for about 20 minutes.
2. Rinse the carrots to remove excess salt and gently squeeze dry. Put in a serving bowl with the spring onions on top.
3. Mix together the ingredients for the dressing, making sure that the sugar is dissolved. Pour over the onions and carrots. Toss well before eating.

Vegetarian ham (Anhui)

230 g (8 oz) bean curd skins (dried weight)

For the seasoning:
1 tbsp light soya sauce
1 tbsp granulated sugar
2 tbsp red fermented bean curd (mashed)
4 tbsp sesame oil, plus a little for sprinkling

1 piece clean muslin
trussing string

1. Save 2 whole pieces of the bean curd skins for wrapping. Pour hot water over the rest of the skins. Rinse, drain and dry. Shred them as fine as chive blades and chop into 2.5 cm (1 in) lengths. Add the seasonings, except the sesame oil, and mix well. Stir-fry the shredded bean curd skins in the sesame oil over a low heat till the seasoning is absorbed.

2. Dip the reserved whole skins in warm water briefly to soften, drain and pat dry with kitchen paper. Lay them on a flat surface in double layers. Place the seasoned bean curd shreds on the skins in a long roll. Roll up into a cylindrical shape. Then wrap in the clean muslin. Starting from one end, tie up with the string and wind to the other end, with turns about 0.6 cm (¼ in) apart, tightly and evenly so that the whole roll is the same width. (*See illustration.*)

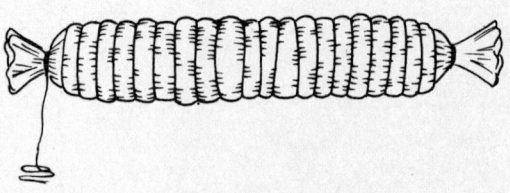

3. Steam in a steaming basket or steamer for about 1 to 1½ hours. Take out, cool and chill in the refrigerator for several hours or overnight. Before serving, remove the string and muslin. Cut into thin slices and arrange on a plate. Sprinkle on some sesame oil.

This looks like pink ham, and has a chewy texture. The fermented bean curd gives it the taste of cured meat. It may be served as an appetizer, forming part of a cold platter, or a side dish in a family meal. Sealed with cling film, it will keep for about a week in the refrigerator.

Vermicelli salad (Shandong)

80 g (3 oz) dried mung bean vermicelli
110 g (4 oz) cooked ham
110 g (4 oz) cooked chicken
110 g (4 oz) charsiu (barbecued pork) or cooked pork
3 eggs (lightly beaten)
4 large caps winter mushrooms (soaked)
110 g (4 oz) hearts of bocai or other greens in season (blanched)
1 tbsp dried shrimps (soaked)

For the dressing:
2 tbsp light soya sauce
1 tbsp vinegar
2 tsp prepared mustard
2 tbsp sesame oil
½ tsp chilli powder (optional)

1. Prepare the mung bean vermicelli (*see page* 235). Drain it and pile in the middle of a large dish.
2. Cook the beaten eggs into an omelette. Cut into juliennes about 5 cm (2 in) long. Cut the winter mushrooms, ham, chicken and pork to a similar size. (For *charsiu see page* 35.) Arrange the 5 juliennes in neat groups around the vermicelli along the edge of the dish. Put the greens on the vermicelli and scatter the soaked shrimps over the top.
3. Mix together the ingredients for the dressing in a little bowl. Take the salad and the dressing to the table separately. Just before serving, pour the dressing over the salad.

MEAT

Beef

Beef cakes in tomato sauce

For the beef cake mixture:
230 g (8 oz) minced lean beef
5 peeled water chestnuts (minced)
1 egg (optional)
1 tsp salt
3 tsp cornflour

For the sauce:
1 small onion (chopped)
2 tsp rice wine
1 tsp chilli powder
1 tsp granulated sugar
1 tbsp dark soya sauce
2 tbsp tomato ketchup
2 tbsp cooking oil

1. Mix together all the ingredients for the beef mixture, except the cornflour, beating in 2 tbsp cold water. Finally mix in the cornflour. Shape into 8 ping-pong size meat balls.
2. Mix together the seasoning for the sauce except the onion, and set aside.
3. Set the wok on a medium heat, and when hot put in the oil. Swirl the wok so that the oil covers an area about 20 cm (8 in) across. Flatten each meat ball and put into the oil. Reduce the heat if it gets too fierce, and cook till both sides are crusty and golden. Lift them to the sides of the wok so that the oil drips to the bottom of the wok.
4. Add the onion to the oil and stir-fry till it changes colour and becomes fragrant. Pour in the seasoning mixture, mix well and put in the meat cakes from the sides. Cook briefly so that the cakes are well flavoured. Dish up.

These beef cakes are succulent and moist, and the water chestnuts give a crunchy texture. The ingredients are simple and the cooking is fast. They go well with plain boiled rice, steamed buns, any of the Chinese pancakes or even potatoes.

Spicy saguo oxtail (Shanghai)

generous 1 kg (2½ lb) oxtail
1 large carrot

Seasoning for the oil:
1 dried red chilli (chopped into 1 cm, ½ in lengths)
1 stalk spring onion (chopped into 2.5 cm, 1 in lengths)
1 slice ginger (bruised)

Seasoning for the casserole:
1 tbsp rice wine
1 tbsp light soya sauce
1 tsp salt
2 tsp granulated sugar
2.5 cm (1 in) length cassia bark
1 pod star anise
1 tsp Sichuan peppercorns (crushed)

2 tbsp lard or cooking oil
1 tbsp sesame oil
pepper to taste

Garnish:
2 tbsp shredded tender leek or spring onions

1. Boil the oxtail in plenty of water with 1 tbsp salt for about 15 minutes. Drain and rinse thoroughly in cold water. Trim off any visible fat.
2. Peel and roll-cut the carrot.
3. Set the wok on a high heat, put in the lard, and stir-fry the carrot for a couple of minutes. Take out and set aside. In the remaining lard stir-fry the red chilli till it turns black, add the spring onion and ginger, and when fragrant stir in the oxtail. Stir-fry briefly, then add the seasoning for the casserole and 1.2 l (2 pt) hot water. Bring to the boil, skim, and pour into a *saguo* (Chinese terracotta pot) and braise on the stove, or in the oven (if a casserole is used) on a low heat till tender, about 2½ to 3 hours. Half an hour before the end of cooking time add the carrot.
4. Before serving, discard all the spices, ginger and onion. Sprinkle with the sesame oil and pepper to taste. Garnish with the shredded leek and take the *saguo* to the table.

This golden, spicy casserole, slightly hot and vaguely sweet, is a popular winter dish. The pre-boiling in salt deodorizes the oxtail. Please remember that the *saguo* is not ovenproof.

Stir-fried beef and apple (Beijing)

170 g (6 oz) lean beef (aitchbone)
1 crisp eating apple
2 stalks spring onions (chopped)

Marinade for the beef:
1 tbsp dark soya sauce
1 tsp sugar
2 tsp rice wine
½ tsp salt
3 tsp cornflour

550 ml (1 pt) cooking oil
60 ml (2 fl oz) stock or water

1. Cut the beef across the grain into thin bite-size slices. Make up the marinade with 2 tbsp cold water, leaving out the cornflour. Mix it into the beef, then mix in the cornflour. In this way the starch seals in the juices. Leave in the refrigerator for 1 to 2 hours.
2. Peel, core and slice the apple.
3. Deep-fry the marinated beef briefly in hot oil to par-cook and seal

the meat. Take out and drain well. Reheat the wok with about 2 tsp oil and stir-fry the spring onion till fragrant. Add the apple and stock, and when it comes to the boil stir in the beef. Cook for a minute to blend well and dish up.

A simple yet delectable dish for the family meal. Sweet and sour, it goes well with boiled rice or steamed buns.

Lamb

Hot braised lamb (Jiangsu)

1–1.5 kg (2½–3 lb) leg of lamb
110 g (4 oz) bamboo shoots
4 small carrots

For the seasoning:
1 stalk spring onion (whole)
1 slice ginger (bruised)
1 tbsp Sichuan chilli paste (or 1 tbsp salted soya bean paste with 1 tsp chilli powder)
1 tsp salt
2 tsp rice wine
2 tsp light soya sauce
1 tsp granulated sugar

3 tbsp cooking oil
2 tsp cornflour with a little water
2 tsp sesame oil

Garnish:
1 leek (shredded)

1. Peel and rinse the carrots, but leave them whole. Roll-cut the bamboo shoots into wedges.
2. Remove every visible trace of fat from the lamb and dice into 5 cm (2 in) cubes. Put into fiercely boiling water and boil for 2 minutes. Drain and rinse in cold water, and dry on kitchen paper.
3. Set the wok over a high heat, and put in 2 tbsp oil. Add the spring onion, ginger and lamb and stir-fry till fragrant. Transfer to a casserole.
4. Reheat the wok, and put in the rest of the oil. Stir fry the Sichuan chilli paste till fragrant, stir in the rice wine, soya sauce, sugar and

salt, and add 550 ml (1 pt) hot water. Bring to the boil and pour on to the lamb in the caserole. Add in the carrots, bring to the boil over a high heat, skim, reduce the heat, cover and simmer till the lamb is tender, about 1 hour. The cooking may be done on the stove or in the oven.

5. Discard the carrots, ginger and spring onion. Add the bamboo shoots and heat through. Thicken with the cornflour mixture. Sprinkle with the sesame oil, garnish with the shredded leek and serve.

Sweet and sour lamb meat balls (Zhejiang)

For the meat ball mixture:
230 g (8 oz) lean lamb (from a leg; weight without bone)
1 egg
8 water chestnuts (peeled)
1 tsp salt
1 tbsp cornflour with a little water

For the sauce:
2 tsp rice wine
1 tbsp light soya sauce
1 tbsp white wine vinegar
2 tbsp granulated sugar
1 tsp cornflour with a little water
140 ml (5 fl oz) stock or water
2 tsp sesame oil

generous 1 l (2 pt) cooking oil

1. Mince the lamb and dice the water chestnuts into rice-size pieces. Lightly beat the egg, and stir in the salt and cornflour mixture. Blend in the minced meat and water chestnuts. Make into quail's-egg-sized meat balls.
2. Deep-fry the meat balls till golden. Drain well on kitchen paper.
3. Mix together all the ingredients for the sauce except the sesame oil. Bring the mixture to the boil in the wok, and stir in the meat balls. Sprinkle with the sesame oil and dish up.

Pork

Barbecue pork spare ribs stuffed with spring onions (Fujian)

450 g (1 lb) pork spare ribs
110 g (4 oz) spring onion whites
1 tbsp white wine vinegar

For coating the ribs:
2 tbsp cornflour
1 tbsp flour

For the sauce:
2 tbsp tomato ketchup
1 tbsp light soya sauce
1 tsp granulated sugar
80 ml (3 fl oz) stock or water
1 tsp cornflour with a little water

600 ml (24 fl oz) cooking oil

1. Mix together all the ingredients for the sauce and set aside.
2. Choose really meaty ribs for this. Trim the joints, separate the ribs, and chop into 4 cm (1¾ in) long pieces. Rinse well and dry. Mix with the vinegar and let stand for 15 minutes. Mix the two coating flours together and roll the marinated ribs in them, covering each completely.
3. Cut the spring onion whites into 5 cm (2 in) long pieces.
4. Deep-fry the ribs on a medium heat till cooked and golden, about 15 minutes. Drain well on kitchen paper. When cooled, slip out the bones, and replace them with one or two spring onion whites. The cooked meat will have shrunk so that the onion whites protrude at both ends.
5. Give the sauce mixture a stir and bring to the boil in the wok. Add the stuffed ribs and mix well. When they are heated through and the sauce has thickened, dish up.

The spring onions may be replaced by par-cooked carrots or bamboo shoots.

Cantonese Gold Coin pork (Guangdong)

280 g (10 oz) lean loin pork
230 g (8 oz) taro (parboiled whole)

For the marinade:
2 tsp rice wine
1 tbsp granulated sugar
2 tbsp dark soya sauce
2 tsp five-spice powder

For the sauce:
1 tbsp Worcester sauce
1 tbsp dark soya sauce
1 tbsp granulated sugar
1 tsp cornflour with a little water
110 ml (4 fl oz) stock or water

850 ml (1½ pt) cooking oil
cornflour for dusting

1. Cut the lean pork into strips about 5 cm (2 in) across. Steam them in the wok or steamer for about 10 minutes to par-cook. Shave off the corners and cut into 24 rounds about 1 cm (⅜ in) thick. Peel the taro and cut into 24 similar sized rounds.
2. Marinate the pork rounds for 30 minutes.
3. Drain and reserve any marinade. Roll the pork rounds in cornflour. Place a taro round on each of the pork ones, pressing them together. Thread the pairs on to skewers, spacing them slightly apart. Dip the skewers in hot oil and deep-fry them till golden and cooked. Slip the cooked 'gold coins' off the skewers, drain well on kitchen paper and put them in a serving dish.
4. Mix the ingredients for the sauce with the remaining marinade. Bring to the boil, adjust seasoning to your taste, and pour over the 'gold coins'.

This attractive dish has a savoury, sweet and piquant sauce. It appears regularly in Cantonese banquets, not least for the auspicious 'gold coins'. The meat rounds with a hole in the centre resemble ancient Chinese coins, which had a hole so that they could be threaded on a string.

Charsiu – Cantonese barbecued pork in the wok (Guangdong)

450–900 g (1–2 lb) leg of pork (skinned and boned)

For the marinade:
1 tbsp light soya sauce
4 tbsp dark soya sauce

1 tbsp rice wine
1 tsp salt
2 tsp hongqu *(dried red fermented rice, ground; optional)*

3 tbsp cooking oil
3 tbsp granulated sugar
2 tsp five-spice powder

Garnish:
cucumber slices

1. Cut the meat into strips about 4 to 5 cm (1½ to 2 in) wide and 2.5 cm (1 in) thick. Mix it with the marinade and leave at room temperature for about 2 to 3 hours or overnight in the refrigerator.
2. Drain the meat. Set the wok on a high heat and when hot put in the oil. Swirl it round to cover a wide area of the wok. Cook the drained pork till it turns a reddish brown and any water from the meat has evaporated; turning the meat over and over to make sure that all sides are nicely coloured. Continue stir-frying till the meat is cooked, when it shrinks considerably and becomes slightly charred. Add the sugar and five-spice powder to the meat, stir-frying to mix well. Reduce the heat if it is too fierce. When the sugar is caramelized and thick and the meat well covered, take out and cool on a cooling tray.
3. When completely cold cut into thin slices, garnish with cucumber slices and serve with plain rice or steamed buns.

The professional Cantonese chefs 'barbecue' this pork over a charcoal fire in an 'earthen oven'. But it is often very successfully imitated in the wok in Chinese homes where the oven is not a common household appliance. The cooking, taking about 25 to 30 minutes, is fast. The meat is red on the outside and white inside, moist and tender. Salty and sweet, it is a popular standby in the house as it may be turned into a filling for steamed buns or an hors d'oeuvre, or stir-fried with noodles or rice, and so on.

Pig's tongue in fermented glutinous rice (Shandong)

550 g (1¼ lb) pig's tongue or tongues

Seasoning for simmering the tongue:
1 tsp five-spice powder
1 stalk spring onion (whole)
1 slice ginger (bruised)
1 tsp salt

For the marinade:
2 tbsp sesame oil
1 tbsp fermented glutinous rice
1 tbsp rice wine
1 teaspoon salt
280 ml (½ pt) stock

1. Prepare the tongue or tongues (*see page* 16). Trim off any gristle, fat and bones. Boil in water for about 5 to 10 minutes. Drain and scrape off the skin with a knife. The skin would not peel off if over-boiled. Rinse thoroughly in cold water.
2. Bring the tongue to the boil together with the seasoning and water to cover. Reduce the heat and simmer till the tongue is tender, about 45 minutes. Take out, cool and cut into bite-size slices.
3. Set the wok on a medium heat, put in the sesame oil and stir-fry the fermented glutinous rice till fragrant. Take the wok off the heat, and add the stock, rice wine and salt. Mix well and strain through a piece of muslin into a dish. Add the tongue slices to the wine mixture, cover and marinate for at least 30 minutes. Use a pair of chopsticks to take out the tongue slices and arrange them on a plate, and serve.

Pork braised with fermented bean curd (Fujian)

generous 1 kg (2½ lb) shoulder of pork

For the seasoning:
2 stalks spring onion whites (whole)
1 slice ginger (bruised)
1 pod star anise
1 piece red fermented bean curd (mashed)
1 tbsp dark soya sauce
2 tsp granulated sugar
2 tsp rice wine

1 tsp cornflour with a little water
2 tsp sesame oil
stock or water

Accompaniment:
450 g (1 lb) bocai *or other greens in season (blanched)*

1. Boil the pork in water for 5 minutes, drain and rinse in cold water.
2. Put the pork together with the ginger, spring onion and anise seed

in a pot. Mix all the rest of the seasoning and pour over the meat. Add stock or water to just cover. Bring to the boil, reduce the heat and simmer on top of the stove or in a slow oven till tender, about 2 hours. The meat should be easy to remove from the bones and the juice reduced until sticky.

3. Transfer the meat to a dish. Thicken the juice with the cornflour mixture and pour over the meat. Surround the meat with the blanched vegetable and sprinkle with the sesame oil.

This is simple to prepare and a popular family dish which goes very well with plain boiled rice.

Stir-fried minced pork

450 g (1 lb) minced lean pork

For the seasoning:
1 tsp salt
2 tsp granulated sugar
2 tbsp dark soya sauce
2 tsp rice wine
1 tbsp sesame oil
1 stalk spring onion (chopped)
1 slice ginger (minced)

Accompaniment:
sesame rolls

Set the wok on a high heat and when hot, without adding oil, dry-fry the minced pork till it turns white and the water evaporates. Stir in the salt, sugar and soya sauce, and continue to stir-fry till the seasoning is completely absorbed by the meat. Stir in the rice wine, sesame oil, spring onion and ginger. Continue stir-frying till fragrant and dry. Dish up. Serve in sesame rolls (*see below*).

SESAME ROLLS

For the bread dough:
generous 1 kg (1¼ lb) strong plain white flour
20 g (¾ oz) fresh yeast or 1½ tsp dried yeast
30 g (1 oz) granulated sugar
330 ml (12 fl oz) tepid water
30 g (1 oz) white sesame seeds on a plate
1 tbsp sesame oil in a saucer

For the syrup:
1 tbsp sugar
2 tbsp water

1. Make an ordinary bread dough with the flour, yeast, 1 tsp of the sugar and the water. Leave to rise till doubled in size. Knock down and knead in the rest of the sugar with 2 tbsp water. Leave to rest for about 30 minutes.
2. Roll the rested dough into a cylinder. Cut off one-fifth of the dough and break it into 14 small pieces. Roll each piece into a ball and set aside. Dissolve the sugar in the water for the syrup and set aside.
3. Cut the rest of the cylinder into 14 equal parts. Flatten a piece into an 8 cm (3 in) round. Dip one of the little balls in the sesame oil and place it in the middle of the round. Gather the edges together and wrap up. Place it gathered-side-down and flatten it lightly into a 5 cm (2 in) round. Brush the top with the syrup. Press the syrup side on to the sesame seeds, pressing lightly to stick. Put it on a greased baking sheet, sesame side up. Continue with the rest in the same way.
4. Bake them in a preheated oven, about 220°C (425°F, gas 7) for about 12 minutes, or till they are golden. Take out and cool on a rack.
5. To eat, make a slit in the side of the roll, remove the little ball inside and fill with fried mince.

Both items may be prepared well in advance. If preferred, reheat by steaming for about 5 minutes over a high heat. The addition of a salad such as shredded carrots, cucumber and lettuce turns this into an excellent light meal. It is rather like a Western hamburger but with a difference. This simple fare used to be one of the imperial breakfasts in the Qing palace. It is said that one night the Dowager Empress Ci-Xi dreamt of such a breakfast and indeed it appeared on the imperial table the next morning. She was more than delighted at the way in which her dream had come true, and the imperial chef who had invented the dish was duly rewarded with silver.

Taro braised pork (Guangdong)

550 g (1¼ lb) belly pork
280 g (10 oz) taro

Seasonings:
1 clove garlic (minced)
1 tsp star anise powder
3 tsp red fermented bean curd (mashed)

1 tsp salt
1 tsp granulated sugar
1 tbsp light soya sauce

Ingredients for the sauce:
4 fl oz stock or water
1 tbsp oil
1 tsp cornflour

generous 1 l (2 pt) cooking oil
dark soya sauce for brushing

1. Mix together all the seasonings, and set aside.
2. Peel the taro and cut into 1 cm (½ in) thick oblong slices.
3. Boil the belly pork till just cooked. To test, stick a chopstick into the meat and lift it out. If not ready the chopstick will not pierce the meat easily, and if overdone the meat will not be lifted out without falling to bits. Brush the meat with the soya sauce.
4. Deep-fry the taro till cooked, when it floats. Drain. Deep-fry the meat till golden. Drain and soak it in cold water for 30 minutes. Drain and cut into slices the same size as the taro.
5. Mix the meat slices with the seasoning mixture and let stand for 20 minutes. Put the meat, skin-side-down, in a bowl, alternating with a piece of taro, sandwich-wise. Steam for 1 hour over a high heat.
6. Take out, place a saucer over the taro and meat, drain and reserve the cooking liquor. Remove the saucer and turn out the sandwiched taro meat on to a serving dish.
7. Bring the reserved liquor and the stock to the boil and thicken with the cornflour. Stir in the oil, and pour over the meat and taro.

If preferred, the deep-frying may be omitted. The taro may be boiled whole and then peeled and sliced.

Turned-over pork with preserved vegetable (Guangdong)

900 g (2 lb) belly pork
230 g (8 oz) meikancai *(preserved vegetable)*

For the seasoning:
1 tbsp dark soya sauce
1 tbsp rice wine
½ tsp salt

110 ml (4 fl oz) stock or water

1 tsp cornflour with a little water

1. Do not wash the pork. Rub some salt all over the skin-side only. Leave it on a rack in a roasting tin. Roast in a preheated oven at about 200°C (400°F, gas 6) for about 30 minutes or till the skin is golden and crackled. Take out and rinse with hot water. Drain well.
2. Rinse the preserved vegetable in several changes of water to remove excess salt and any grit. Separate the leaves from the stem. Pour hot water over and soak for 10 minutes, then rinse again in cold water. Chop finely.
3. Cut the meat into slices about 1 cm (⅜ in) thick and 8 cm (3 in) long. Lay them in two rows skin-side-down in a bowl or pudding basin. Mix the seasoning with the stock and pour over the meat. Cover the meat completely with the chopped vegetable. Steam in the wok or steamer for 2 to 3 hours on a medium heat. You can use a pudding basin, placed directly in the wok or pot, but on a folded piece of muslin which stops it from moving and rattling.
4. Remove from the wok. Invert a saucer over the vegetable and tip all the cooking liquor into a saucepan. Remove the saucer and turn the meat and vegetable into a serving bowl, skin-side-up. Bring the cooking liquor to the boil and thicken with the cornflour mixture. Pour over the turned-over meat and serve.

POULTRY AND GAME

Chicken

Almond chicken (Guandong)

230 g (8 oz) skinned chicken breast

For the marinade:
1 tbsp light soya sauce
2 tsp rice wine
1 tsp salt
1 tsp ginger juice
pepper to taste

1 tsp cornflour with a little water

For the coating:
60 g (2 oz) toasted almonds (crushed)
1 egg (lightly beaten)

Garnish:
2 tomatoes (in wedges)

850 ml (1½ pt) cooking oil

1. Cut the chicken meat into 1 cm (⅜ in) thick bite-size slices. Beat them lightly with the back of a chopper to loosen the fibres. Marinate for about 20 minutes.
2. Mix the beaten egg into the marinated chicken. Put the crushed almonds on a plate. Cover each piece of chicken meat in the almond chips, pressing them in to make them stick.
3. Deep-fry in hot oil till golden. Drain well on kitchen paper. Place in a dish and garnish with the tomato wedges.

Cantonese salt-baked chicken (Guandong)

1 plump chicken, about 1.4–1.6 kg (3–3½ lb)

For the seasoning:
2 tsp salt
2 tbsp melted lard or peanut oil
1 tbsp sesame oil
2 tsp sajiang (dried ginger) powder

For the dip:
1 tbsp salt
2 tsp sajiang (dried ginger) powder
2 tbsp groundnut oil

1. Bring about 2 l (4 pt) water (or enough to cover the chicken) to the boil. Reduce the heat to medium and put in the chicken. Keep the water gently bubbling – it must not be fast boiling or the meat would not be smooth, firm and crisp. Poach the chicken until cooked, about 35 to 40 minutes. Take out and leave to cool slightly. Mix together all the seasoning ingredients. When cool enough to handle, rub the cooked chicken all over and inside the cavity with some of the mixture. Leave to cool.
2. Prepare the dip: dry-fry (without oil) the salt and the *sajiang* powder till fragrant. Put in 4 individual saucers. Heat the oil and divide it between the saucers.

3. Chop the seasoned and cooled chicken into bite-size pieces and arrange neatly in a plate. Pour the rest of the seasoning mixture over. Serve with the dip.

The famous Cantonese salt-baked chicken is usually cooked in hot salt, but this alternative way of cooking has been adopted for nearly seventy years in Guangzhou (Canton) restaurants for the simple reason that it is faster and simpler, so that the clients' fluctuating orders can be handled. This is also true of restaurants in the West. The secret of success lies in the choice of a plump, tender chicken and in the poaching. The indispensable ingredient is the *sajiang* powder, which is not the same as the ordinary dried green ginger powder, and which gives this dish its authentic taste and flavour.

Chicken cake (Sichuan)

For the chicken cake mixture:
230 g (8 oz) chicken breast meat (skinned and boned)
80 g (3 oz) pork fat
2 tsp rice wine
2 tsp spring onion and ginger juice
1 tsp salt
pepper to taste
2 egg whites (lightly beaten)
1 tbsp cornflour with a little water to mix

Garnish:
170 g (6 oz) salad cabbage (finely shredded)
1 red chilli pepper (finely shredded)
3 tbsp tomato ketchup

Dip:
Sichuan pepper salt

cornflour for dusting
850 ml (1½ pt) cooking oil

1. Finely mince the chicken meat and pork fat separately. Mix them with the rest of the ingredients for the chicken cake mixture. Blend well.
2. Toss the cabbage and chilli pepper in the tomato ketchup with a pinch of salt. Set aside.
3. Grease a sandwich cake tin or a dish, fill with the chicken cake mixture and level the top. Steam in the wok or steamer over a high

43

heat till cooked, about 10 minutes. Cool and cut into bite-size oblongs. Roll each oblong in cornflour till completely covered.

4. Deep-fry the chicken cakes till golden and crusty. Take out, and drain on kitchen paper. Arrange them in the middle of a plate and surround them with the cabbage salad just before serving. Eat with the Sichuan pepper salt as dip.

Crisp and succulent, this is suitable for either entertaining or a family meal. It also goes very well with potatoes and salad. Without the pork fat it would be too dry. The steaming makes sure that the cakes are cooked and moist, and the deep-frying crisps them.

Mango chicken (Guangdong)

450 (1 lb) skinned chicken meat
2 mangoes

For the marinade:
1 tbsp light soya sauce
1 tsp salt
pepper to taste
2 tsp cornflour

For the sauce:
1 small onion (sliced)
1 slice ginger (minced)
2 shallots (chopped)
2 tsp rice wine
2 tsp granulated sugar
1 tbsp light soya sauce
1 tsp salt
pepper to taste

110 ml (4 fl oz) stock or water
850 ml (1½ pt) cooking oil

1. Slice the chicken and mix with the marinade. Leave for 10 minutes. Peel the mangoes and cut the flesh into 20 cherry-sized cubes, or use a melon ball cutter. Set them aside for garnish. Purée the rest of the mango and add to the stock.
2. Deep-fry the chicken meat till golden. Drain well on kitchen paper.
3. Set the wok on high heat, put in 1 tbsp oil and when hot, stir-fry the onion, ginger and shallots till fragrant. Put in the chicken and the stock mixture with the seasonings for the sauce. Mix well, cover and

cook for 2 minutes for the flavour to blend. Transfer to a serving
dish and arrange the mango balls around the edge as a garnish.

In sub-tropical Guangdong fruits are often cooked or served with meat.
Choose firm mangoes for this dish, over-ripe mangoes are too soft.

Orange and pineapple chicken (Guangdong)

1 small chicken, about 1 kg (2 lb)
2 oranges
110 g (4 oz) pineapple (fresh or canned)
60 g (2 oz) bamboo shoots

For the sauce:
2 shallots (chopped)
1 slice ginger (minced)
1 tbsp light soya sauce
1 tsp granulated sugar
2 tsp sesame oil
pepper to taste
140 ml (5 fl oz) stock or water

generous 1 l (2 pt) cooking oil
cornflour for dusting
light soya sauce for brushing

1. Peel the oranges and remove all the pith. (Steeping them in boiling
   water for a minute and plunging in cold water makes peeling
   easier.) Slice one orange into rounds and cut each round in two.
2. Arrange the orange semi-circles in a ring round a serving plate. Dice
   the other orange and the pineapple and bamboo shoots into 1 cm
   (½ in) cubes and set aside.
3. Scald the chicken by pouring boiling water all over it. Wipe dry with
   kitchen paper and brush it all over with some light soya sauce.
   Chop it into 10 pieces. Cover them with cornflour. Deep-fry till
   golden and drain well on kitchen paper.
4. Set the wok on a high heat, put in 1 tbsp oil and when hot, stir-fry
   the onions and ginger till fragrant. Stir in the chicken, the fruits and
   the bamboo shoots. Turning to mix well, add in the stock and the
   rest of the seasoning. Cover and cook for about 5 minutes or till the
   sauce begins to thicken and the chicken has absorbed the flavour.
   Transfer to the plate which has previously been prepared, with the
   orange slices around the edge.

This is attractive enough for a dinner party. Only a very young, meaty and small chicken should be used. Two English spring chickens would be an excellent substitute.

Steamed chicken with fermented bean curd (Zhejiang)

1 young chicken, just over 1 kg (2½ lb)
110 g (4 oz) bamboo shoots

For the marinade:
1 tsp hongqu (dried red fermented rice; pounded)
1 square red fermented bean curd (mashed)
1 tbsp rice wine
1 tsp sugar
¼ tsp salt

Garnish:
230 g (8 oz) seasonal greens (blanched)
1 stalk spring onion (chopped)

1 tsp cornflour with a little water
2 tsp melted lard

1. Mix together the ingredients for the marinade. Chop the chicken into 4 cm (1½ in) squares and mix them with the marinade. Leave for about 30 minutes.
2. Roll-cut the bamboo shoots into wedges.
3. Arrange the marinated chicken skin side down in a bowl in two layers, with the best pieces first. Lay the bamboo shoots on the chicken. Pour on the marinade.
4. Steam in a wok or steamer for about 25 minutes or till cooked.
5. Place a saucer over the bamboo shoots and drain the juice into a saucepan. Turn the meat on to a dish. Bring the juice to the boil and thicken with the cornflour mixture. Pour over the chicken. Sprinkle with the melted lard and then the spring onion. Surround the chicken with the blanched greens.

This simple dish has a reddish sauce and a delicious cheesy flavour. It goes well with either boiled rice or steamed buns.

White chopped chicken (Guangdong)

1 plump chicken, about 1.4–1.6 kg (3–3½ lb)

46

For the dip:
30 g (1 oz) ginger (minced)
30 g (1 oz) spring onion whites (minced)
1 tbsp salt
3 tbsp groundnut oil
sesame oil for brushing

1. Prepare the dip: mix the minced ginger and the onion whites with the salt and divide into 4 saucers. Heat the oil till really hot and pour into the saucers.
2. Bring 3 l (5 pt) of water (enough to cover the chicken) to a gentle boil, add 2 tsp salt and put in and completely immerse the chicken. Cover. After 5 minutes take it out and pour out the water that has collected in the cavity. This is to ensure that the temperature inside the chicken is the same as outside. Repeat the process once. Replace the chicken in the pot, cover and leave to cook in gently boiling water for another 15 minutes or till cooked.
3. Put the chicken in a colander, and pour cold water all over to rinse off any grease. Let it drip dry. Brush with the sesame oil and chop into bite-size pieces. Arrange them neatly on a plate with the best pieces on top. Serve with the dip and plain boiled rice.

This is the white chicken that one sees hanging in Chinese restaurants. White chopped chicken is a versatile basic ingredient for many dishes but its success depends on using the best and most tasty chicken. Frozen chickens are not suitable for this exacting cooking.

Duck

Braised Eight Treasures duck (Fujian)

1 duck, about 1.8 kg (4 lb)

For the stuffing:
1 duck's gizzard, liver and heart
110 g (4 oz) lean pork
30 g (1 oz) cooked ham or smoked back bacon
30 g (1 oz) dried shrimps (soaked)
4 caps winter mushrooms (soaked)
60 g (2 oz) carrots
60 g (2 oz) bamboo shoots
60 g (2 oz) lotus seeds (soaked and boiled)

For the seasoning:
2 stalks spring onion (chopped)

2 slices ginger (minced)
2 tbsp dark soya sauce
1 tbsp rice wine

dark soya sauce for brushing
1 tbsp cooking oil

1. Bone the duck whole (*see page* 229). Set aside. Cover the bones with boiling water with 1 tsp of salt for the stock.
2. Prepare the filling: dice the first 7 ingredients into pea-size pieces. Set the wok on a high heat, put in the oil and stir-fry the spring onions and ginger till fragrant. Add the pork and when it turns white, put in the gizzard, liver and heart. Stir-fry till they lose their redness. Add in the rest of the ingredients and stir-fry till fragrant. Stir in the rice wine and soya sauce. Pour in 60 ml (2 fl oz) water, cook briefly to blend in the flavour and set aside.
3. Sew up the rear opening of the boned duck with cotton. Fill the cavity with the prepared stuffing from the neck end. Sew up the neck opening with cotton, leaving a long end for easy removal. Pour boiling water all over the duck to tighten the skin. Pat dry.
4. Preheat the oven to 230°C (450°F, gas 8). Brush the duck all over with soya sauce. Put on a rack in a roasting tin with 1 cm (½ in) water. Roast in the preheated oven for 15 minutes each side to brown the skin. Take out and pour away the fat.
5. Put the browned duck, breast up, in a casserole and pour on the duck stock to cover. Cover and braise in the oven at 190°C (375°F, gas 5) for 1½ hours or till tender.
6. Drain the cooking liquor into a saucepan and skim off the fat. Reheat and pour it on to the duck in the casserole. Serve whole in the casserole. To eat, tear open the breast with the servers, and spoon out the stuffing with some juice to serve first. Then serve the meat with some juice.

The stuffing may be varied according to preference. Pig's heart, kidney, boiled pig's tripe, and green peas are often included. To make the meat go further a few ounces of glutinous rice may be added. The duck may be steamed, as was originally done, but this takes about 3 hours. No salt is required as the ham, shrimp and soya sauce make it salty enough.

Cantonese roast duck (Guangdong)

1 duck about 2 kg (4½ lb)
1 tin (440 g, 15½ oz) litchis

For the basting syrup:
1 tbsp honey
1 tbsp vinegar
2 tsp cornflour

For the sauce:
2 tbsp dark soya sauce
110 ml (4 fl oz) stock or water

dark soya sauce for brushing

1. Pour hot water all over the duck. Pat dry with kitchen paper. Brush dark soya sauce all over the skin. Hang the duck up by the neck in a cool and airy place, with a basin below to catch any drops. Leave to dry for about 2 hours or longer. Mix together the honey, vinegar and cornflour and set aside.
2. Preheat the oven to about 230°C (450°F, gas 8). Seal the rear and neck openings with cotton or wooden cocktail sticks. Place the duck breast up on a rack in a roasting tin with ½ cup water. Roast for 30 minutes. Turn it over, and brush the back with some more soya sauce. Roast for a further 30 minutes.
3. Turn the duck over again and brush the breast all over with the basting mixture. Reduce the heat to 200°C (400°F, gas 6) and roast for 10 minutes, by which time the breast should have become a dark mahogany red. Turn over and brush the back with the basting mixture. Roast for a further 10 minutes or till cooked. Test with a fine skewer on the thickest part of the leg, and if the juice runs clear it is ready.
4. Take the duck out and leave to cool completely on a rack in a tray or hang up on a meat hook. This stops the steam from condensing on the duck and moistening it. Remove the thread or cocktail sticks and pour away the water collected inside the cavity. Bone and cut into neat, bite-size pieces, and arrange in a circle on a plate. Drain and pile the litchis in the centre.
5. Pour away all the fat in the roasting tin. Dilute the juice with the stock. Deglaze, and stir in 2 tbsp soya sauce. Bring to the boil and strain. Serve separately.

This duck looks attractively waxy and is dark mahogany red in colour (as often seen hung up in Chinese restaurant windows). A traditional Cantonese roast duck, it is often used as a basic ingredient for many other dishes: stir-fried with noodles, vermicelli or vegetables, as part of a cold starter or chopped and served plain with boiled rice or noodles. The combination with litchi is typically Cantonese; fruit is often served with

49

meat, producing a deliciously sweet and salty taste. Other fruits such as pineapple cubes, loquats (*pipa*) and fresh or tinned longans are suitable. The sauce is particularly useful if rice or noodles are served with the duck.

Clove-spiced crispy duck (Jiangsu)

1 duck, about 2 kg (4½ lb)

For the marinade:
2 tsp ground cloves
2 stalks spring onion (minced)
2 slices ginger (minced)
1 tbsp rice wine
2 tbsp dark soya sauce
2 tsp salt
1 tbsp granulated sugar
pepper to taste

Garnish:
450 g (1 lb) salad cabbage (finely shredded)
2 tomatoes (sliced)

For the dressing:
1 tbsp granulated sugar
1 tbsp vinegar
1 tbsp sesame oil
1 tsp salt

1. Pour hot water all over the duck to tighten the skin. Wipe dry with kitchen paper. Hang it up in a cool and airy place for 1 hour to dry.
2. Mix together the ingredients for the marinade. Rub the duck all over and inside the cavity with the marinade. Leave it on a rack over a tray for about 1 hour for the flavours to penetrate. Hang it up to dry again for about 1 hour.
3. Blend together the ingredients for the dressing. Toss the cabbage with the dressing, and set aside.
4. Preheat the oven to 230°C (450° F, gas 8). Place the duck, breast up, on a rack in a roasting tin with ½ cup water in it. Roast for 30 minutes. Turn over and roast for another 40 minutes. Turn it breast up and roast for a further 20 minutes, or till cooked. Cool completely and chop into bite-size pieces. Arrange them neatly on a large serving plate surrounded by the cabbage salad, and garnish with the tomato slices.

In the original recipe the duck is steamed after marinating and dried, then deep-fried till the skin is crisp.

Plum duck (Guangdong)

1 duck, about 1.6–1.8 kg (3½–4 lb)

Seasoning for the duck cavity:
2 cloves garlic
4 whole pickled plums (stoned and chopped)
60 g (2 oz) rock sugar or granulated sugar
2 tbsp salted soya beans (finely ground)
1 tbsp dark soya sauce
½ tsp salt

Seasoning for braising:
2 stalks spring onion (minced)
2 slices ginger
1 tbsp rice wine

dark soya sauce for brushing
1 tsp cornflour with a little water
2 tsp sesame oil
1 tbsp cooking oil

Garnish:
coriander leaves or parsley

1. Preheat the oven to 200°C (400°F, gas 6). Souse the duck all over with hot water. Drain and wipe dry with kitchen paper. Brush the duck all over the skin with dark soya sauce.
2. Place the duck on a rack in a roasting tin with a little water. Roast in the preheated oven for about 10–15 minutes on each side till it becomes a dark red. Take out, and drain away the fat. Leave to cool.
3. Set the wok on a medium heat, put in the cooking oil and stir-fry the garlic till fragrant. Stir in the rest of the seasoning for the cavity. When the sugar dissolves, remove the wok from the heat. Fill the duck cavity with the plum mixture.
4. Place the duck in a casserole or roasting dish. Sprinkle with the seasoning for braising. Pour in 400 ml (¾ pt) of water down the side, cover and cook in the oven at 200°C (400°F, gas 6) for about 45 minutes or till cooked.
5. Remove the duck and let it cool slightly. Pour the cooking liquor into a basin. Skim off all the fat. Strain through a sieve. Bring the

liquor to the boil, reduce slightly and thicken with the cornflour mixture. Remove from the heat, stir in the sesame oil, cover and keep warm.

6. Chop the duck and arrange on a serving dish. Ladle some sauce over the duck and serve the rest separately. Garnish before serving.

Roast duck in fermented bean curd (Guangdong)

1 duck, about 1.8 kg (4 lb)

For the fermented bean curd mixture:
2 squares red fermented bean curd
½ tsp salt
1 tbsp rice wine
pepper to taste

For the honey syrup:
1 tbsp honey
2 tbsp water

For the sauce:
60 g (2 fl oz) stock or water
1 tbsp dark soya sauce
½ tsp salt
1 tsp granulated sugar

1. Mash the fermented bean curd and mix together with the rest of the ingredients for the mixture. Blend the honey and water over a low heat, and leave to cool.
2. Souse the duck all over with hot water (not boiling) so that the skin tightens slightly. Wipe dry with kitchen paper. Rub the cavity of the duck with the fermented bean curd mixture. Seal the openings with thread or wooden cocktail sticks. Brush the skin all over with the honey syrup.
3. Leave the duck on a rack in a tray to dry in a cool and airy place for about 1 to 2 hours, which allows the skin to dry and crisp better during roasting and the marinade to be absorbed.
4. Preheat the oven to 230°C (450°F, gas 8). Place the duck on a rack in a roasting tin with a little water. Roast in the oven for 30 minutes on each side and another 20 minutes back on the first side. Take out and cool. Remove the thread or cocktail sticks. Pour out the juice and reserve. Bone the duck and slice into bite-size pieces. Arrange them on a plate.

5. Skim the fat off the reserved juice and mix the juice with the ingredients for the sauce. Bring to the boil and pour over the meat.

This rich and cheesy flavoured duck is equally excellent with boiled rice or steamed buns.

Teochiew crispy stuffed duck (Guangdong)

1 duck, about 1.8 kg (4 lb)

For the filling:
1 duck's gizzard
60 g (2 oz) lean pork
30 g (1 oz) cooked ham or smoked back bacon
4 caps winter mushrooms (soaked)
30 g (1 oz) dried shrimps (soaked)
60 g (2 oz) lotus seeds (soaked and boiled)
15 g (½ oz) dried brill (optional)
110 g (4 oz) glutinous rice

Seasoning for the filling:
2 stalks spring onion whites (chopped)
1 tsp salt
1 tsp granulated sugar
2 tsp sesame oil
pepper to taste

Garnish:
coriander leaves
dark soya sauce for brushing
1 tbsp cooking oil
1 tbsp cornflour with a little water

1. Bone the duck whole (*see page* 229), taking care to keep the skin intact.
2. Rinse the glutinous rice and soak for about 1 hour. Steam the rice on a medium heat in a steaming basket (or steamer) lined with a piece of muslin, for about 30 minutes or till cooked, when it becomes transparent.
3. Meanwhile, dice the gizzard, pork, ham and mushrooms into pea-size pieces. Deep-fry the dried brill (if used) till golden and pound into a powder.
4. Set the wok over a medium heat, put in 1 tbsp oil and stir-fry the spring onion whites till fragrant. Add the ingredients for the filling, except the glutinous rice. Stir-fry till fragrant, then add the rice, mix

well and stir in the rest of the seasoning. Mix well, take out and leave to cool.

5. Sew up the rear opening of the duck. Fill the cavity with the rice mixture from the neck opening. Sew up the neck opening.
6. Pour boiling water all over the duck, wipe dry and prick in several places with a fine skewer to prevent bursting when cooking. Steam over a high heat in a steaming basket or steamer for 1 hour, till the juices run clear when the leg is pricked.
7. Take out, and lightly press the duck to flatten it. Brush all over with the soya sauce and then the cornflour mixture.
8. Deep-fry the duck till golden and crisp. Drain well on kitchen paper. Allow it to cool. To serve, cut along the back, scoop out the stuffing and put it on a serving plate. Cut the duck into 4 strips and each strip into bite-size pieces. Arrange them neatly on another plate. Garnish with coriander leaves. Serve together.

If more convenient, the duck may be roasted standing on a rack in a roasting tin filled with ½ cup water. This rich and filling recipe comes from the Chouzhou (Teochiew) clan in Shantou (Swatow).

Goose

Goose in vinegar sauce (Zhejiang)

700 g (1½ lb) cooked goose meat
110 g (4 oz) bamboo shoots

For the sauce:
1 tbsp light soya sauce
2 tbsp white wine vinegar
1 tsp cornflour with a little water

For the seasoning:
1 stalk spring onion (chopped)
1 tbsp rice wine
2 tbsp vinegar
1 tbsp light soya sauce
1 tsp salt

Garnish:
2 stalks spring onion (shredded)
110 ml (4 fl oz) pork stock or water
2 tbsp lard or vegetable oil

1. Dice the goose meat into oblong slices about 4 cm (1½ in) long and 2.5 cm (1 in) wide. Roll-cut the bamboo shoots into wedges.
2. Mix together the ingredients for the sauce and set aside.
3. Set the wok on a high heat, and put in 1 tbsp of the lard. Stir-fry the spring onion till fragrant. Add the goose and bamboo shoots, and stir-fry briefly. Sprinkle in the rice wine, vinegar, soya sauce and salt. Mix well and pour in the stock. Bring to the boil, stir the sauce mixture and add to the wok. Stir well and when thickened add the rest of the lard, mix well and dish up. Garnish with the shredded spring onion.

Quail

Minced quails in lettuce leaves (Guangdong)

For the minced quails mixture:
8 quails, about 900 g (2 lb) in all
1 tbsp raw chicken fat or pork fat
2 egg yolks
2 tsp cornflour

170 g (6 oz) bamboo shoots or celery
30 g (1 oz) smoked back bacon
4 caps winter mushrooms (soaked)

For the seasoning:
1 clove garlic (minced)
1 slice ginger (minced)
2 tsp rice wine
2 stalks spring onion (chopped)

For the sauce:
2 tbsp oyster sauce
1 tbsp sesame oil
1 tsp granulated sugar
1 tbsp dark soya sauce
pepper to taste
2 tbsp stock or water
2 tsp cornflour with a little water

Garnish:
60 g (2 oz) rice sticks
3 tbsp groundnut or vegetable oil
24 leaves lettuce

1. Skin and bone the quails. Dice the chicken or pork fat. Chop the quail meat together with the fat till fine. Mix in the egg yolks and then the cornflour. Mix well and set aside.
2. Dice the bamboo shoots, mushrooms and bacon into rice-sized pieces. Rinse the lettuce thoroughly, shake dry and pile on two plates. Deep fry the rice sticks (without rinsing) till light and puffy. (This may be done well in advance and kept in an airtight container.) Drain well and spread out on a serving plate.
3. Mix together all the ingredients for the sauce and set aside.
4. Set the wok over a medium heat and dry-fry (without oil) the bamboo shoots till dry, then add 1 tbsp oil. Stir-fry till fragrant and remove from the wok. Reheat the wok and put in the rest of the oil. Stir-fry the garlic and ginger till fragrant. Put in the quail meat mixture and stir-fry to mix well. Add the bacon and mushrooms, and continue to stir-fry till the meat is fragrant and the grains are separated. Stir in the precooked bamboo shoots. Sprinkle with the wine and spring onion and mix well. Give the sauce mixture a stir and add to the wok. Continue to stir-fry till all ingredients are well coated with a glistening glaze. Dish up and pile into a mound on the rice sticks in a plate with about 2.5 cm (1 in) of the rice sticks showing all round.
5. To serve, take the minced quails and lettuce leaves to the table. To eat, spread a lettuce leaf on the plate. Take a spoonful of quail, wrap up and eat with the fingers.

This dish, called *caibao* in Mandarin, meaning 'vegetable parcels', has evolved from a less sophisticated, self-contained, convenience food in which cooked rice is mixed into a cooked meat mixture and eaten wrapped up in lettuce leaves. It used to be particularly popular in Beijing where *caibao* was eaten in the spring with lettuce leaves and in the autumn with Chinese 'celery' cabbage leaves, dipped in a 'tiger sauce' – a mixture of minced garlic and salted soya bean paste. *Caibao* was served during the Ming period (1368–1644) in the imperial palace in the spring. It appears from literary sources that it was also a popular convenience food among the common people. It must be said that this mode of eating existed amongst the Manchurians too. This probably explains its waning popularity since the foundation of the Republic in 1912; for it was associated with the overthrown Manchus, the final imperial house. However, the sophisticated version is now regaining popularity and the classic stuffing is pigeon with dried oysters. The round lettuces with soft leaves are preferred for this dish for the reason that they wrap better.

Stuffed quails (Sichuan)

4 quails

For the marinade:
1 tsp salt
1 tbsp rice wine
1 stalk spring onion (minced)
2 slices ginger (minced)
pepper to taste

For the filling:
110 g (4 oz) minced pork
30 g (1 oz) smoked back bacon
4 caps winter mushrooms (soaked)
60 g (2 oz) button mushrooms
4 peeled water chestnuts
2 tbsp garden peas
1 tsp salt
pepper to taste
2 tsp cornflour with a little water

Garnish:
coriander leaves or parsley
cucumber slices

For the dip:
Sichuan pepper salt

cornflour for dusting
generous 1 l (2 pt) cooking oil

1. Defrost the quails thoroughly if frozen. Rinse and wipe dry. Bone the quails whole (*see page* 229). Rub well inside and out with the marinade. Leave for about 30 minutes.
2. Dice the bacon, mushrooms and water chestnuts into pea-size pieces. Mix them with the rest of the ingredients for the filling.
3. Turn the boned quails inside out and dust them with some cornflour. Turn them right side out again, sew up the rear openings with cotton, and fill each bird with a quarter of the filling mixture from the neck opening. Then sew up the neck opening.
4. Steam the stuffed birds in a wok or steamer over a high heat for 40 minutes. Take out, drain and dust thoroughly with cornflour.
5. Deep-fry in hot oil till golden and crisp. Take out and drain well on kitchen paper. Cut each bird open from the back centre and spread

on a serving dish in pairs, cut side down. Garnish with coriander leaves and cucumber slices. Serve with Sichuan pepper salt as a dip.

The stuffing enhances the taste of the quails considerably. These attractive and delicious quails may be eaten in the western manner with a salad or vegetables and potatoes.

FISH

Five Willows fish (Guangdong)

700 g (1½ lb) sea bass or pomfret

Seasoning for poaching the fish:
1 tsp salt
2 tsp lard or cooking oil
1 stalk spring onion (cut into 2.5 cm, 1 in, lengths)
1 slice ginger (bruised)

For the sauce:
2 slices ginger (shredded)
1 tbsp bamboo shoots (shredded)
1 tbsp soaked winter mushrooms (shredded)
1 tbsp red chilli pepper (shredded)
140 ml (5 fl oz) sweet and sour sauce
1 tsp cornflour with a little water

Garnish:
2 stalks spring onion (shredded)

3 tbsp groundnut oil
2 tsp sesame oil
pepper

1. For the sweet and sour sauce, *see page* 240. Scale, gut and rinse the fish thoroughly and leave whole.
2. Put a generous 1 l (2 pt) of water with the seasoning, for poaching in a wok, and bring to the boil. Put in the fish, lower the heat, cover and cook for about 10 minutes or till cooked, when the eyes turn opaque and protude. Drain and transfer to a serving dish. Sprinkle pepper on the fish and scatter over the spring onion garnish.

3. Set the wok over a high heat, put in 2 tbsp groundnut oil and when smoking hot pour over the fish. Return the wok to a medium heat and stir in the shredded vegetables, ginger and the sauce. Thicken with the cornflour mixture. Take off the heat and stir in the sesame oil and the rest of the groundnut oil. Mix well and pour over the fish. Serve immediately.

In China the favourite fish for this dish is tench, but that is seldom on sale in Britain. 'Five Willows' refers to the five kinds of shredded vegetables in the ingredients. In Guangdong grocers specializing in sauces and preserved foods supply a 'Five Willows' pickle cut into juliennes the width of willow leaves. Hence, 'willow' is a Chinese culinary term meaning finely shredded or cut into juliennes.

Fish slices in tomato sauce (Hunan)

230 g (8 oz) white fish meat (monkfish, halibut or turbot)

For the marinade:
½ tsp salt
1 tbsp light soya sauce
2 tsp rice wine
1 tbsp ginger juice
pepper to taste

For the sauce:
1 stalk spring onion (chopped)
4 tbsp tomato ketchup
1 tsp salt
80 ml (3 fl oz) chicken or pork stock or water
1 tsp cornflour with a little water

450 ml (1 pt) cooking oil
cornflour for coating

1. Cut the skinned and filleted fish into slices about 0.6 (¼ in) thick. Mix the marinade, coat the fish in it, then in cornflour.
2. Mix together the ingredients for the sauce, except the spring onion and the ketchup.
3. Deep-fry the fish slices briefly in hot oil to par-cook and crisp the outside. Drain well on kitchen paper.
4. Remove all but 2 tsp of the oil from the wok, put it back over a medium heat and stir-fry the spring onion till fragrant. Add the tomato ketchup and the par-cooked fish. Stir-fry briefly to mix well.

Give the sauce mixture a stir and add to the wok. When thickened and heated through dish up.

The white fish in a red sauce makes a very attractive dish, simple yet delicious, which goes equally well with rice or French fried potatoes and salad. Or serve with prawn crackers, *see page 236*.

Fried pomfret in spicy sauce (Guangdong)

1 pomfret, about 550 g (1¼ lb)

For the sauce:
4 tbsp strong stock or water
2 tbsp Worcester sauce
½ tsp salt
2 tsp granulated sugar
1 tbsp dark soya sauce
1 tbsp light soya sauce
1 tsp sesame oil
pepper to taste
1 tsp cornflour with a little water

For the seasoning:
1 clove garlic (minced)
1 stalk spring onion (chopped)
1 slice ginger (minced)
1 tbsp rice wine

For the marinade:
1 tbsp light soya sauce
1 tbsp ginger wine

140 ml (5 fl oz) cooking oil

1. Gut, rinse and dry the pomfret thoroughly. Make 4 slashes across the back, about 2.5 cm (1 in) apart, on both sides. Pour the marinade over, making sure the cuts are soaked. Leave for about 30 minutes.
2. Mix together all the ingredients for the sauce and set aside.
3. Set the wok on a medium heat. Add in 2 tbsp oil and when hot drain and dry the pomfret. Pan-fry the fish till golden on one side, dribbling in the oil 1 tbsp at a time all round. Turn it over and cook the other side. Finally pour in the rest of the oil and fry till crisp. Take out and drain well on kitchen paper.
4. Pour away all the oil. Reheat the wok without rinsing. Stir-fry the

garlic, onion and ginger till fragrant. Tip in the wine and then the sauce mixture. Stir in 1 tsp oil and pour over the fish.

This simple dish is crusty, red and golden and its sauce piquant and delicious.

Pan-fried fish in fermented glutinous rice (Jiangsu)

450–550 g (1–1¼ lb) white fish in a single large cutlet

For the marinade:
1 tbsp rice wine
2 tsp salt
2 tbsp fermented glutinous rice

For the sauce:
1 tbsp rice wine
1 slice ginger (minced)
2 tbsp bamboo shoots (shredded)
4 caps winter mushrooms (soaked and shredded)
1 tbsp light soya sauce
1 tsp granulated sugar
110 ml (4 fl oz) water
1 tsp cornflour with a little water

3 tbsp lard or cooking oil
1 stalk spring onion (chopped)

1. Rub the fish cutlet all over with the marinade. Cover, and marinate for 2 hours. Rinse off the marinade. Pat dry with kitchen paper.
2. Set the wok over a high heat, put in 2 tbsp of the lard. Reduce the heat and pan-fry the fish till both sides are golden. Sprinkle with the rice wine and ginger, cover and cook for ½ minute. Add the vegetables and then the rest of the ingredients for the sauce, except the cornflour mixture. Cover, and cook for about 8 minutes. Take out the fish and put in a warmed dish. Raise the heat and reduce the liquid slightly, thicken with the cornflour mixture and pour over the fish.
3. Rinse the wok, and set over a medium heat. Put in 1 tbsp lard and stir-fry the spring onion till fragrant. Pour over the fish.

This is a local flavour from Wuxi in Jiangsu province.

Ruyi fish rolls (Zhejiang)

For the egg skins:
2 eggs plus 2 extra yolks
½ tsp salt

For the fish paste:
170 g (6 oz) raw white fish (skinned and boned)
60 g (2 oz) boiled pork fat
1 tsp salt
40 ml (1½ fl oz) water
2 tsp rice wine
1 egg white (lightly beaten)
1 tbsp cornflour with a little water

For the sauce:
80 ml (3 fl oz) chicken stock
1 tsp salt
1 tsp cornflour with a little water
2 tsp rendered chicken fat

2 stalks spring onion (minced)
30 g (1 oz) cooked ham (minced)

cooking oil

Garnish:
coriander leaves or parsley

1. Mince the fish and pork fat separately and finely. Mix them together. Add the salt and water. Stir in one direction till the mixture is sticky. Mix in the rice wine and the lightly beaten egg white in the same direction until they are completely absorbed into the fish paste. Finally, stir in the cornflour mixture, in the same direction.
2. Beat the eggs and yolks with the salt. Set an omelette pan on a low heat and grease it lightly. When heated, pour in half the egg mixture. Swirl the pan round to make an egg skin about 20 to 22 cm (8 to 9 in) across. When the egg is firm turn it on to a plate. Make another one in the same way.
3. When cooled, trim off the edges to make a square. Spread half the fish paste to cover the egg skin completely. Put half the spring onion on one edge of the square in a row; and half the minced ham on the opposite side.
4. Roll both the spring onion end and the ham end towards the middle

of the square so that both meet in the centre. Place it rolled-side-down on a plate. Make another one in the same way. Steam them in a wok or steamer for 15 minutes over a medium heat. Take out, drain off any liquid and cool.

5. Cut each roll into bite-size slices and arrange them cut side up on a serving plate. Steam again for 2 minutes over a high heat to heat through. Drain off any liquid collected in the plate.
6. Mix together all the ingredients for the sauce, bring to the boil and when thickened pour over the rolls. Garnish with the coriander leaves round the edges.

These rolls look like double Swiss rolls, one with a pink, the other with a green centre, and are very attractive as well as being tasty and light. This kind of roll is known as *ruyijuan* or 'lucky' roll. (*See page 204 for illustrations.*)

Steamed fish en papillote

550 g (1¼ lb) skinned and boned white fish (monkfish, haddock or cod)
40 tender pods mangetout peas
60 g (2 oz) bamboo shoots
60 g (2 oz) peeled carrots

For the seasoning:
1 tsp salt
1 tbsp rice wine
pepper to taste
2 tbsp light soya sauce
2 tsp cornflour with a little water

Garnish:
coriander leaves or parsley

10 squares greaseproof paper, 20 × 20 cm (8 × 8 in)
cooking oil for greasing

1. Slice the fish into 10 pieces, mix in the seasoning and leave to marinate for about 20 minutes.
2. Rinse and top-and-tail the peas. Slice the bamboo shoots and carrots into juliennes and blanch them in boiling water, then refresh in cold water.
3. Lay out a greaseproof square on a flat surface. Oil it all over. Lay a piece of the marinated fish in the centre. Lay one tenth of the carrot and bamboo shoots on it with 2 pods of mangetout. Wrap up

63

envelope-wise (*see illustrations*). Make nine more in the same way.

4. Place the parcels in one layer in a preheated steamer or steaming basket and cook over a high heat for about 10 to 12 minutes.

5. Remove the steamer from the heat and transfer the parcels with a wok spatula or a pair of long chopsticks to a serving plate. Garnish round the edge with coriander or parsley. To eat, open the parcel and eat straight from the paper.

(a)   *(b)*   *(c)*

Sweet and sour pomfret (Zhejiang)

1 pomfret, about 700 g (1½ lb)

For the sauce:
1 tbsp dark soya sauce
2 tbsp sugar
4 tbsp vinegar
2 stalks spring onion (chopped)
1 tsp cornflour with a little water
110 ml (4 fl oz) water

1 tbsp rapeseed oil or other cooking oil
2 tbsp cooked garden peas
2 tsp melted lard

1 tbsp dark soya sauce for marinade

1. Gut and thoroughly rinse the pomfret. Make 2 slashes on each side, as far as the bones. Rub the fish with the soya sauce and let it soak for 10 minutes.

2. Pat dry with absorbent kitchen paper. Set a thick, flat-bottomed frying pan on a medium heat till hot. Put in the oil, and then the fish. Reduce the heat to low if it gets too fierce, and cook till both sides are golden-red. Take out, drain well on kitchen paper and put on a warmed serving plate.

3. Mix together all the ingredients for the sauce and bring to the boil. Stir in the peas and lard and pour over the fish.

If preferred, the fish may be deep-fried.

SEAFOOD

Guoba prawns in tomato sauce (Zhejiang)

280 g (10 oz) fresh uncooked prawns (weight without shells)
110 g (4 oz) guoba (dried cooked rice)

For the sauce:
4 tbsp tomato ketchup
2 tsp rice wine
1 tbsp light soya sauce
½ tsp salt
280 ml (½ pt) stock or water
3 tsp cornflour with a little water

2 tbsp cooking oil
2 stalks spring onion (chopped)

1. Devein the shelled prawns by making a slit along the back with a sharp knife. Rub them with some salt, rinse well and dry on kitchen paper. This crisps them when cooked.
2. Deep-fry the *guoba* till well puffed up and a pale golden colour. Drain well and put in a large serving bowl.
3. Mix together all the ingredients for the sauce, except the cornflour mixture.
4. Set the wok on a high heat and when very hot, put in the oil and stir-fry the spring onion till fragrant. Add the prawns and stir-fry till they curl up into round balls and turn pink. Pour in the sauce mixture, and when it comes back to the boil stir in the cornflour mixture. When thickened, dish up immediately. There should be a lot of sauce. Take to the table immediately with the *guoba* in a separate bowl.
5. Pour the prawns with the sauce onto the *guoba* at the table, and wait for a crackling or hissing noise.

This dish is cooked very fast and must be served immediately, or the crackling noise would be lost. The *guoba* may be deep-fried well in advance and kept in an airtight container till required. It keeps for several weeks. Just before cooking the prawns, crisp the *guoba* in a hot oven for 2 minutes. The crisp and hot *guoba* will make a better crackling noise at table. This is a traditional *guoba* dish from the Yangzi delta, and the crackling noise is appreciated as much as the taste.

Mussels in spring onion sauce

850 g (1½ lb) fresh mussels
1 tbsp rice wine

For the sauce:
2 stalks spring onion (chopped)
1 slice ginger (minced)
1 tbsp rice wine
pepper to taste
1 tsp cornflour with a little water

1 tbsp cooking oil

1. Cover the mussels with water and feed them overnight with rolled oats or flour in a cool dark place. This will fatten and clean them at the same time. Before cooking, scrub each one thoroughly with a stiff brush and rinse well. Pull off any beard and rinse well.
2. Set the wok on a high heat and when hot put in the prepared mussels with 1 tbsp rice wine. Cover and cook for about 2 minutes. When they are open remove the wok from the heat. Take out the mussels and reserve the cooking liquor. Leave the mussels in their half shells and discard the other halves. Arrange them in a serving plate in one layer.
3. Strain the reserved liquor through muslin over a fine sieve. Rinse the wok and set over a medium heat. When hot, put in the oil and stir-fry the ginger and spring onion till fragrant. Add the wine, pepper and the reserved liquor. Thicken with the cornflour mixture and pour over the mussels.

This simple dish is very attractive visually, with the coral-coloured meat cradled in black shells speckled with the emerald green of the spring onions. Although fresh mussels are seldom eaten in mainland China, in Hong Kong and among the overseas Chinese they have been added to the cuisine. Hong Kong nowadays imports a great deal of seafood from Australia, including mussels.

Oysters

Oysters are a speciality in Fujian province. Both Fujian and the island of Formosa (Taiwan) produce oysters but those from Ming Jiang, Jinmen (Quemoy island) and the Xiamen (Amoy) area are deemed to be the best as they are plump and tender. Xiamen is famed for her oyster pancakes or *ojien*.

Oysters do not like the open sea because the water is too salty, nor fresh water which is saltless, so their natural habitat is where the rivers and the sea meet along the coastlines. A land of rivers, China has many suitable breeding grounds for the oysters, in particular the estuaries of Jiulong Jiang and Min Jiang in Fujian, and the Zhujiang (Pearl River) in Guangdong. Every summer, the fry (young oysters) are washed on to the shores, where they cling to the rocks and begin to multiply. The Chinese have the tradition of encouraging growth by cultivating oysters on bamboo stands which are about knee high, low enough to be immersed by the tide.

The oyster harvest season is in the autumn. Apart from being eaten fresh, oysters are made into a sauce for seasoning, or sun-dried for use at other times of the year, and for consumption by people living inland or overseas. In Fujian, in the oyster season, the fisherwomen sell fresh oysters in bamboo baskets suspended from poles. The oysters are opened on purchase and are thus very fresh. Since oysters are a common food, there are many simple ways of enjoying them.

Larded oysters: heat plenty of lard till very hot and drop in freshly shelled oysters. Mix well and eat with plain hot rice. In this method the oysters are virtually raw.

Roasted oysters: oysters in their shells are roasted in a little charcoal stove till they are about to open. They are then prised open and eaten with a sauce made from minced ginger, spring onion, soya sauce and vinegar. This is absolutely delicious.

Oyster fritters: fill a ladle with some rice batter (made with rice flour and water) and drop in a few shelled oysters; cover them with some more batter. Dip the ladle into hot oil. When the batter is cooked it comes away from the ladle. The fritter is left to cook in the oil till golden and then eaten on the spot. This is a common snack sold by hawkers in the street.

Pickled oysters: freshly shelled oysters are marinated in rice wine, minced ginger, spring onion, soya sauce, pepper and salt for about 2 to 3 hours and served as an appetizer.

Stir-fried oysters with eggs: stir-fry the shelled oysters with ginger and spring onion till just cooked, then add the beaten eggs and stir-fry till the eggs are cooked. This is a snack to go with drinks.

Doufu and oyster soup: *doufu* and shelled oysters are cooked with ginger and leeks in a stock and thickened with a starch.

Pan-fried oysters – ojien (Fujian)

For the oyster mixture:
350 g (12 oz) shelled oysters
110 g (4 oz) minced pork
60 g (2 oz) Chinese chives or leeks or spring onions (chopped)
2 tsp ginger (minced)
1 tsp salt
140 g (5 oz) potato flour
280 ml (½ pt) cold water
pepper to taste

For the egg mixture:
2 eggs (duck or chicken)
110 g (4 oz) dressed crab meat (white only)

2 tbsp cooking oil
1 tbsp rice wine
1 tbsp coriander leaves (chopped)
pepper

Dip:
minced garlic, vinegar and chilli sauce (to taste)

1. Mix together all the ingredients for the oyster mixture and set aside.
2. Beat the eggs lightly until smooth and mix in the crab meat.
3. Set a thick flat-bottomed frying pan over a medium heat and when smoking hot, put in 1 tbsp oil. Pour in half the oyster mixture and spread into a round. Cook each side for about 3 minutes, and when the moisture has evaporated and the surface appears dry, pour in half the egg mixture and cook for another 2 minutes. Sprinkle with the rice wine. Fold over into a semi-circle and cook for another 2 minutes. Sprinkle with coriander leaves and pepper, and dish up. Cook another one in the same way. Serve with the dip.

This delicious omelette is a famous traditional oyster dish from Xiamen (Amoy) in Fujian. It makes an excellent snack with drinks, or goes well with a salad.

Phoenix Tail prawns (Jiangsu)

450 g (1 lb) fresh uncooked prawns
60 g (2 oz) garden peas

For the coating:
1 egg white (lightly beaten)
½ tsp salt
2 tsp cornflour

For the seasoning:
1 stalk spring onion white (chopped)
2 tsp rice wine
½ tsp salt
4 tbsp chicken stock or water
1 tsp cornflour with a little water

140 ml (5 fl oz) rendered duck fat or cooking oil

1. Blanch the peas and refresh in cold water.
2. Shell the prawns and remove the heads, but leave the tails on. Devein by slitting the back with a sharp knife and removing the black vein. Rub them with some salt and rinse well. Dry on kitchen paper.
3. Mix together the ingredients for the coating and add the prawns. Mix well.
4. Set the wok on a high heat, and put in most of the duck fat or oil (reserve 2 tsp). When hot add the prawns, stirring all the time. When the prawns turn opaque and the tails red they are cooked. Take out and drain well.
5. Pour away the fat and reheat the wok over a high heat. Add in the reserved 2 tsp duck fat, stir-fry the spring onion white and peas briefly, pour in the chicken stock and the rest of the seasoning and finally the cornflour mixture. When the sauce thickens, stir in the prawns, mix well and dish up immediately.

This is a traditional Nanjing dish. The duck fat is used for its flavour. The cooking is fast, as overcooking would toughen the prawns. When cooked, the prawns curl up and the tails stand up, looking like a bird – hence 'phoenix tail'.

Prawn parcels (Henan)

For the prawn mixture:
280 g (10 oz) uncooked prawn meat
30 g (1 oz) boiled pork fat
30 g (1 oz) bamboo shoots
30 g (1 oz) cooked ham
30 g (1 oz) coriander leaves

1 egg white (lightly beaten)
1 tsp salt
2 tsp rice wine
1 tsp granulated sugar
2 tsp cornflour

For the wrappers:
12 circles rice paper

850 ml (1½ pt) cooking oil

1. Dice the bamboo shoots and cooked ham into rice-size pieces. Chop the coriander leaves. Chop the prawns and pork fat finely. Mix together all the ingredients for the prawn mixture. Divide into 12 equal portions.
2. Lay a circle of the rice paper on a flat surface. Put a portion of the prawn mixture in the centre in a row about 8 cm (3 in) long. Fold the rice paper into a semicircle. Wrap up envelope-wise, forming a parcel about 10 cm (4 in) long and 5 cm (2 in) wide. Make another 11 in the same way.
3. Deep-fry in two batches in hot oil over a medium heat for about 1½ minutes, when the parcels will float to the top of the oil and the prawns turn pink. Take out with a brass wire mesh strainer and drain well on kitchen paper. Serve immediately.

(For illustration on wrapping up envelope-wise *see* 'Steamed fish en papillote' *page* 63.)

Spicy stuffed baby squid (Guangdong)

9–10 baby squid (each about 50 g, 2 oz, cleaned weight including head)

For the filling:
170 g (6 oz) white fish (skinned and boned)
3 oz raw prawn meat
1 tsp salt
½ tsp granulated sugar
2 tsp rice wine
1 tbsp spring onion and ginger juice
pepper to taste
2 tsp cornflour with a little water

For the sauce:
1 stalk spring onion (chopped)
1 slice ginger (minced)

1 tbsp salted black beans
1 red chilli pepper (chopped into 1 cm, ½ in rounds)
2 tsp rice wine
110 ml (4 fl oz) stock or water
1 tsp cornflour with a little water

Garnish:
coriander leaves or parsley

1 tbsp cooking oil

1. Clean the squid. Pull the head out of the body sac. Reserve the head. Pull out and discard the transparent jelly-like fin in the sac. Empty the sac completely and rinse thoroughly. Pull off the membrane covering the body and discard. Rinse and drain well.
2. Mince the fish and prawns finely. Mix in the rest of the ingredients for the filling, except the cornflour mixture, and stir in one direction till sticky. Blend in the cornflour mixture till absorbed. Divide into 9 or 10 equal portions.
3. Fill each cleaned baby squid with a portion of the fish mixture, to about three-quarters full only. Replace the head and secure it with a wooden cocktail stick. Fill the rest in the same manner. Prick each stuffed squid in several places to prevent bursting.
4. Put them in a sandwich cake tin or on a plate, and steam in a wok over a high heat for about 8 minutes, or till cooked, when they shrink slightly and feel firm to the touch. Take out immediately. Transfer to a serving dish, and arrange neatly. Carefully remove the cocktail sticks.
5. Rinse the salted black beans. Set the wok over a medium heat, and when hot put in the oil. Stir-fry the spring onion, ginger and salted black beans till fragrant. Add the chilli rounds and rice wine, stir-fry briefly and pour in the stock. Thicken with the cornflour mixture and pour over the squid. Garnish with coriander leaves.

Stir-fried dried squid (Fujian)

2 dried squids, about 170 g (6 oz) dry weight (soaked)
80 g (3 oz) bamboo shoots
2 tomatoes
4 stalks spring onion (cut into 2.5 cm, 1 in lengths)

For the sauce:
2 tsp granulated sugar
1 tbsp light soya sauce

2 tsp vinegar
4 tbsp stock or water
1 tsp cornflour with a little water

1 clove garlic (minced)
2 tbsp cooking oil
2 tsp sesame oil

1. Score the soaked squid criss-cross on the underside and cut into 5 ×
   2.5 cm (2 × 1 in) oblongs. (*See page* 228 *for soaking.*) Slice the
   bamboo shoots into bite-size pieces. Skin and deseed the tomatoes,
   and cut into slices.
2. Mix together the ingredients for the sauce.
3. Set the wok on a high heat and when hot, put in the cooking oil.
   Stir-fry the garlic till fragrant, then add the squid and bamboo
   shoots. Stir-fry for a minute, and add the spring onion and tomato
   slices. Mix well and stir in the sauce mixture. As soon as the sauce
   thickens and the squid curl up, take off the heat and dish up.
   Sprinkle with the sesame oil and serve.

This dish is very quickly cooked: all ingredients should be to hand, as
over-cooking would toughen the squid. If liked, tomato ketchup may be
added.

Stir-fried inkfish with shredded pork (Shanghai)

230 g (8 oz) cleaned inkfish
110 g (4 oz) lean pork (shredded)
60 g (2 oz) bamboo shoots (shredded)

For the seasoning:
2 tsp rice wine
1 tbsp light soya sauce
½ tsp salt
1 tsp granulated sugar

80 ml (3 fl oz) stock or water
1 tsp cornflour with a little water
2 tsp sesame oil

Garnish:
1 stalk spring onion (chopped)

2 tbsp lard or vegetable oil

1. Make criss-cross scores on the underside of the inkfish (*see page* 228) and cut across into matchstick shreds.
2. Set the wok on a high heat, and when hot put in the lard. Stir-fry the shredded inkfish briefly and add the pork. Stir-fry till the pork is white. Take out and drain in a colander.
3. Return the wok to a high heat without rinsing. Put in the pork and inkfish, together with the bamboo shoots. Stir-fry briefly, then add in the seasoning and stock. Thicken with the cornflour mixture. Stir in the sesame oil. Dish up and sprinkle with the chopped spring onion.

This tasty dish looks slightly pink; the fish is crisp and the pork tender. The cooking is very fast as overcooking would toughen the inkfish.

DOUFU – BEAN CURD

The soya bean has been thoroughly exploited as a food by the Chinese, especially in the form of soya bean curd or *doufu*. In the West the commonest known type of *doufu* is the soft, tender cream-coloured one, sold in square blocks of about 450 g (1 lb) in weight and kept in cold water. *Doufu* itself is almost tasteless. This bland, neutral quality of course makes *doufu* an ideal material for combining with other ingredients with a stronger taste. Thus *doufu* is a versatile ingredient, both as a protein food in its own right – and as an extender for others such as meat. Little wonder that during the Ming dynasty (1368–1644) *doufu* was dubbed 'young lamb' – a reference to its nutritious quality. It may be cooked or blended with meat, fish, seafood, eggs or vegetables; each combination is a new dish, a new taste which is never dull.

In China different provinces have each developed their own *doufu* speciality. Smelly *doufu*, or *choudoufu* originated by accident in Beijing in 1669, during the Qing dynasty. It is said that a vendor had a glut and rescued the fermented *doufu* with salt and spices and it became an instant success. Nowadays, *choudoufu* is made by steeping *doufu* for about 1 to 5 hours in a fermenting liquor prepared from salted black soya beans, winter mushrooms, bamboo shoots, rice wine and coarse salt boiled in water and left to ferment for about 15 days. After steeping, the smelly *doufu* is deep-fried in tea oil until it becomes crisp on the outside. A hole is then made in each piece and filled with a mixture of chilli powder, soya sauce and sesame oil. The resulting smelly *doufu* has the mouldy, green colour of old copper. It is tender inside and crusty on the outside, rather like the tropical fruit, durian, which to the uninitiated is merely smelly but in fact tastes delicious. The above smelly *doufu* is now a speciality of Hunan. Other provinces such as Jiangxi, Jiangsu and Hebei also have their special recipes for *choudoufu*, with differences in preparation and cooking. *Choudoufu*, like *doufu*, is a versatile food: it may be eaten as an accompaniment to tea or wine, as a vegetable with porridge or rice, or on its own as a snack.

Another unusual bean curd is frozen *doufu*, or *dongdoufu*, a favourite in northern China, where the bean curd is left out overnight in the severe cold so that it freezes and becomes spongy, rather like the flesh of the angled luffa vegetable. A speciality of Hubei, *dongdoufu* is a famous dish served to visitors at the mountain resort of Wudang Shan (Wudang mountain). It is said to have been invented by a Daoist monk, when he ran out of food, to feed the visitors to his monastery. After the *doufu* was frozen in the cold night, he tore it into shreds to extend the food. In the event, rather like the biblical loaf, there was an endless supply of *dongdoufu* for everyone. In China, in areas where there is no refrigeration, *dongdoufu* is made only in the winter months, then it is wind-dried and stored for future use. With a refrigerator or freezer it is easy to freeze *doufu* overnight. On freezing the *doufu* turns porous and spongy and reverts to its beige soya colour. It should be thawed, torn into shreds and then braised or stir-fried with meat or other ingredients.

Anhui province is noted for its 'hairy' *doufu* or *maodoufu*. As the name implies, it is covered with 2.5 cm (1 in) long, fine, white, furry hair, which is really a white mould. To cook *maodoufu*, slice it and pan-fry in oil until golden. As soon as the skin begins to wrinkle it is seasoned and braised briefly. It is usually served with soya sauce mixed with chilli sauce.

Also from Anhui is 'mildewed' *doufu* or *meidoufu*. The bean curd is cut into eight squares, spread out in a dish and covered. It is left in the hot sun for a day and then removed to the kitchen or a warm place to preserve the heat. After two to three days a fragrant or mildew smell (a matter of taste) begins to appear. Sometimes it may need a couple more days before it is ready. This *meidoufu* is pan-fried till crisp and golden, and with its fragrant (or mildew) aroma it is scrumptious. The less gastronomically adventurous may wish to prevent bean curd from getting smelly, mouldy or hairy. To do this, first dissolve 30 g (1 oz) salt in 550 ml (1 pt) of boiling water, enough to cover 450 g (1 lb) *doufu*. When completely cold, immerse the *doufu* in the brine. Provided that it is covered and left in a refrigerator, it should keep for 3 to 4 days without spoiling. If a longer storage time is needed, double the amount of salt. This is sufficient to preserve the *doufu* for about 2 weeks in a refrigerator. Rinse well to remove excess salt before cooking, and go easy on salting the dish.

Agate doufu

For the doufu mixture:
230 g (8 oz) doufu
110 g (4 oz) shelled uncooked prawns
60 g (2 oz) boiled pork fat
1 egg white (lightly beaten)
2 tsp rice wine
1 tsp salt
1 tbsp cornflour

For the egg white coating:
2 egg whites (lightly beaten)
2 tsp cornflour with a little water

2 raw salted egg yolks
850 ml (1½ pt) vegetable oil
1 tsp Sichuan pepper salt

Garnish:
sweet and sour carrot salad

1. For the salad *see page* 27, and for salted egg yolks *see page* 84. Wrap the *doufu* in a piece of muslin and squeeze gently into a lump, removing excess water at the same time.
2. Mince the prawns and the pork fat separately and finely. Add them to the *doufu* paste together with the egg white, rice wine and salt. Mix well and stir in the cornflour.
3. Grease a dish (or a sandwich cake tin) and spread the *doufu* mixture in it. Level the top. Use your fingers to pinch the raw salted egg yolk into pea-size pieces, and press them lightly on to the top of the *doufu*, so that you have an 'agate' decorated *doufu*.
4. Steam in a wok over a medium heat for about 10 minutes, until it is cooked and feels firm to the touch. Leave it to cool completely, then cut into 3 pieces. Up to this stage it may be prepared in advance and kept wrapped up in the refrigerator for a couple of days.
5. Mix the egg whites and cornflour into a batter.
6. Cut the 'agate *doufu*' into pieces the size of a fish finger. Dip them in the egg batter and deep-fry till golden. Drain well on kitchen paper. Arrange them neatly on one end of an oval plate. Pile the salad on the other end. Sprinkle the 'agate *doufu*' with the Sichuan pepper salt and serve.

The term 'agate' refers to the bright orange colour of the salted egg yolks. This is the Ritz of fish fingers. The skin is crisp and the inside creamy and extremely tasty.

Deep-fried doufu balls (Hunan)

For the doufu mixture:
230 g (8 oz) doufu
30 g (1 oz) mung bean vermicelli (dry weight)
60 g (2 oz) flour
30 g (1 oz) cornflour
1 egg (lightly beaten)
1 stalk spring onion (chopped)
1 tsp salt
pepper to taste

For the sauce:
1 tsp salt
2 tsp light soya sauce
pepper to taste
1 stalk spring onion (chopped)
60 ml (2 fl oz) stock or water
1 tsp cornflour with a little water

850 ml (1½ pt) cooking oil

1. Soak the vermicelli in boiling water for 5 minutes. Drain and chop them finely. Set aside.
2. Mash the *doufu* with a potato masher. Mix in the chopped vermicelli and the rest of the ingredients for the *doufu* mixture into a firm dough.
3. Heat the oil on a medium heat. Use two dessert spoons to scoop out walnut-size balls of the mixture. As each one is made, drop it into the hot oil. Deep-fry till they are golden. Take out with a brass wire mesh strainer, drain on kitchen paper and place on a serving plate. This amount makes 24 balls.
4. Mix together the ingredients for the sauce and bring to the boil. When thickened, pour over the *doufu* balls.

The vermicelli give the *doufu* balls body. If preferred, tomato ketchup, sweet and sour sauce or even oyster sauce may be added to vary the dish. These scrumptious, crusty *doufu* balls may be eaten hot or cold with a salad and they are equally attractive on the buffet table. If preferred, in step 3, the balls may be made in the 'tiger's mouth' method, *see* 'Deep-fried vegetable and *doufu* balls', *page 77*.

Deep-fried vegetable and doufu balls (Sichuan)

For the doufu mixture:
230 g (8 oz) doufu
60 g (2 oz) carrots (finely grated)
60 g (2 oz) potatoes (finely grated)
1 small egg
30 g (1 oz) cornflour
60 g (2 oz) flour

For the seasoning:
2 tsp light soya sauce
1 tsp salt
2 tsp rice wine
½ tsp Sichuan peppercorns (ground)
1 tbsp sesame oil

850 ml (1½ pt) cooking oil

1. Use a potato masher to turn the *doufu* into a paste. Add the rest of the ingredients for the *doufu* mixture, together with the seasoning. Mix well and set aside.
2. Heat the oil. Take a handful of the *doufu* mixture in your left hand and squeeze till a ball appears between your left thumb and index finger (called the 'tiger's mouth' in the Chinese culinary term). Scoop the ball out with a spoon and drop into the hot oil at once. Cook till golden. Take out with a brass wire mesh strainer and drain well on kitchen paper. Make the rest in the same way.

These *doufu* balls may be served with a Chinese or Western salad. They are moist and crispy at the same time, and quite delicious.

Doufu-stuffed green peppers

8 small green peppers

For the filling:
110 g (4 oz) doufu
110 g (4 oz) skinned chicken breast meat
30 g (1 oz) boiled pork fat
2 egg whites
1 tsp salt
1 tsp granulated sugar

pepper to taste
2 tsp cornflour with a little water

For the sauce:
110 ml (4 fl oz) stock or water
1 tbsp light soya sauce
1 tsp cornflour with a little water

Garnish:
30 g (1 oz) cooked ham (minced)

2 tbsp cooking oil
cornflour for dusting

1. Mash the *doufu* into a paste. Mince the chicken meat and the pork fat separately and finely. Add them to the *doufu* together with the egg white, salt, sugar and pepper. Mix in one direction till the mixture becomes sticky (this may be done in a food processor). Add the cornflour mixture.
2. Rinse and cut the peppers into halves lengthwise. Deseed and remove any pulpy parts. Dust the inside with the cornflour. Fill each with the *doufu* mixture.
3. Set the wok over a medium heat, put in the oil and when hot, pan-fry the stuffed peppers, filled side down, till the filling turns a pale golden colour. Take them out with a perforated spoon or wok spatula, and arrange on a serving plate.
4. Pour the stock and soya sauce into the wok, adjust the seasoning and thicken with the cornflour mixture. Pour over the peppers and serve.

The number of green peppers used depends very much on their size. Small, tender ones are best for this purpose.

Huaiyang doufu in oyster sauce (Jiangsu)

450 g (1 lb) doufu

For the seasoning:
1 stalk spring onion (chopped)
1 slice ginger (minced)
1 tbsp oyster sauce
110 ml (4 fl oz) chicken stock or water
1 tsp salt
1 tsp sugar
pepper to taste

1 tsp cornflour with a little water to mix

2 tbsp lard or vegetable oil

1. Cut the *doufu* into 4 squares and each square into 3 oblongs. Place them, a few at a time, in a brass wire mesh strainer and dip them in boiling water for about ½ minute. Take out and drain in a colander.
2. Set a wok over a high heat, put in 1½ tbsp lard, reduce the heat and stir-fry the spring onion and ginger till fragrant. Add the oyster sauce, then the stock, salt, sugar and pepper. Bring to the boil and add the *doufu*, neatly arranged in the wok. Cover and cook over a low heat for 5 minutes. Adjust the seasoning, and thicken with the cornflour mixture. Sprinkle with the rest of the lard and dish up.

This well-known Huaiyang style of cooking is clear and tasty, rich but not greasy. The culinary map of Huaiyang covers a wide area from Huaiyin in the north of Jiangsu province to Yangzhou and Zhenjiang in the south. The term 'Huaiyang' is a combination of the first syllables of 'Huaiyin' and 'Yangzhou'.

Steamed fish doufu (Guangdong)

230 g (8 oz) doufu

For the minced fish mixture:
230 g (8 oz) white fish (boned and skinned)
1 tsp salt
2 egg whites
pepper to taste
1 tbsp spring onion and ginger juice
2 tsp cornflour with a little water

For the flavouring:
1 Chinese sausage (diced)
1 tbsp dried shrimps (soaked and diced)
1 stalk spring onion (minced)
1 slice ginger (minced)
1 tbsp sesame oil

For the topping:
1 tsp pepper (or to taste)
1 tbsp light soya sauce
1 tbsp heated groundnut oil

lard or white vegetable fat for greasing

79

Garnish:
1 tbsp coriander leaves (chopped)

1. Prepare the minced fish mixture (*see* 'Fish paste', *page* 232).
2. Mash the *doufu* and gradually work into the fish mixture, stirring in one direction all the time. Add the flavouring ingredients.
3. Grease a bowl and fill with the fish *doufu* mixture. Level the top and steam in a wok or steamer over a high heat for about 15 minutes or till cooked.
4. Take out, drain off any water collected in the bowl. Turn it out on to a serving dish. Sprinkle with pepper and the heated groundnut oil. Garnish with the chopped coriander leaves sprinkled in the middle. Just before eating pour the soya sauce over.

This dish looks like a mousse, beautifully creamy white and marbled with red and green. It has a smooth texture and a delicate flavour, with no fishy taste at all. It is normally served hot and heavily peppered. In step 3, it is important to grease the bowl with solid fat or it will not turn out well.

Stir-fried doufu brain – 'doufunao'

230 g (8 oz) doufu *(mashed)*

For the seasoning:
1 stalk spring onion (minced)
1 slice ginger (minced)
1 tsp salt
2 tsp rice wine
60 ml (2 fl oz) stock or water
2 tsp cornflour with a little water
1 tsp rendered chicken fat or sesame oil

1 tbsp lard or vegetable oil

Garnish:
1 tbsp coriander leaves or parsley (chopped)

1. Set the wok on a high heat, put in the lard and when hot, stir in the spring onion and ginger. Cook briefly and, before it changes colour, pour in the mashed *doufu*. Stir-fry for about 2 minutes, then add the salt, rice wine and stock. Continue to cook till it has the consistency of a thick batter.
2. Stir in the cornflour mixture and, when thickened, sprinkle with the chicken fat and dish up. Garnish with chopped coriander leaves and serve.

The Chinese name for this dish is *doufunao*, literally '*doufu* brain', as it has much of the colour and texture of cooked pig's brain and is similarly odourless. *Doufunao* is popularly translated as 'jellied bean curd'. This used to be one of the favourite 'soft foods' of the Qing Dowager Empress, Ci-Xi, in her old age. She died in 1908. As it has a 'melt-in-the-mouth' softness, it is deemed to be easily digestible and readily absorbed, and hence a popular food for the elderly. A native of Manchuria – the land of soya beans – it is not surprising that Ci-Xi had a preference for *doufu*. During the Qing dynasty, and particularly during her reign, *doufu* was given a fillip. The imperial chefs were encouraged to invent, innovate or improve existing *doufu* dishes. More than this, *doufu* was regarded as a beauty food for the Dowager Empress's skin, and was said to preserve her youthful looks.

Stir-fried doufu mince

450 g (1 lb) doufu

For the seasoning:
1 stalk spring onion (minced)
1 slice ginger (minced)
1 tsp salt
4 tbsp dark soya sauce
2 tsp rice wine
2 tbsp dried shrimps (soaked and pounded)
1 tbsp red chilli pepper (chopped)

Garnish:
coriander leaves or parsley (chopped)

4 tbsp sesame oil

1. Place the *doufu* in a piece of muslin, squeeze out the excess water and work it into a mash with the consistency of curd cheese.
2. Set the wok over a high heat and when hot, put in 1 tbsp of the sesame oil. When the oil is hot add the *doufu*. Stir-fry till the *doufu* looks like breadcrumbs; if the heat is too fierce, reduce it to medium. Draw the *doufu* aside, put in another 1 tbsp of the sesame oil, and stir-fry the shrimps till fragrant. Mix in the *doufu*.
3. Draw the *doufu* and shrimps aside, put in the rest of the oil, and stir-fry the spring onion, ginger and chilli till fragrant. Return the *doufu* and shrimps to the centre. Stir-fry for about 2 minutes, sprinkle with the salt, soya sauce and rice wine, stir-fry till absorbed by the *doufu*, and dish up. Garnish with coriander leaves.

Dark golden and delicious, this dish has a resilient texture. It may be eaten in sesame rolls instead of stir-fried minced pork (*see page* 38). The Chinese emperors used to abstain from meat foods before an important state function or feast days, and this recipe (minus the shrimps) used to feature regularly on the Qing imperial household menu.

Stir-fried doufu with carrots and pork

170 g (6 oz) doufu
170 g (6 oz) carrots
170 g (6 oz) pork
1 tbsp dried shrimps (soaked)

For the seasoning:
2 stalks spring onion (chopped)
1 slice ginger (minced)
1 tbsp salted soya bean paste
2 tsp rice wine
1 tsp salt
1 tbsp dark soya sauce

2 tbsp vegetable oil
2 tsp sesame oil

1. Wrap the *doufu* in a piece of muslin. Place it on a chopping board and put a dinner plate on top to press out excess water. Raise one end of the board slightly to allow the water to run away. Leave it for about 1 hour.
2. Dice the pork, carrots and pressed *doufu* into peanut-size pieces.
3. Set the wok on a high heat and stir-fry the carrots in the vegetable oil till par-cooked. Draw them to the side of the wok to allow the oil to drip back to the bottom. Take out the carrots. Stir-fry the pork till the water evaporates and the oil begins to run.
4. Add the spring onion, ginger and bean paste. Continue to stir-fry till the meat has absorbed the paste. Add the rice wine, salt and soya sauce. Stir-fry briefly. Add the *doufu*, shrimps and carrots. Continue to stir-fry till all is nicely brown. Sprinkle with sesame oil, mix well and dish up.

The sweet carrots and the salty seasoning combined with the contrasting textures and tastes of the other ingredients make this an exquisite dish. It used to be on the menu for the Qing imperial family meals.

EGGS

Chrysanthemum eggs (Fujian)

6 eggs (duck or chicken)

For the filling:
140 g (5 oz) raw prawn meat
60g (2 oz) boiled pork fat
2 caps winter mushrooms (soaked)
4 peeled water chestnuts

For the seasoning:
1 tsp salt
1 tsp granulated sugar
2 tsp rice wine
1 egg white (lightly beaten)
2 tsp cornflour with a little water

For the sauce:
110 ml (4 fl oz) stock or water
2 tsp lard or cooking oil
2 tsp rice wine
1 tsp salt
pepper to taste
1 tsp cornflour with a little water

Garnish:
coriander leaves or parsley

1. Boil the eggs for about 5 minutes, till just hard. (To prevent cracking during boiling add a pinch of salt.) Plunge them into cold water. Tap lightly with the back of a teaspoon around the middle of each egg. Break along the cracked shell and slip out the egg. Rinse the eggs to remove any fragments of shell. Cut a tiny slice off both ends of each egg so that when they are halved, each half will stand up. Use the sharp end of a paring knife to cut a series of 'V' shapes round the middle of the egg (*see illustrations page* 84) to make a pair of 'egg cups' with serrated edges – 12 in all. Take out and chop the egg yolks and reserve.
2. Mince the pork fat and the prawns separately and finely. Dice the water chestnuts and mushrooms into rice-size pieces. Mix them

83

together with the seasoning and half of the chopped yolks. Shape into 12 equal-sized balls and put one in each 'egg cup'. Shape the top in a mound. Sprinkle with some chopped yolks.

3. Put the filled 'egg cups' in a plate or a sandwich cake tin. Steam in a wok or steamer over a high heat for about 10 minutes. Transfer to a serving dish.

4. Mix together the ingredients for the sauce. Bring to the boil, and when thickened pour around the eggs from the edge of the plate. Decorate each egg with a sprig of coriander or parsley.

These beautiful and tasty eggs make a decorative piece for the buffet table.

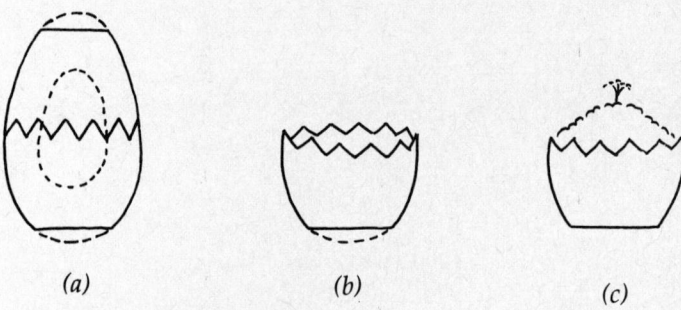

(a) (b) (c)

Salted eggs

12 duck's eggs
110 g (4 oz) salt
550 ml (1 pt) water

1. Add the salt to the water and bring to the boil, stirring to dissolve the salt. Leave to cool completely.

2. There is no need to wash the eggs if they are very clean. With free-range duck's eggs, however, scrub them carefully with a nail brush and rinse thoroughly. Wipe dry with a clean tea towel.

3. Wash a glass jar or earthenware crock with liquid detergent and rinse thoroughly, making sure it is spotlessly clean and free from grease. Dry it well. Pack the eggs in the jar or crock. Pour the cold brine on to the eggs. Cover tightly and leave in a cool, dry place for 30 to 40 days.

4. To cook, boil for 10 minutes or till completely hard. Cool in cold water and cut into two or quarters. The white should be salty and the yolk golden and delectable.

Hen's eggs may be salted but the shells are more fragile to handle. If stored in an airtight container, completely immersed in the brine, and taken out every time with clean hands, the salted eggs may be kept for up to 3 months. After this they will deteriorate: the whites will begin to harden, the yolks will dry out and the taste will suffer. Some commercially prepared salted eggs are covered in black sooty earth which should be removed before they are rinsed and cooked in the usual way.

Steamed eggs with barbecued pork (Guangdong)

For the egg custard:
8 eggs plus 2 extra yolks
½ tsp salt

For the sauce:
2 egg whites (lightly beaten)
110 ml (4 fl oz) stock or water
1 tsp salt
1 tsp oil
1 tsp cornflour with a little water

Garnish:
60 g (2 oz) charsiu *(barbecued pork) or cooked ham (finely diced)*
1 tbsp chopped parsley

cooking oil for greasing

1. Beat the eggs and yolks with the salt until well blended. Grease 12 Chinese tea cups or dariole moulds. Divide the beaten eggs equally among the cups. Put the cups in a dish and steam on a medium heat in a wok or steamer till just set, about 10 minutes. Take them out and unmould on to a serving dish.
2. Beat the stock and the rest of the ingredients for the sauce into the egg whites. Bring the mixture to the boil, stirring well. When thickened pour onto the custards. Sprinkle with the *charsiu* and then the parsley. (For *charsiu see page* 35.)

If preferred, the eggs may be steamed and served in individual bowls and topped with the sauce and garnish.

Quail's eggs in golden threads (Beijing)

2 dozen quail's eggs

For the egg skins:
3 large hen's eggs plus 2 extra yolks

For the meat mixture:
350 g (12 oz) pork
4 caps winter mushrooms (soaked)
1 stalk spring onion (finely chopped)
2 tbsp soya sauce
1 tsp salt
1 tsp granulated sugar
2 tsp cornflour with a little water
pepper to taste

cooking oil

1. Beat the hen's eggs and the yolks to blend. Heat the wok and make thin egg skins with the beaten eggs (for the method, *see page* 26). When cooled cut into fine shreds and spread them out on a plate.
2. Boil the quail's eggs for about 3 to 4 minutes. Plunge into cold water and shell. Rinse well to remove any bits of shell. Remove the whites (reserve them for other cooking in salad or soup), taking care to keep the yolks whole.
3. Mix together the ingredients for the meat mixture. Divide into 24 equal portions. Wrap a quail's egg yolk with a portion of the meat mixture, like a Scotch egg, and shape into a round ball. Roll it in the shredded eggs so that it is completely covered. Repeat with the rest of the quail's eggs.
4. Put them in a greased dish and steam in a wok or steaming basket for about 10 minutes over a high heat, or till cooked. Transfer them to a dish and serve hot.

This recipe comes from the well-known Tan family style of cooking in Beijing. Originally the Tan family's ancestors were high officials from Guangzhou (Canton). In later years fortune deserted their descendants, who eventually opened up a small family restaurant serving the Tan family's traditional dishes, a kind of Beijing hybrid of Cantonese food with a character of its own.

VEGETABLES

Angled luffa and eggs

1 angled luffa, about 350–450 g (12 oz–1 lb)

2 eggs (lightly beaten)
1 clove garlic
1 tsp salt
pepper to taste

2 tbsp cooking oil

1. Shave the ridges off the luffa. Then peel the rest of the skin. Rinse and roll-cut into wedges.
2. Set the wok on a high heat, and when hot put in the oil. Stir in the garlic, salt and pepper, and when fragrant add the luffa. Stir-fry till the luffa changes colour, about 1 minute. Pour in about 50 ml (2 fl oz) water. Cover and cook for about ½ minute. Stir in the beaten eggs, and when it thickens, dish up.

This simple but sweet and tasty dish is a kind of fast food for family eating. The luffa is a very fast-cooking vegetable; overcooking would rob it of its sweetness.

Aubergine salad

2 aubergines

For the dressing:
3 cloves garlic (minced)
1 tbsp coriander leaves or spring onion (chopped)
½ tsp salt
1 tbsp dark soya sauce
1 tbsp sesame oil

1. Rinse and halve the aubergines lengthwise. Grease a baking sheet and place the aubergines on it, cut-side-down. Bake in a preheated oven at 200°C (400°F, gas 6) for about 30 minutes, or till they are soft enough for a dent to be left when they are pressed.
2. Take out and cool slightly. Peel off the skins. Lift the peeled aubergines with a fish slice and place on a dish, laying them neatly side by side. Use a fork or a pair of chopsticks to tear them lengthwise into strips, leaving the strips in place.
3. Mix the ingredients for the dressing and pour on the aubergines.

This may be eaten as a side dish with rice, steamed bread or sesame bread. It is also suitable as a starter.

Braised stuffed fuzzy melon (Guangdong)

450–550 g (1–1¼ lb) fuzzy melon

For the filling:
170 g (6 oz) minced pork (¼ fat)
3 caps winter mushrooms (soaked and finely diced)
1 tbsp dried shrimps (soaked and pounded)
15 g (½ oz) dried brill (optional; grilled and pounded)
1 tsp salt
pepper to taste
2 tsp cornflour with a little water

400 ml (¾ pt) chicken or pork stock or water
cornflour for dusting
850 ml (1½ pt) cooking oil

Garnish:
1 tbsp dongcai (preserved vegetable; rinsed)
1 stalk spring onion (chopped)

1. Choose slender melons of about 6 to 8 cm (2½ to 3 in) diameter. Cut away both ends of the melon to neaten, and slice into rings about 5 cm (2 in) thick. Stand them upright, use a paring knife to cut round the pulp and seeds, and discard them. Pare off the skins thinly. Rinse and drain.
2. Mix together all the ingredients for the filling.
3. Dust the inside of each ring with cornflour. Fill each with a portion of the meat mixture. Level the top to smooth, and dust well with cornflour.
4. Deep-fry the stuffed melon rings in hot oil till they colour. This causes a thin film to form round the melon and prevents it from disintegrating on cooking. Drain well on kitchen paper.
5. Place the melon rings in a single layer in a casserole. Pour on the stock and bring to the boil on high heat. Skim, reduce the heat to medium, cover and cook till tender, about 30 minutes.
6. Sprinkle with the rinsed *dongcai* and spring onions and serve in the casserole.

This is an all-in-one, self-contained family dish which comprises meat, vegetable and soup, and is eaten with plain boiled rice. It may be augumented with a green leafy vegetable. Young, slender courgettes may be substituted, though there is a subtle difference in flavour. If preferred, the deep-frying may be left out.

Cucumber in milk sauce (Jiangsu)

1 cucumber

For the milk sauce:
2 tsp rice wine
1 tsp salt
pepper to taste
110 ml (4 fl oz) stock or water
3 tbsp milk
1 tsp cornflour with a little water

2 tbsp cooking oil

Garnish:
2 tbsp cooked ham (minced)

1. Peel and quarter the cucumber lengthwise. Remove the seeds and soft parts. Slice into 8 cm (3 in) lengths. Blanch them in boiling water. Drain well.
2. Set the wok over a high heat, put in the oil and when hot, stir-fry the cucumber briefly. This helps to extract the water from the cucumber and prevents it from disintegrating during cooking. Drain in a colander.
3. Bring the stock to the boil in the wok, and add the drained cucumber, the seasoning, rice wine and milk. Bring to the boil and cook for 1 minute. Thicken with the cornflour mixture. Transfer to a dish and sprinkle with the cooked ham.

This simple dish is quite attractive with the green cucumber bathed in white sauce and speckled with pink ham and it is a pleasant way of eating the cucumber. Vegetables in milk sauce is one of the 'Huaiyang' styles of cooking from Jiangsu, *see* 'Huaiyang *doufu* in oyster sauce' *page 78*.

Deep-fried sandwiched aubergines

2 large aubergines, about 450–550 g (1–1¼ lb)

For the filling:
170 g (6 oz) white fish (skinned and boned)
30 g (1 oz) peeled cooked prawns (chopped)
30 g (1 oz) boiled pork fat (minced)
3 caps winter mushrooms (soaked and minced)
pepper to taste

850 ml (1½ pt) cooking oil
cornflour for dusting

1. Cut the aubergines into rounds about 2.5 cm (1 in) thick, and slash each into two without cutting right through so that they are joined together by about one-fifth. Sprinkle with some salt and leave in the colander for about 30 minutes.
2. Mince the fish till sticky, and mix it with the rest of the ingredients for the filling.
3. Thoroughly rinse the aubergines to remove the salt, and pat dry with kitchen paper. Divide the mixture into as many portions as there are aubergine rounds. Dust each round between the two slices with some cornflour and fill with a portion of the fish mixture. Press lightly to spread the filling and stick the slices together. Cover both outer surfaces with some more cornflour.
4. Deep-fry in hot oil till golden and just tender. Take out and drain well on kitchen paper.

This is a delicious and satisfying way of eating aubergine. If preferred, it may be pan-fried in a thick, flat-bottomed pan till both sides are golden.

Eight Treasures tomatoes (Zhejiang)

10 firm tomatoes (about 50 g, 2 oz each)

For the filling:
60 g (2 oz) soaked sea cucumber
60 g (2 oz) cooked chicken meat
1 cooked chicken liver
1 cooked chicken gizzard
60 g (2 oz) boiled pork fat
30 g (1 oz) bamboo shoots
4 caps winter mushrooms (soaked)
30 g (1 oz) peeled cooked shrimps
30 g (1 oz) garden peas
2 tsp rice wine
60 ml (2 fl oz) chicken stock
1 tsp cornflour with a little water

For the sauce:
110 ml (4 fl oz) chicken stock
1 tsp salt
1 tsp cornflour with a little water
extra chicken stock

1. Plunge the tomatoes into boiling water for ½ minute, drain and drop into cold water. Skin them. Stand the tomatoes stalk-side-down and cut a quarter from the top of each to serve as a cover. Use a sharp paring knife to remove the seeds and pulp. Soak the tomato shells in cold chicken stock to flavour.
2. Finely dice the first 8 items for the filling.
3. Put 60 ml (2 fl oz) of chicken stock in a wok over a high heat. Add the diced items and the peas. Then add the wine and the cornflour mixture. Mix well and when thickened, dish up.
4. Drain the tomatoes, and arrange them neatly in a greased dish. Fill each with the hot cooked Eight Treasures stuffing. Replace the lids. Cover the dish with cling film and steam in the wok or a steamer to reheat, about 10 minutes.
5. Meanwhile, make the sauce. Bring the chicken stock to the boil. Adjust the seasoning and thicken with the cornflour mixture. Take out the tomatoes and pour the sauce over them.

Mouli cakes in tomato sauce

For the cake:
450 g (1 lb) mouli
230 g (8 oz) doufu
1 tsp salt
2 tsp ginger (minced)
1 tbsp cornflour with a little water

For the sauce:
2 tbsp tomato ketchup
1 tsp salt
1 tbsp granulated sugar
1 tbsp white wine vinegar
2 tsp lard or sesame oil

2 tbsp vegetable oil

1. Peel the mouli and grate into fine shreds. Scald in boiling water. Drain and soak in cold water for about 2 hours. Drain and squeeze dry. Season with the salt and minced ginger.
2. Mash the *doufu* to a paste and mix it with the mouli. Add the cornflour mixture, mix well and shape into walnut-sized balls.
3. Set a thick, flat-bottomed frying pan over a medium heat. Put in the oil, and when hot put in the mouli balls. Flatten them lightly into cakes. Lower the heat and cook slowly till both sides are golden.

Take out and drain on kitchen paper.

4. Pour away any excess oil from the pan. Add in the tomato ketchup. Season with the salt, sugar and vinegar. Mix well and put in the mouli cakes. Lower the heat and let them cook in the sauce for about 5 minutes on a low heat. Stir in the lard and dish up.

Red peppers stuffed with pork (Hunan)

6 small red peppers

For the pork filling:
230 g (8 oz) minced pork (¼ fat)
1 tbsp peeled cooked shrimps
3 caps winter mushrooms (soaked)

For the seasoning:
1 egg (lightly beaten)
½ tsp salt
1 tbsp light soya sauce
pepper to taste
2 tsp cornflour with a little water

For the sauce:
60 ml (2 fl oz) stock or water
1 tsp cornflour with a little water

30 g (1 oz) garlic (peeled and sliced)
850 ml (1½ pt) cooking oil
2 tsp sesame oil
cornflour for dusting

1. Dice the shrimps and mushrooms into rice-size pieces. Mix them with the minced pork and the seasoning. Divide into 12 equal portions.
2. Rinse the red peppers and slice each into two lengthwise. Deseed and cut out the pulpy bits. Dust inside each pepper with some cornflour. Fill each with a portion of the pork mixture, level the top and dust with cornflour.
3. Deep-fry the sliced garlic till golden, take out and set aside. Deep-fry the red peppers till par-cooked. Take out and drain well on kitchen paper.
4. Place the par-cooked peppers, meat-side-down, on a plate, sprinkle with the fried garlic and steam in the wok for about 20 minutes or till cooked. Transfer the peppers and garlic to a serving plate with a

perforated spoon, meat side up. Reserve any liquor. Sprinkle the sesame oil on the peppers.

5. Set the wok on a medium heat, bring the stock and the reserved liquor to the boil, thicken with the cornflour mixture, and pour over the red peppers.

Stuffed sweet peppers in milk sauce (Jiangsu)

5 or 6 small sweet green peppers

For the filling:
230 g (8 oz) fresh prawns
1 egg white (lightly beaten)
2 tsp rice wine
1 tbsp cornflour
1 tsp salt
pepper to taste

For the sauce:
½ tsp salt
½ tsp granulated sugar
4 tbsp milk
2 tsp rice wine
110 ml (4 fl oz) stock or water
1 tsp cornflour

cornflour for dusting
2 tsp sesame oil

1. Rinse the peppers and quarter them lengthwise. Deseed and remove any pulpy bits. Blanch them in boiling water with a little salt added. Drain and refresh in cold water. Drain again thoroughly. Dust the inside of each pepper with some cornflour.
2. Shell the prawns and devein them by cutting along the back. Rub them with some salt, rinse and dry with kitchen paper. Mince the prawns finely and mix in the rest of the filling ingredients.
3. Fill each floured pepper slice with the prawn mixture, and smooth the top. Place them in a plate (or sandwich cake tin) and steam in a wok or steamer for about 10 minutes or till cooked, when the filling appears pink and feels firm. Transfer to a serving dish and keep warm.
4. Mix together all the ingredients for the sauce, and bring to the boil.

Stir well, and when thickened pour over the peppers. Sprinkle with the sesame oil.

Fast-cooking prawns are used as a filling so that the peppers are not over-cooked. This is another 'Huaiyang' dish in milk sauce, *see* also note on 'Cucumber in milk sauce', *page* 89. Choose small, tender peppers of similar size.

Tomatoes in milk sauce (Jiangsu)

700 g (1½ lb) tomatoes

For the sauce:
140 ml (5 fl oz) chicken stock or water
1 tsp salt
2 tsp rice wine
1 tsp cornflour with a little water
60 ml (2 fl oz) milk
2 tsp rendered chicken fat

1. Put the tomatoes in boiling water for 1 minute, drain and plunge into cold water. Skin, quarter and deseed. Drain well.
2. Bring the chicken stock, rice wine, salt and tomatoes to the boil. Adjust the seasoning. Thicken with the cornflour mixture. Add the milk and when it is almost boiling again, stir in the chicken fat and dish up immediately.

This is another 'Huaiyang' vegetable dish, simple, attractive and tasty. *See* also 'Cucumber in milk sauce' *page* 89.

Water spinach salad with ginger juice (Sichuan)

450–700 g (1–1½ lb) Chinese water spinach (kongsincai)

For the dressing:
30 g (1 oz) ginger
1 tbsp vegetable oil
1 tbsp sesame oil
1 tsp salt
1 tbsp vinegar

1. Discard any soiled or yellow leaves from the water spinach. Break

the stems into 2.5 cm (1 in) long pieces with a couple of leaves attached. Rinse in several changes of water.

2. Scrape the ginger, pound it finely. Squeeze out and reserve the juice.

3. Scald the spinach in boiling water, drain well in a colander and spread out to disperse the heat and to prevent over-cooking.

4. Toss the scalded spinach in the vegetable oil, then add the sesame oil, ginger juice and salt, and mix well. Just before eating, toss in the vinegar, which if added too early would turn the spinach an unpleasant blackish-green colour.

Chinese *bocai* or another tender, sweet vegetable of the spinach type may be used instead.

SOUPS

Beef and egg broth (Guangdong)

230 g (8 oz) beef (topside or aitchbone or lean braising steak)
3 eggs (lightly beaten)

Marinade for the beef:
1 tbsp light soya sauce
¼ tsp bicarbonate of soda (optional)
2 tsp cornflour with a little water
2 tsp groundnut oil

For the seasoning:
1 tbsp rice wine
1 tsp salt
pepper to taste
2 tsp sesame oil
1 tbsp cornflour with a little water

1 tbsp lard or vegetable oil
850 ml (1½ pt) stock

1. Remove any fat or gristle from the beef, and cut the meat into thin bite-size slices. Mix in the light soya sauce, then the soda (if used) and cornflour mixture. Finally mix in the groundnut oil. Leave to marinate for 30 minutes.

2. Scald the marinated beef in fast-boiling water for ½ minute, or till it loses its redness. Drain immediately.
3. Set a thick-bottomed pot on a medium heat, and put in 2 tsp lard. Add the rice wine and stock. Season with salt, pepper and sesame oil. Bring to the boil and thicken with the cornflour mixture. Stir to mix well, and when it turns clear add the par-cooked beef. Take the pot off the heat immediately.
4. Slowly pour in the beaten eggs with one hand and stir in one direction with the other hand. The soup should be glutinous and thick. Add the rest of the lard. Pour into a soup tureen and serve.

The taste of this soup is clear, the meat tender and smooth, the egg fragrant and slippery. The bicarbonate of soda is used here as a tenderizer with the cheaper, tougher cut of meat i.e. braising steak.

Clam and furong soup (Fujian)

8 fresh clams
1 tbsp rice wine

For the egg furong:
4 egg whites
110 ml (4 fl oz) stock
1 tsp salt
pepper to taste

For the seasoning:
2 tbsp rice wine
1 tbsp light soya sauce
1 tsp salt

850 ml (1½ pt) clear chicken stock

1. Scrub the clams and rinse in cold water. Pour boiling water over them. Leave for 1–2 minutes. Prise each one open with a knife. Reserve the juice. Cut the clam meat into two, rinse off any sand or earth. Scald in boiling water for ½ minute to par-cook. Marinate in 1 tbsp of the rice wine.
2. Lightly beat the egg whites and add the stock, salt and pepper. Mix well and skim off any froth. Steam in a bowl for about 5 minutes, until just set. This is the *furong*.
3. Drain the clams, keep the marinade and mix it with the reserved clam juice. Put the clams in a soup bowl.
4. Bring the stock and the clam juice mixture to the boil. Season, bring

to the boil again and pour over the clams. Scoop the *furong* out with a spoon and slip into the soup. Serve immediately.

Crab ball soup (Guangdong)

For the crab meat mixture:
170 g (6 oz) dressed crab meat (white only)
110 g (4 oz) shelled uncooked prawns (finely minced)
30 g (1 oz) boiled pork fat (finely minced)
2 peeled water chestnuts (finely diced)
egg white (lightly beaten)
1 tsp salt
pepper to taste
2 tsp cornflour

For the coating:
3 large caps winter mushrooms (soaked and finely diced)
80 g (3 oz) cooked ham (finely diced)

For the seasoning:
1 tsp salt
2 tsp light soya sauce
2 tsp sesame oil
pepper to taste

850 ml (1½ pt) strong clear chicken or pork stock
oil for greasing

1. Mix together the diced mushrooms and ham, and put on a plate.
2. Mix the finely minced prawns with the salt and egg white until sticky. Add the crab meat, pork fat and water chestnuts and mix well. Make into 24 crab meat balls. Take a handful of the mixture in your left hand and squeeze till a ball appears between your left thumb and index finger. Scoop out the ball with a spoon and drop it into the ham and mushroom mixture on the plate.
3. Roll the crab balls in the ham and mushroom mixture to cover completely. Put them on a greased plate or in a sandwich cake tin and steam over a high heat in a wok or steamer for about 7 minutes. Transfer to a soup tureen.
4. Bring the stock, together with the seasoning, to the boil and pour over the crab balls in the tureen.

This delectable seafood soup is a traditional dish from Chouzhou (Teochiew) in Guangdong province. The crab balls may be prepared to the end of step 3 in advance and kept refrigerated. Re-steam to heat through just before required.

Crystallized chicken soup (Sichuan)

170 g (6 oz) chicken breasts (skinned and boned)
30 g (1 oz) tender garden pea shoots
30 g (1 oz) bamboo shoots
30 g (1 oz) cooked ham

For the seasoning:
1 tsp salt
pepper to taste
2 tsp rice wine

generous 1 l (2 pt) clear strong chicken stock
cornflour for dusting

1. Slice the bamboo shoots and ham into bite-size, oblong slices and set aside. Rinse the pea shoots.
2. Slice the chicken breast into thin lengthwise slices. Dust a flat surface with some cornflour. Place a slice of chicken breast on it. Cover the chicken slice with some more cornflour. With a rolling pin, roll the chicken into a very thin slice. The pressure must be even and light so that the chicken slice will have a uniform thickness.
3. When all the slices have been rolled out, scald them in boiling water. Take out with a brass wire mesh strainer, and leave in cold water to cool completely. Cut to the same size as the bamboo shoots and ham.
4. Bring 280 ml (½ pt) of the chicken stock to the boil, and briefly scald the chicken slices, bamboo shoots, ham and pea shoots to heat through. Drain well and transfer into a soup tureen.
5. Bring the rest of the stock together with the seasoning to the boil, and pour into the soup tureen.

This traditional banquet soup from Sichuan is equally suitable for a dinner party or a family meal. The chicken is transparent, hence the name 'crystallized'. The chicken slices may be prepared in advance up to step 3 and kept refrigerated after cooling.

Duck's tongue soup (Beijing)

20 duck's tongues

60 g (2 oz) cucumber or garden pea shoots
1 tbsp dried silver wood ears (soaked)

For the soup:
generous 1 l (2 pt) strong chicken stock
1 tsp salt
1 tbsp rice wine

1. Scald the tongues in boiling water for ½ minute. Take out and scrape off the skins. Rinse well and boil in water for about 20 minutes. Drain and refresh in cold water. Pull out the soft bones inside the tongues from the open ends. Rinse out the grease inside the tongues.
2. Rinse the cucumber, deseed and cut into julienne strips. (Or rinse the pea shoots if used.)
3. Bring 280 ml (½ pt) of the stock with a pinch of salt and 2 tsp of the rice wine to the boil. Add the tongues and wood ears. Boil for 1 minute, drain, and put in a soup bowl. Place the cucumber slices on top.
4. Bring the rest of the stock with the seasoning to the boil, skim and pour on to the tongues from the side of the bowl.

This is food fit for an emperor. Duck's tongues were one of the eight delicacies supposed to be eaten only by the Son of Heaven. The list includes bear's paw, deer's tail, torpedo roe, camel's hump, monkey's lips, carp's tail and beef marrow. As the ingredients changed from dynasty to dynasty, the more common items were discarded and rarer ones added. As time went on, the eight delicacies became nutritional food for the infirm and the elderly. Today, to qualify as one of the eight items, the food has to be either unobtainable or non-existent!

Gluten dumpling soup (Jiangsu)

280 g (10 oz) raw wheat gluten

For the pork filling:
280 g (10 oz) minced pork (¼ fat)
1 stalk spring onion (minced)
1 tbsp rice wine
3 tbsp light soya sauce
1 tbsp icing sugar or granulated sugar

Seasoning for the soup:
2 tsp salt
2 tsp rice wine

1. Mix the minced pork together with the rest of the ingredients for the pork filling. Mix well and divide into 25 equal portions.
2. Shape the raw gluten into a long strip and cut into 25 equal parts. Roll each piece into a ball. Soak them in cold water in the summer, but warm water in the winter, for about 10 minutes. Take one gluten ball and use your fingers to flatten it into a small round, and wrap a portion of the meat mixture in it. Make another 24 dumplings in the same way.
3. Bring a generous 1 l (2 pt) of water to the boil, season with the salt and add the dumplings. Bring to the boil again, reduce the heat and cook for 5 to 6 minutes. Skim and add in the rice wine. Pour into a soup tureen.

This is a speciality of the county of Wuxi in Jiangsu province.

Pearly chicken soup

12 quail's eggs (hard-boiled and shelled)

For the chicken paste:
140 g (5 oz) raw chicken breast (skinned and finely minced)
2 tsp rice wine
1 tsp salt
1 tsp cornflour with a little water
2 egg whites
pepper to taste

850 ml (1½ pt) clear chicken stock
1 tbsp cornflour with a little water
2 tsp sesame oil

Garnish:
1 tbsp cooked ham (minced)

1. Mix together all the ingredients for the chicken paste with 1 tbsp cold water.
2. Bring the stock and the shelled quail's eggs to the boil. Adjust the seasoning and thicken with the cornflour mixture. Trickle in the chicken paste gradually, and when it is white and the soup thickens, stir in the sesame oil. Pour into a soup tureen and sprinkle with the ham.

The pearl-like eggs floating in the snow-like chicken meat with specks of red ham make this a very attractive soup, which also tastes delicious.

Quail's egg and silver wood ear soup (Jiangsu)

12 quail's eggs
1 tbsp dried silver wood ears (soaked)
30 g (1 oz) cooked ham or smoked back bacon

For the soup:
850 ml (1½ pt) strong clear chicken or pork stock
2 tsp rice wine
2 tsp sesame oil
1 tsp salt

sesame oil for greasing

Garnish:
coriander leaves or parsley

1. Dice the ham into rice-size pieces. Rinse the coriander leaves and break into small sprigs.
2. Grease 12 Chinese saucers or wine cups (or dariole moulds). Break one quail's egg into each greased saucer. Scatter some minced ham on to the white of each egg. Put the saucers in a dish or a sandwich cake tin. Steam in a wok or steamer over a high heat for about 3 minutes.
3. Meanwhile, bring the stock to the boil with the pre-soaked silver wood ears. Season with the salt and rice wine. Pour into a soup bowl. Slip the steamed eggs out of the saucers and slide on to the soup. Sprinkle with the sesame oil and coriander or parsley, and serve.

This light, tasty and attractive soup is called 'moonshine over the peonies' in Chinese. The floating discs of eggs are the moons and the crinkly-looking balls of wood ears resemble the petals of peonies.

Sea cucumber and pork ball soup (Guangdong)

50 g (2 oz) dried sea cucumber (dry weight; soaked)

For the meat ball mixture:
170 (6 oz) minced pork (¼ fat)
3 caps winter mushrooms
1 tbsp dried shrimps (soaked)

1 egg
1 tsp salt
2 tsp cornflour

Seasoning for the soup:
2 tsp lard
2 tsp rice wine
2 tsp oyster sauce
1 tsp granulated sugar
1 tbsp dark soya sauce
pepper to taste
2 tsp cornflour with a little water
2 tsp sesame oil

Seasoning for steaming the meat balls:
2 tsp rice wine
80 ml (3 fl oz) chicken stock

850 ml (1½ pt) cooking oil
850 ml (1½ pt) strong chicken stock

1. Slice the soaked sea cucumbers (for soaking *see page* 238) into bite-size pieces.
2. Dice the mushrooms and soaked shrimps into rice-size bits. Mix them together with the minced pork, egg, salt and cornflour. Blend well, and shape into 12 balls.
3. Deep-fry the meat balls till golden. Take them out, drain and scald in boiling water for ½ minute to remove the grease. Drain well. Place them in a dish with the seasoning for steaming. Steam in a wok or steamer over a high heat for about 30 minutes. Drain and reserve the liquor for other cooking.
4. Set the wok on a medium heat, and when hot put in 2 tsp lard and 2 tsp rice wine. Pour in the chicken stock, oyster sauce and sugar. Add the sea cucumbers. Cover and cook for about 10 minutes. Put in the steamed meat balls, soya sauce and pepper to taste. Cover and cook for another 3 minutes. Thicken with the cornflour mixture and stir in the sesame oil. Take off the heat and sit the wok on a woven basket. Use a perforated spoon to pick out the meat balls and put them in a soup bowl. Pick out the sea cucumbers and lay them over the meat balls. Pour the soup into the bowls from the side.

This is a traditional Cantonese banquet dish. For a simpler family meal, if preferred, the meat balls may be steamed without deep-frying first.

DESSERTS

Crystal cake

7 g (¼ oz) agar agar
850 ml (1½ pt) water
4 eggs
230 g (8 oz) granulated sugar

1. Soak the agar agar in cold water till saturated. Drain and put in a pot with the cold water. Bring to the boil, reduce the heat and simmer on a low heat till completely dissolved, stirring continuously to prevent sticking. Add 110 g (4 oz) of the sugar, stir till the sugar dissolves and strain through a fine sieve into a clean pot. Put this on a very low heat and leave to simmer.
2. Beat the eggs and the rest of the sugar together in a heatproof dish till well blended and creamy. Leave the froth to subside or skim off.
3. Bring the agar agar mixture to the boil again on a low heat, and pour the boiling mixture gradually into the egg and sugar mixture, off the heat, stirring all the time to mix thoroughly and cook through. Pour into an 18 cm (6 to 7 in) cake tin or dish. There is no need to grease it. Cool thoroughly and chill in the refrigerator. Cut into diamond-shaped pieces and serve.

This cake has a layer of yellow custard on the top and a crystal-clear base, hence the name.

Egg custard tarts – danta (Guangdong)

For the pastry:
230 g (8 oz) strong plain white flour
110 g (4 oz) lard or white vegetable fat
30 g (1 oz) granulated sugar
2 tbsp water

For the custard:
140 g (5 oz) granulated sugar
2 eggs plus 1 yolk (lightly beaten)
110 ml (4 fl oz) water
2 tbsp top of milk

½ tsp salt

2 tartlet tins

1. The pastry is similar to Western shortcrust. Rub the fat into the flour till it resembles breadcrumbs (this may be done in a food processor). Stir in the sugar, then the water. Mix into a dough; do not overwork. Wrap in cling film and leave in a cool place to rest for about 30 minutes.
2. Meanwhile, prepare the custard. Dissolve the sugar in the water over a low heat and let boil for a minute. Cool completely. Gradually add the beaten eggs and the milk to the cooled syrup, taking care not to beat up bubbles. Stir in the salt and strain through a fine sieve. Set aside.
3. Preheat the oven to 200°C (400°F, gas 6). Roll the rested pastry into a 6.25 mm (¼ in) thick sheet on a floured surface. Stamp out rounds with an 8 cm (3 in) cutter. Line the tartlet tins with the pastry rounds. Do not prick the base or the tarts will stick to the pans. Fill each round to three-quarters full and bake in the preheated oven for about 20 minutes or till the custard is set. Lift each tart out with a palette knife and cool on a cake rack.

These delicious tarts show an Occidental influence. *Danta* means 'egg tarts'.

Frosted pork spare ribs (Anhui)

generous 1 kg (1¼ lb) pork spare ribs
2 tsp crystallized peel (chopped)

Marinade for pork:
1 tsp salt
1 tbsp dark soya sauce
2 tsp rice wine

Sugar syrup:
110 g (4 oz) rose sugar, or granulated sugar plus 1 tsp dried rose petals
60 ml (2 fl oz) water

cornflour for coating
generous 1 l (2 pt) cooking oil

1. Choose meaty pork ribs for this dish. Chop the ribs into 4 cm (1½ in) lengths. Rinse and dry. Marinate for at least 1 hour at room temperature.

2. Steam in a wok or steamer over a high heat for 15 minutes or till just cooked. Drain off any liquor. Roll each piece in cornflour to cover completely.
3. Dissolve the sugar in the water in a saucepan and leave on a very low heat.
4. Meanwhile, deep-fry the ribs in batches in hot oil till golden and crusty on the outside. Take out and drain well. Raise the heat, and boil the sugar syrup till bubbles appear all over. Pour in the fried spare ribs and the peel. Remove from the heat immediately, and stir well so that each piece is covered with the syrup. Pour into a dish to cool. Separate the pieces with a pair of chopsticks. When cold and frosted, transfer to a serving dish.

This is a Chinese sweetmeat served as a dessert at a banquet. In the original recipe crystallized kumquats and dried cassia flowers are used, but they are not easily available here.

Sandwiched bananas (Shanghai)

12 oz bananas

For the coating:
2 egg whites
2 tsp cornflour with a little water

For the filling:
110 g (4 oz) red bean paste

cornflour for dusting
icing sugar for sprinkling
850 ml (1½ pt) groundnut or other vegetable oil

1. Peel the bananas. Slice each into halves lengthwise. With the back of a knife, gently press each piece into a flattened strip. Put a portion of red bean paste on half of the flattened strips, and spread out to cover completely. Place the other halves on top, forming banana sandwiches.
2. Slice the sandwiched strips diagonally into 5 cm (2 in) pieces. Roll them in the cornflour to cover completely.
3. Lightly beat the egg whites, and stir in the cornflour mixture to make an egg paste.
4. Heat the oil and when fairly hot, dip each floured banana sandwich in the egg paste and deep-fry till they turn milky-white. Take out with a brass wire mesh strainer, and drain well on kitchen paper.

Transfer to a serving plate and sprinkle with icing sugar.

This is a simple and truly delicious sweet.

Steamed honey date bread (Beijing)

For the bread dough:
450 g (1 lb) strong plain white flour
20 g (¾ oz) fresh yeast or 1½ tsp dried yeast
1 tsp sugar
280 ml (½ pt) tepid water

For the rice flour mixture:
170 g (6 oz) soft dark brown sugar
60 g (2 oz) rice flour
2 tsp rose water
80 ml (3 fl oz) hot water

20 honey dates

1. Rinse the dates, stone and cut each into 4 lengthwise. Grease a cake tin of 22 or 25 cm diameter (8½ to 10 in).
2. Make a basic bread dough with the flour, yeast, sugar and water. Cover and leave to rise till doubled in size.
3. Dissolve the brown sugar in the hot water. Stir in the rose water. Mix in the rice flour. Use your hand to work the rice flour mixture into the risen dough till it is well blended; dip your hand in water if sticky. The mixing may be done with a cake mixer. The dough when picked up should look like a piece of soft wet rag.
4. Break the dough into two equal parts. Pull one out to about the size of the cake tin and lay it at the bottom. Pat it out to level it and cover the base completely; dip your hand in water if it sticks.
5. Sprinkle some of the dates on top. Cover the whole with the rest of the dough, patting it level. Press in the rest of the dates in neat parallel rows across the whole surface of the dough.
6. Preheat a steaming basket or steamer, and steam the bread over a high heat for about 50 minutes to 1 hour. Test with a skewer; if it comes out clean the bread is cooked. Let it cool completely, and cut into slices.

This bread-cake is quite similar to the English walnut bread except that it is steamed. It looks like a jewel-encrusted, shiny ivory slab – rather unusual. It does not taste like bread at all. This used to be one of the tea cakes in the Chinese imperial palace. If it is steamed in a lined steaming basket or a cake tin with a perforated base, this cuts the cooking time considerably, as the holes allow the steam to penetrate better.

Thousand layer cake (Beijing)

For the dough:
450 g (1 lb) strong plain white flour
20 g (¾ oz) fresh yeast or 1 tsp dried yeast
110 g (4 oz) granulated sugar
280 ml (½ pt) tepid water
30 g (1 oz) lard or white vegetable fat

For the filling:
3 raw salted egg yolks (optional)
60 g (2 oz) crystallized kumquats or peel
8 glacé cherries
60 g (2 oz) crystallized angelica or greengages

60 ml (2 fl oz) vegetable oil for brushing

1. Make the dough: dissolve the yeast in 280 ml (½ pt) tepid water (half boiling and half cold) with 2 tsp of the sugar. Leave in a warm place until frothy. Put the flour on a flat surface, make a well in the centre and pour in the frothy yeast mixture. Mix into a dough, knead till smooth and leave to rise in a warm place, covered with a damp cloth or cling film till doubled in size.
2. Meanwhile, chop the fruits and egg yolks into mung bean size, mix them together and divide into 4 equal portions.
3. Knock down the risen dough and mix in the rest of the sugar, lard and 4 tbsp water. Knead till smooth, and leave to rest for 15 to 20 minutes. To test, cut the dough in two; if it is full of holes it is ready.
4. On a floured, flat surface roll the dough into an oblong about 1 cm (⅜ in) thick, 40 cm (16 in) long and 25 cm (10 in) wide. Brush it all over with the oil. Sprinkle with the mixed fruits on two-thirds of the oblong, starting from the top end farthest from you. Fold the empty third nearest to you over to the middle and over again, making a three-layered oblong. Give it a quarter turn and roll out again as before, brush with the oil, fill with the fruits and fold as before. (*See illustrations page* 108.)
5. Repeat the above process a third time, but roll the oblong narrower so that when folded in three, it turns into a square. Cover the top of the square completely with the rest of the mixed fruits, pressing in lightly.

6. Put the dough in a greased, loose-bottomed 20 cm (8 in) square cake tin. Leave to rest for about 15 minutes. Preheat a steaming basket or steamer on a high heat. Steam the cake over a high heat for about 25 to 30 minutes. Take out and cool completely before cutting into diamond shaped pieces.

If made in advance, the cake may be cut and resteamed for 5 minutes in a plate in the steaming basket. This delicious and attractive cake was originally a dessert served in the Qing imperial palace.

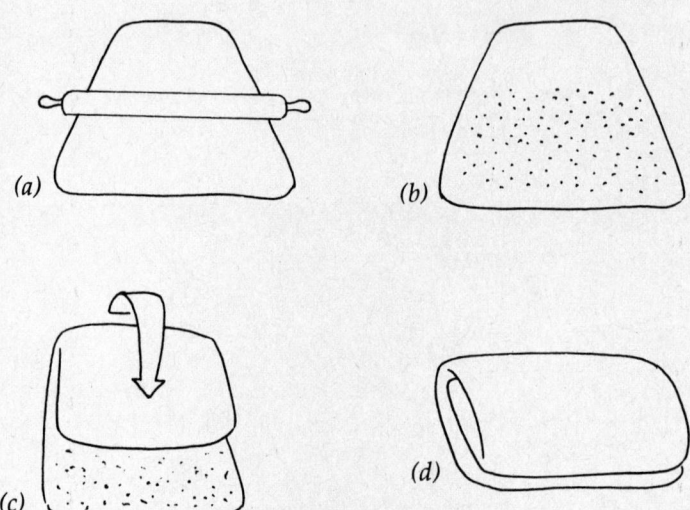

(a)   (b)   (c)   (d)

Festive Cooking

The Chinese culinary calendar is punctuated with festive meals. Throughout the year there are festivals at regular intervals, beginning with the Winter Solstice (around 22 to 25 December); followed by *Laba* Day (8th day of the 12th lunar month, roughly our January); the New Year celebration in February; the Spring Equinox; *Qingming* or 'pure and bright' festival in the 3rd lunar month, when the graves of ancestors are swept; the Dragon Boat Festival (5th day of the 5th lunar month); the Celebration of the Meeting of the Cowherd Boy and the Weaver Girl (7th day of the 7th lunar month); the Feast of the Fifteenth Day of the 7th lunar month for the underworld; the August Moon Festival; and the Chongyang festival of the ninth lunar month, besides celebrations for birthdays, births and marriages. For these occasions (apart from the normal banquet dishes) special cakes or dumplings or titbits are eaten to mark the event. The following is a selection of some of this interesting traditional fare.

BOBING AND CHUNBING – SPRING PANCAKES

The *chunbing* or spring pancake is a meal in itself, usually eaten on the day of the Spring Equinox some time in the second lunar month (our March). The *chunbing* has evolved from the spring platter or *chunpen* of the Jin dynasty (AD 265–420), when five kinds of spring vegetables, mainly of the Allium family were eaten with pancakes on that day. This practice had a healthy intention, in that the hot and pungent vegetables were supposed to stimulate the guts. From that time it was the custom for the imperial palace to offer ministers and high officials *chunpen* on that day. The ritual of *chunpen* eating was also observed by the common people. Later the meal became more elaborate as further ingredients were added, and there is now a vast array of shredded, cooked and raw vegetables with cold cooked meat and seafood served with sauces as dips and pancakes as wrappers.

This is one of the rare Chinese meals where everything is served at room temperature. The diners select foods and wrap them in pancakes before eating. The pancake itself is similar to that eaten with the Beijing duck, which is translated into 'Mandarin pancake'. In mainland Fujian and the island of Formosa (Taiwan) the pancake is called *bobing*, 'thin pancake', as it is almost transparent; poets often compare them to cicada's wings. Whenever a *chunbing* or *bobing* is deep-fried (as happens to the left-overs) it is called spring roll, *chunjuan*. The most familiar in the West is the Cantonese spring roll, which is specially made, traditionally wrapped in bean curd skin and coated in batter before frying.

Bobing – Fujian spring pancakes (Fujian)

30 spring pancakes (see page 112)

For the cooked filling:
450 g (1 lb) bean curd
450 g (1 lb) skinned and boned belly pork (par-boiled)
450 g (1 lb) bamboo shoots
230 g (8 oz) carrots
450 g (1 lb) peeled (cooked) shrimps
30 g (1 oz) dried bream (optional)
1 tbsp salted soya bean paste or light soya sauce
2 tsp salt
2 tsp granulated sugar
pepper to taste
280 ml (½ pt) pork stock or water

For the accompaniments:
4 eggs (lightly beaten)
230 g (8 oz) mung bean sprouts (tailed and blanched)
60 g (2 oz) coriander leaves (chopped)
170 g (6 oz) peanut brittle (pounded)
2 lettuces
2 tbsp prepared mustard
2 tbsp chilli sauce
60 ml (2 fl oz) Hoisin sauce or plum sauce

spring onions made into brushes (one for each diner)

sesame oil and cooking oil

1. Wrap the bean curd in a piece of muslin and weigh it down with a dinner plate for about 2 hours to remove excess water. Cut the pressed bean curd, pork, bamboo shoots and carrots into matchstick-sized pieces. Deep-fry or grill the dried bream till fragrant and pound finely.
2. Set the wok on a medium heat till hot, and put in 2 tbsp cooking oil. When the oil is hot, stir-fry the bean curd till pale golden, take out and set aside.
3. Add 1 tbsp oil to the wok, stir-fry the salted bean paste and the pork till fragrant, then add the bamboo shoots, carrots and bean curd. Stir-fry for about 2 minutes. Pour in the stock, season with the salt and sugar. Cover, reduce the heat and cook till just moist, about 15 minutes. Stir in the shrimps and pounded bream. Sprinkle with pepper. Mix well and transfer into a serving dish to cool.
4. Make thin omelettes with the eggs, and shred these finely. Put in a dish and set aside.
5. Season the blanched bean sprouts with salt and sesame oil to taste, and place in a serving dish. Separate the lettuce leaves and cut each into two. Rinse well and pile on a plate.
6. Put the pounded peanut brittle, prepared mustard, chilli sauce and *Hoisin* sauce in separate little bowls or saucers.
7. To serve, take the cooked filling, shredded omelettes, bean sprouts, lettuce, pounded peanut brittle, mustard, the two sauces, coriander leaves, spring onion brushes and pancakes (11 items) to the table. Arrange them in a circle with the cooked filling in the middle, with one plate and a pair of chopsticks for each diner.
8. To eat, lay a piece of the pancake on the plate. Spread on a little chilli sauce on one half and *Hoisin* sauce on the other with an onion brush. Spread a piece of the lettuce over the sauces in the middle of the pancake. Arrange some cooked filling in a row on the lettuce. Top it with some bean sprouts, coriander leaves and shredded omelette. Sprinkle with some of the pounded peanut brittle. Use the onion brush to spread some *Hoisin* sauce round the edges of the pancake – this helps to stick the roll together – and add mustard if you prefer it hot. Fold up the pancake envelope-wise into a flattened roll about 5 cm (2 in) wide and 12 to 15 cm (5 to 6 in) long. Either eat it in your fingers or slice it into 4 or 5 pieces and eat with chopsticks.

For the bobing (pancake):
230 g (8 oz) strong plain white flour
1 tsp salt
170 ml (6 fl oz) water

1. Make a thick batter with the flour, salt and water. Beat well, cover and leave in a warm place till bubbles appear round the edges.
2. Use your hand to gather the batter from the edges and push it into the middle. Repeat till the batter is elastic and may be picked up like a piece of wet rag.
3. Saturate a folded piece of kitchen paper with cooking oil and have a piece of damp tea towel ready. Set a griddle or thick, flat-bottomed frying pan on a low heat. Wipe it with the oiled kitchen paper.
4. With your hand, pick up a handful of the elastic batter and wipe the heated surface of the griddle swiftly in a circular motion, making a circle about 18 to 20 cm (7 to 8 in) across. Return the rest of the batter to the bowl. When the edges of the pancake begin to curl up (very quickly), lift it out, put it on a plate and cover immediately with slightly dampened tea towel to prevent it from hardening. If the griddle or pan gets too hot the pancake will become coloured and burnt. In this case, wipe the surface with the damp cloth to reduce the heat and grease it with the oiled kitchen paper before proceeding. Stack the pancakes as you go along. This amount makes around 30, or 40 with practice.

Usually the pancakes are made a day in advance, wrapped and stored in a cool, dry place. The cooked filling may also be prepared in advance, as it is served at room temperature. For the buffet table these pancakes may be served ready filled and rolled up. (For the peanut brittle *see page* 207 and for spring onion brushes *see page* 239).

Chunbing – spring pancakes (Beijing)

For the pancakes:
230 g (8 oz) strong plain white flour
1 tsp salt
2 tsp vegetable oil
110 ml (4 fl oz) boiling water

oil for brushing

1. Sift the flour together with the salt on to a flat surface. Make a well in the centre, and put the vegetable oil and boiling water into it. Using a wooden spoon mix it into a dough. Knead till smooth.

Divide into 40 equal-sized pieces. Flatten each with the heel of your hand into a disc about 5 cm (2 in) across. Brush each lightly with oil and sandwich them in pairs, oiled sides together. With a rolling pin, roll each pair into a thin circle about 18 cm (7 in) across.

2. As you roll, cook each pair in a dry, heavy-based frying pan or griddle on a medium heat till bubbles appear; reduce the heat if it gets too hot. Turn over, and when bubbles appear again they are ready. Take them out, separate and stack together, oiled sides up. Cover them with a clean tea towel to keep them soft.

3. To serve, fold each pancake in half twice to make a quadrant. Arrange them, overlapping, in a circle on a plate.

For the mixed vegetable and cold meat platter:
1 cucumber (peeled and shredded)
140 g (5 oz) lettuce (shredded)
2-egg omelette (shredded)
2 sticks celery (shredded)
60 g (2 oz) coriander leaves (rinsed and whole)
170 g (6 oz) charsiu (barbecued pork; shredded)
110 g (4 oz) cooked ham (shredded)
170 g (6 oz) peeled cooked shrimps

Arrange the shredded vegetables, omelette, shrimps and meats in individual dishes or on a large platter.

STIR-FRIED BEAN SPROUTS AND CHINESE CHIVES

450 g (1 lb) mung bean sprouts
110 g (4 oz) Chinese chives
1 tsp salt
2 tbsp cooking oil

1. Pick over the chives, discard any soiled leaves and break off any brown ends. Rinse well and chop into 2.5 cm (1 in) lengths. Tail the sprouts and discard any bad ones. Rinse well and drain.

2. Set the wok on a high heat, and when very hot put in the oil and salt. Stir-fry the sprouts for about 2 minutes. Add the chives and stir-fry till they change colour. Remove from the wok, drain away any liquid and put in a dish.

STIR-FRIED PORK WITH BAMBOO SHOOTS

170 g (6 oz) lean pork (shredded)
110 g (4 oz) fatty pork (shredded)
110 g (4 oz) bamboo shoots (shredded)

4 caps winter mushrooms (soaked and shredded)
1 stalk spring onion (shredded)

Marinade for the pork:
1 tsp salt
2 tsp rice wine
2 tsp cornflour with a little water

For the seasoning:
1 slice ginger (minced)
1 stalk spring onion (minced)
2 tsp rice wine
1 tbsp light soya sauce
1 tbsp oyster sauce
2 tsp granulated sugar
pepper to taste
2 tbsp sesame oil
1 tsp cornflour with a little water

2 tbsp cooking oil

1. Marinate the lean pork. Mix together all the seasoning ingredients except the ginger, spring onion and rice wine, and set aside.
2. Set the wok on a high heat till hot, and put in the cooking oil. Stir-fry the ginger and spring onion till fragrant, add the fatty pork and stir-fry till the oil begins to run out. Add the marinated lean pork. Stir-fry till it loses its pink colour, then add the bamboo shoots and mushrooms. Mix well and sprinkle with the rice wine. Stir-fry to mix well and pour in the seasoning mixture. Mix well, and when the sauce thickens dish up on to a serving plate.

Dips in small bowls:
plum sauce
Hoisin *sauce*
sweet salted soya bean paste
chilli sauce
10 spring onion brushes

To serve, arrange the platter of pancakes and the meat and vegetable platters in a circle on the table with the small bowls of sauces dotted round. Each diner has a plate and a pair of chopsticks. To eat, spread a pancake on the plate, brush on a little sauce (or sauces combined, i.e. a sweet one with a hot one or a salty one) with a spring onion brush. Select a few items from the dishes and lay them neatly on the pancake. Fold up three sides envelope-wise, roll up and eat with your fingers.

The pancakes may be made in advance, wrapped and stored in the refrigerator. To refresh, steam in a wok or steaming basket over a high heat for about 5 minutes. As the meal is served at room temperature, the meat and vegetable dishes may also be prepared in advance. You may reduce or increase the items, but the classic *chunbing* should include bean sprouts and chives, pork and bamboo shoots. You may introduce stir-fried squid, or substitute beef or lamb for pork. In Beijing, where the eating of *chungbing* is taken seriously, there are two ways, formal and informal. For the formal one there must be included an assortment of eight kinds of sliced cooked meat, usually supplied by a specialist food shop. An informal one can be as simple as stir-fried sprouts and chives with stir-fried pork and bamboo shoots. (For *charsiu see page* 35. For spring onion brushes *see page* 239.)

Cantonese spring rolls (Guangdong)

For the wrappers:
4 sheets bean curd skin

For the filling:
350 g (12 oz) lean pork (shredded)
450 g (1 lb) Chinese celery cabbage (shredded)
110 g (4 oz) peeled cooked shrimps

For the seasoning:
2 tsp rice wine
1 tbsp dark soya sauce
2 tsp granulated sugar
1 tsp salt
2 tsp five-spice powder
60 ml (2 fl oz) stock or water
1 tsp cornflour with a little water

For the egg paste:
1 egg white
2 tsp cornflour with a little water

For the batter:
230 g (8 oz) self-raising flour
2 eggs
170 ml (6 fl oz) cold water
½ tsp salt

generous 1 l (2 pt) cooking oil

1. Set the wok over a high heat till hot, and put in 1 tbsp oil. Stir-fry the pork till it loses its pink colour, and add the rice wine and soya sauce. Stir-fry till cooked, and transfer to a dish.

2. Reheat the wok till hot, put in 1 tbsp oil and stir-fry the shredded cabbage for about 2 minutes. Add in the salt, sugar, five-spice powder and stock. When it comes back to the boil, stir in the pork. Thicken with the cornflour mixture. Add in the peeled shrimps, mix well and dish up. Cool and divide into 12 equal portions.

3. Lightly beat the egg white, and mix with the cornflour mixture into a thin paste.

4. Dip one sheet of bean curd skin at a time in hot water to soften, drain and pat dry with kitchen paper. Cut each piece into three squares of 12 × 12 cm (5 × 5 in), and trim off any hard edges. Spread one piece on a flat surface and brush it all over with some egg paste. Put a portion of the filling diagonally in the middle of the square. Fold in three corners envelope-wise and roll up, sealing the flap with more paste. Put on a plate folded-side-down. (*See illustrations.*) Make another 11 in the same way.

5. Make a batter with the flour, eggs, salt and cold water. It should be of a thick coating consistency.

6. Dip each spring roll in the batter, and deep-fry in hot oil till golden and crisp. Take out and drain on kitchen paper.

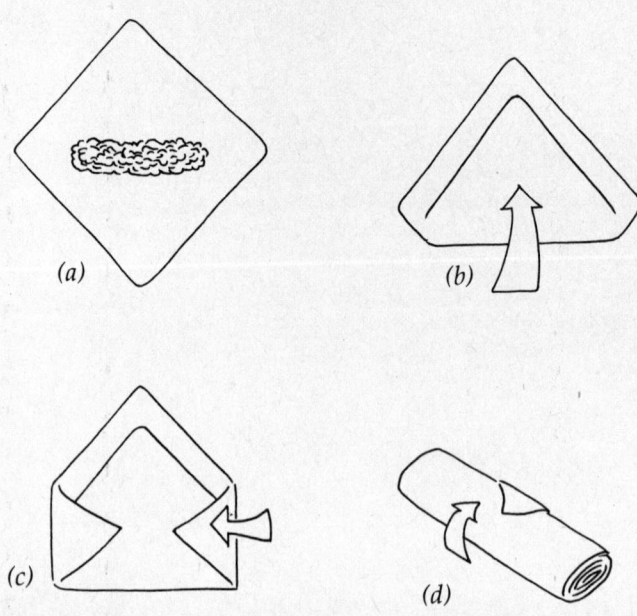

(a)

(b)

(c)

(d)

If more convenient, ready-made spring roll wrappers may be used without the batter, though the traditional Cantonese spring rolls are made with bean curd skins and coated with batter.

DUMPLINGS

Mandarin New Year dumplings (Hubei)

For the dumplings:
6 fresh mandarins or tangerines (or 1 can)
230 g (8 oz) glutinous rice flour
60 g (2 oz) granulated sugar
280 ml (½ pt) hot water

For the syrup:
110 g (4 oz) granulated sugar
850 ml (1½ pt) water
2 tsp cornflour with a little water

1. Peel the mandarins, separate the segments and remove every trace of pith. If there are any seeds, cut each segment into two and discard the seeds.
2. Dissolve the sugar in the water. Put the glutinous rice flour in a mixing bowl, make a well in the centre and pour in some of the sugared water. Gradually draw in the flour and mix, adding more of the sugared water till all is used up. Knead the dough till smooth.
3. Bring 850 ml (1½ pt) water to the boil. Break the dough into almond-size pieces and roll in your palms into round balls. Drop them into the boiling water as they are made. When cooked they will float to the surface. When all are done add the sugar, stir to dissolve and put in the mandarin segments. Bring to the boil again. Thicken with the cornflour mixture. Pour into a bowl and serve.

Rice dumplings in syrup are an ubiquitous dessert on New Year's Eve and also on the last, 15th day of the Spring Festival. This particular version is unusual in that it is cooked with mandarins, the creamy pearl-like dumplings contrasting with the bright orange mandarin segments. Sweet and sour with a clear, uncloying taste, it is a traditional banqueting dessert from Jiangling Xian in Hubei province for the Spring Festival celebration. The mandarin, or *ji*, is also traditionally a symbol of luck and fruitfulness in China, as the word *ji* is a homonym to both 'luck' and 'fruitfulness'. Besides, Jiangling Xian is renowned for its mandarins and other citrus fruits. For centuries successive poets such as Bai Juyi (Pai Chuyi), Dufu (Tufu) and the like have sung the praises of the Jiangling citrus fruits, comparing them to pearls. But the most flattering of praises comes from the historian, Sima Qian of the Han dynasty (202 BC–AD 220), who described Jiangling Xian as a place where 'every tree is a mandarin, and every person and household a marquis'.

Zongzi – glutinous rice dumplings in bamboo leaves

Zongzi, a pyramid-shaped glutinous rice dumpling wrapped in bamboo or reed leaves, is normally eaten during the Dragon Boat Festival on the 5th day of the 5th lunar month (roughly our June). On this day there is a very long-standing tradition of feasting, the eating of *zongzi*, and dragon boat racing. It is thought, from archaeological evidence, that this festival derives from prehistoric practices. A Stone Age people living in south China with a dragon totem probably celebrated a dragon's day, on which cooked foods in bamboo tubes or other leaves were made as offerings.

This festival later became a commemoration of the patriotic poet and minister, Qu-yuan, who took his own life by drowning on the 5th day of the 5th lunar month in the year 278 BC, during the era of the Warring Kingdoms. At the time his country was on verge of ruin and his counsel was ignored by the king, who took instead the advice of traitors. Thus his suicide was looked upon as a great patriotic gesture, for he would rather be dead than alive in a decadent age.

In the beginning these dumplings were cooked in bamboo tubes. Later the fragrant leaves of the mugwort (*Artemisia vulgaris*) were used; hence they were also known as 'mugwort perfumed dumplings' in the Song time (906–1279). By the Ming dynasty (1368–1644), reed leaves had become popular. From around Qing Qianlong's time (1736–1796) to the present day bamboo leaves have been preferred. The overseas Chinese, who live in tropical South-East Asia, prefer sweet fragrant screwpine (*pandan*, botanical name *Pandanus odoratissimus*) leaves for the sweet variety of dumplings, and reserve bamboo leaves for the savoury kinds.

In Britain, dried bamboo leaves imported from China are available all the year round. They come in bundles in assorted sizes, about 3 in to 4 in wide and 12 in to 17 in long. If stored in a plastic bag in a cool, dry place they keep almost indefinitely. An alternative leaf is the screwpine or *pandan*, mentioned above, which is imported fresh, but at a price.

Today these dumplings come in myriad varieties from different provinces, but generally there are three main types: plain dumplings made with lye water and eaten with honey or sugar syrup; a savoury kind with a delicious meat filling; and dumplings stuffed with mixed fruits such as chestnuts, dried persimmons and almonds.

Pork dumplings in bamboo leaves – Bazhang (Fujian)

For the dumplings:
700 (1½ lb) glutinous rice
2 shallots (chopped)
2 tsp granulated sugar
2 tsp salt
2 tbsp light soya sauce
280 ml (½ pt) stock or water
2 tbsp cooking oil

For the filling:
350 g (12 oz) belly pork with skin (parboiled)
20 chestnuts (boiled)
5 large caps winter mushrooms (soaked and quartered)
40 dried shrimps (soaked)

Seasoning for the pork:
280 ml (½ pt) pork stock or water
1 tbsp granulated sugar
2 tbsp dark soya sauce
2 tsp rice wine
2 tsp five-spice powder

20 trussing strings, each about 80 cm (32 in) long
40 bamboo leaves

1. Rinse the rice and soak for about 2 hours.
2. Tie the trussing strings into bunches of five each. Boil the bamboo leaves in batches in water till they turn dark green. Soak them in cold water till required. If soaked overnight, they revert to their fresh state.
3. Dice the parboiled pork into 20 pieces. Put them in the wok on a high heat, and add the stock and the seasoning for the pork. Bring to the boil, cover and simmer over a medium heat till the juice is sticky and almost dried up. Mix well, transfer to a dish and leave to cool.

4. Drain the soaked rice in a fine sieve. Set the wok on a high heat till hot and put in the oil. Cook the shallots till fragrant, add the sugar, salt, soya sauce and then the rice. Stir-fry till well mixed. Add in the stock or water, lower the heat, cover and cook for 5 minutes. Transfer to a dish and let cool. (The rice will be just flavoured and par-cooked.)

5. Have ready the soaked bamboo leaves, par-cooked rice, seasoned pork, boiled chestnuts, mushrooms and shrimps. Sling the strings across the back of a wooden chair or over a clothes airer. The best position is to sit in front of the strings.

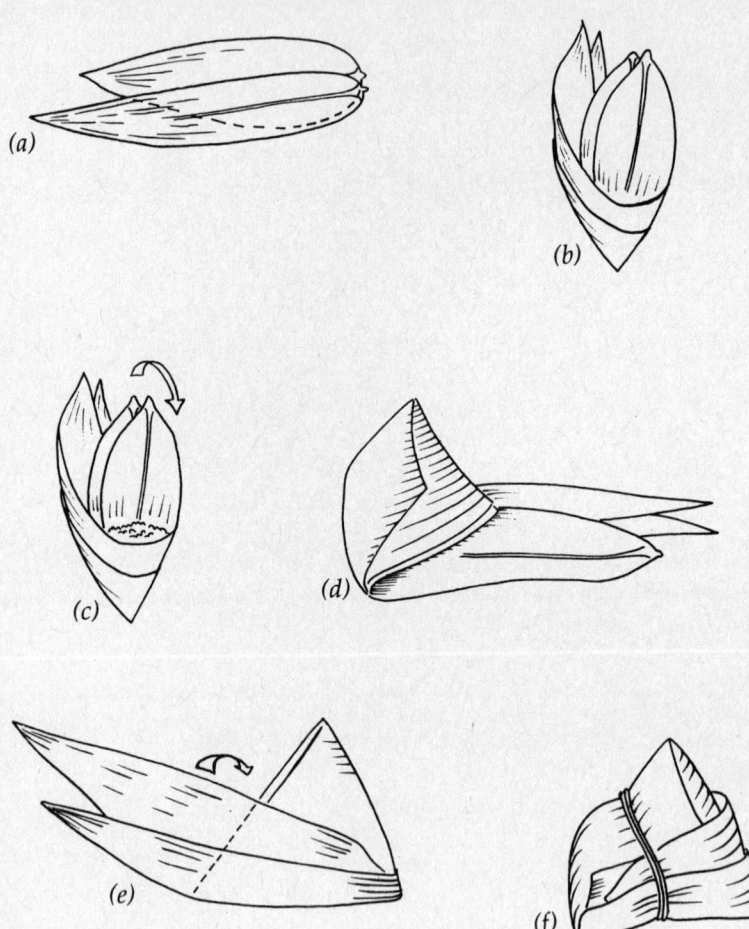

(a)

(b)

(c)

(d)

(e)

(f)

6. Take 2 bamboo leaves (try to use one large and one smaller one), arrange them smooth sides facing up, stalk ends together and overlapping for two-thirds of their width all along the length. (This is to strengthen and widen the leaves.) Fold them into a cone shape, with the left end longer than the right. Half fill the cone with the rice, make a dent in the rice, and put in 1 piece each of the pork, mushrooms, chestnuts and 2 shrimps. Cover with some more rice, pressing in to firm and shape into a pyramid. If the rice sticks to your fingers, dip them in water. (*See illustrations* a to c.)

7. Fold over the ends of the leaves on to the base of the pyramid. Fold up the edges along the two sides of the triangle. Bend the end of the leaves round the pyramid tightly. Wind a string round the pyramid twice, taking care to catch the ends of the leaves, and tie securely. Trim the ends to neaten. (*See illustrations* d to f.)

8. When all the dumplings are made, boil them in plenty of water to cover for about 1½ hours on a medium heat, topping up the water if necessary. Take out and hang up to cool and dry. Eat hot or cold, after removing the wrappings which are inedible. To reheat, steam them thoroughly.

Normally soaked but uncooked rice is used, but more skill is needed in the wrapping and tying and the cooking time would be at least 1 hour more. It is easier and faster to par-cook the rice by steaming or cooking as above. These dumplings are usually made in great numbers several days in advance. They keep well in a cool, dry place, usually hung up. To prevent them from spoiling they are steamed or boiled every few days, which improves the taste. The above recipe is a well-known speciality of Quanzhou on the coast of Fujian province. Quanzhou had early contacts with the outside world, and Marco Polo rated it the *largest* port he had seen. It is also a city with Moslem relics and monuments, and indeed the fourth disciple of Muhammad is buried there.

Lye water dumplings in bamboo leaves (Guangdong)

700 g (1½ lb) glutinous rice
2 tsp lye water mixed with 10 ml (4 fl oz) water
2 tsp bicarbonate of soda (optional)
2 tsp vegetable oil

40 bamboo leaves
20 trussing strings, each about 80 cm (32 in) long

1. Rinse the rice and soak for about 2 hours.
2. Drain it and steam in a steaming basket or in the wok for about 20 minutes. Take out and mix in the lye water mixture. Put it back to steam for another 10 minutes. Take out, mix in the oil and bicarbonate of soda, and cool.
3. Wrap the rice in bamboo leaves (*see* the previous recipe), omitting the filling.
4. Boil the dumplings in plenty of water for 1½ to 2 hours, adding more boiling water if necessary. Take out and dry.
5. To eat, unwrap the leaves and dip the dumplings in honey or sugar.

Care should be taken in measuring the lye water, as too much would render the dumplings unpalatable. This is a plain lye water dumpling, but sometimes they are stuffed with a walnut-size piece of sweet red bean paste and cooked in the same way.

Mixed fruit dumplings in bamboo leaves

For the rice dumpling:
generous 1 kg (1¼ lb) glutinous rice
30 g (1 oz) lard
110 g (4 oz) granulated sugar

For the filling:
110 g (4 oz) crystallized winter melon (chopped)
60 g (2 oz) crystallized pineapple (chopped)
30 g (1 oz) crystallized angelica (chopped)
30 g (1 oz) glacé cherries (chopped)
10 walnuts (skinned and chopped)
10 dried chestnuts
30 g (1 oz) melon or pumpkin seeds
30 g (1 oz) sultanas

40 bamboo leaves
20 trussing strings, each about 80 cm (32 in) long

1. Rinse the glutinous rice, and soak for several hours.
2. Prepare the bamboo leaves (*see page 119*).
3. Boil the chestnuts for about 10 minutes. Drain, remove any bits of red skin, and chop. Mix them together with the rest of the fruits and nuts. Divide into 20 equal portions.
4. Steam the rice in the wok or in a steaming basket lined with a piece of muslin for 30 minutes over a high heat, or till tender. Take out, and while still hot mix in the lard and sugar.

5. Wrap the rice and filling in the bamboo leaves (*see page* 120).
6. Boil the wrapped dumplings in plenty of water to cover for about 1 hour on a medium heat, topping up the pot with boiling water when necessary.

The fruits and nuts may be varied to taste. Melon seeds are dried cooked water melon seeds. Both pumpkin and melon seeds are available ready prepared.

Jiaozi – wheat dough dumplings

Jiaozi are half-moon shaped dumplings with a meat or vegetable filling. 'Jiaozi' is also a homonym for 'being with child', a fortunate association indeed in the Chinese mind. In the North where wheat is the staple food, *jiaozi* are a must for the first five days of the New Year and the Spring Festival celebrations. They are produced in great numbers in advance and frozen raw. When required they can be boiled, steamed, fried or deep-fried without first thawing, so they are a convenience food during festivities. At other times of the year, particularly in the North, the eating of *jiaozi* is a custom full of symbolic meaning, since it represents reunion, harmony and happiness. Family, relatives or friends gather together chatting, making and eating *jiaozi* over a holiday or weekend lunch. In Beijing people say, 'There is nothing as delicious as *jiaozi* and nothing as comfortable as lying down.'

Historical records show that *jiaozi* were consumed in the Three Kingdoms period (221–280 BC) and the Northern Qi era (550–589). But an ancient myth relates the origin of this humble fare. There once existed a goddess with a human head but the body of a snake. She was Nü Wa, the sister of Fuxi, the first of the five emperors of the legendary period (circa 2953–2828 BC). A superwoman, she performed great feats and is said to have smelted stones and repaired the sky when it crumbled. Her favourite pastime was to fashion human beings from yellow earth. But in the winter the clay people's ears fell off because of the frost. So she made holes in their ear lobes and threaded them with cotton, the ends of which were left in their mouths, so that the ears were secured. The term for 'biting the threads' is another homonym for *jiaozi*. Since the day of the Winter Solstice was in the depth of winter, when ears were most likely to fall off, it was a folk custom to eat the half-moon shaped *jiaozi* to forestall the disaster.

Later *jiaozi* were eaten not only at the Winter Solstice, but also at the Spring Festival and on other holidays. The popularity of *jiaozi* is said to have increased during the Qing dynasty (1644–1912), as the Manchurian imperial family loved a kind of *jiaozi* called *bobo* (dumpling) in Manchurian. Legend has it that Nurhachi (1559–1626), who consolidated the petty tribes and founded Manchu power, killed a marauding tiger during his tour of a tribal village. In gratitude villagers ground the tiger's meat, wrapped it in wheat dough, cooked and presented it as *bobo* to Nurhachi. Ever since, the Manchurians have eaten *bobo* every New Year. We know that there was a custom on New Year's Day for the palace ladies to dine in the inner palace of the dowager Empress Ci-Xi and to sample the New Year dishes created by the imperial chefs. Great fortune was considered to befall on anyone who found a coin in the *jiaozi* or *bobo*. Hence the eating of *jiaozi* in the imperial palace was a very important annual ritual for the palace ladies. (It must be said that this custom had existed since the Tang dynasty (618–906).) For this reason *jiaozi* was also known as *jiaochun*, or 'biting the spring', to celebrate the start of the year.

Another reason for *jiaozi* to be associated with good fortune is that its half-moon shape is similar to that of an ancient Chinese silver piece; thus to eat a *jiaozi* is to assimilate good fortune – particularly auspicious on New Year's Day. The parallel of this dumpling in the South is the Cantonese *won ton*, which literally means 'swallowing the clouds'. This refers to the ability of Chinese sages to ride above difficulties. Little wonder that there are now at least 100 varieties of *jiaozi*. There is no hard and fast rule in the making of this dumpling; the ingredients for the filling may be varied to suit one's preference. And, just as in ancient times, it may be frozen raw and then steamed, boiled, pan-fried or deep-fried when required.

Aubergine dumplings

For the dough:
130 g (8 oz) strong plain white flour
1 tsp sesame oil or vegetable oil
170 ml (6 fl oz) boiling water

For the filling:
450 g (1 lb) aubergines
170 g (6 oz) minced pork (¼ fat)
1 stalk spring onion (minced)
1 slice ginger (minced)
1 tsp salt
2 tsp granulated sugar
1 tbsp light soya sauce
1 tbsp sesame oil or vegetable oil

2 tsp cornflour with a little water
pepper to taste

cornflour or potato flour for dusting
oil for greasing

1. Put the flour on a flat surface. Make a well in the centre, and put in the sesame oil. Pour in the boiling water. Use a wooden spoon to mix in the flour. When cool enough to handle, knead it into a smooth dough with your hands. Dust with cornflour or potato flour. Cover with an upturned bowl. Leave to rest for at least 30 minutes.
2. Peel the aubergines, quarter lengthwise and boil till tender. Drain and cool. Put the cooled aubergine in a piece of muslin and squeeze out excess water, so that there is only about 170 g (6 oz) of aubergine purée.
3. Mix the aubergine purée with the minced pork. Add the rest of the ingredients for the filling, and mix well. Divide into 40 equal portions thus: cut the mixture into 4 equal parts. Take one part in your left hand, and squeeze a ball out between your left thumb and left index finger, scoop it out with a teaspoon and put it on a plate. Make 10 balls from each part.
4. Roll the rested dough into a cylinder, and cut into 40 equal portions. Take one piece of the dough, flatten it with your palm and use your fingers to shape it into a round, with the edges thinner than the centre. Place a portion of the aubergine mixture in the centre, and fold over the pastry into a semicircle. Pinch the edges to seal. Make another 39 in the same way. (*See illustrations.*)

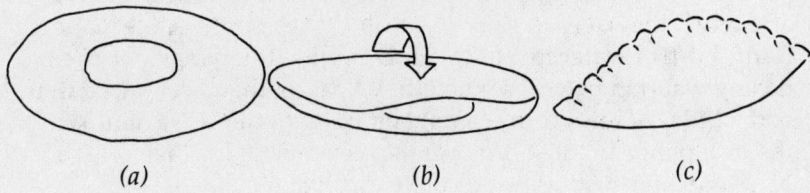

(a) (b) (c)

5. Steam them in a greased steaming basket over a high heat for about 8 minutes or till cooked. Remove the basket from the heat, brush each dumpling lightly with oil and take out with a spatula.

Boiled cabbage and meat dumplings (Beijing)

For the dough:
450 g (1 lb) strong plain white flour
230 ml (8 fl oz) cold water
1 tsp salt

For the filling:
230 g (8 oz) Chinese celery cabbage
230 g (8 oz) minced pork
2 tsp rice wine
1 tsp salt
2 tsp granulated sugar
1 tbsp sesame oil
1 stalk spring onion (minced)
1 slice ginger (minced)

For the dip:
chilli sauce
light soya sauce

extra flour for dusting

1. Shred the cabbage finely, then chop finely. Squeeze dry. Mix the chopped cabbage with the rest of the ingredients for the filling. Divide into 64 equal portions.
2. Gradually mix the flour with the salt and cold water into a pliable dough. Divide into 2 equal parts. Roll each into a cylinder and cut each into 32 equal portions. With the rolling pin, roll each on a floured surface into a circle of about 5 cm (2 in) diameter. Place a portion of the meat mixture in the centre, fold over into a semicircle and pinch the edges to seal. Make all the rest in the same manner.
3. Bring a pot of water to a fast boil. Drop the dumplings into the boiling water in batches. When they float on the water and puff up, add a little cold water to the pot and bring to the boil again. When the dumplings become transparent they are ready. Take out with a brass wire mesh strainer and place on a plate.
4. To eat, dip in a chilli and soya sauce mixture.

Carrot dumplings

For the dough:
350 g (12 oz) strong plain white flour

110 g (4 oz) carrot purée
1 tsp salt
60 ml (2 fl oz) hot water
2 tsp granulated sugar
2 tsp lard or vegetable oil

For the filling:
350 g (12 oz) skinned and boned chicken (finely diced)
4 caps winter mushrooms (soaked and finely diced)
110 g (4 oz) celery (finely diced)
2 stalks spring onion (finely chopped)
1 tbsp light soya sauce
1 tsp salt
pepper to taste
1 tbsp sesame oil
1 tsp cornflour with a little water

2 tbsp cooking oil
potato or cornflour for dusting
extra oil for greasing and brushing

1. Mix the flour, salt and sugar on a flat surface. Make a well in the centre and put in the lard and carrot purée. Use your hand to draw in the flour and mix gradually, adding the hot water a little at a time. Mix into a pliable dough and knead till smooth. Cover with a bowl and leave to rest.
2. Meanwhile, cook the filling. Set the wok on a high heat till hot, and put in the oil. Stir-fry the chicken meat, celery and winter mushrooms till the meat turns white. Add the spring onions, soya sauce, salt and pepper. Stir-fry briefly. Thicken with the cornflour, sprinkle with the sesame oil and transfer to a dish. Leave to cool completely.
3. Roll the rested pastry on a lightly floured surface. Cut into 30 equal parts. With your fingers, shape each into a round of about 6 cm (2½ in) diameter, with the edges thinner than the middle. Fill with 2 tsp of the meat mixture. Fold into a semicircle. Pinch the edges together to seal. Make another 29 in the same manner.
4. Steam the dumplings in batches in a greased and preheated steaming basket over a high heat for about 8 minutes or till cooked. Remove the basket from the heat and brush each dumpling lightly with some oil, then take them out with a spatula.

These tasty dumplings have the combined flavour of carrot, chicken and celery. They are a bright golden colour. They may be frozen uncooked and steamed from frozen over a high heat for 15 minutes. Take off the heat and leave to cool slightly before taking out.

Potato 'lohan' dumplings

For the dough:
350 g (12 oz) peeled potatoes
170 g (6 oz) strong plain white flour
1 tsp salt
2 tbsp vegetable oil

For the filling:
350 g (12 oz) minced pork
110 g (4 oz) bamboo shoots (finely diced)
4 caps winter mushrooms (soaked and finely diced)
2 stalks spring onion (chopped)

For the seasoning:
2 tbsp light soya sauce
1 tbsp rice wine
2 tsp granulated sugar
1 tsp salt
pepper to taste

1 tbsp cooking oil
potato flour or cornflour for dusting
extra oil for greasing and brushing

1. Set the wok on a high heat till hot and put in the oil. Stir-fry the pork till it loses its pink colour. Pour in the seasoning, and stir well. Add in the bamboo shoots and mushrooms, and when well mixed add in the spring onion and remove to a dish. Let it cool completely.
2. Boil and mash the peeled potatoes. Mix in the salt and oil and blend well. Let the mixture cool slightly before adding the flour. Knead on a lightly floured surface till smooth. Divide into 4 equal parts. Shape each into a cylinder and cut into 9 equal parts (about 15 g, ½ oz, each), making 36 pieces in all.
3. Take a piece of the potato dough, and use your fingers to shape it into a round of about 8 cm (3 in) diameter, thinner at the edge than in the middle. (Dip your fingers in the flour if they get sticky). Fill the centre with 2 tsp of the meat mixture. Fold into a semicircle. Gather and pinch the edges together to seal. Make the rest in the same way.

4. Steam the dumplings in batches in a greased and preheated steaming basket over a high heat for 8 minutes. Remove the basket from the heat, and brush each dumpling lightly with some oil. Transfer with a spatula on to a greased serving plate.

Do not attempt to roll out this dough or use a pastry cutter as it is too delicate for such treatment. In fact, it is faster to do it with your fingers. The eighteen *lohans* are the disciples of Buddha. These meat dumplings are named after the vegetarian *lohans* in spite of the meat filling, for the bulging shape resembles the pot belly of a monk.

Tomato dumplings

For the dough:
280 g (10 oz) strong plain white flour
1 tsp salt
2 tsp lard or cooking oil
140 g (5 oz) canned tomatoes

For the filling:
170 g (6 oz) skinned chicken breast or lean pork (minced)
30 g (1 oz) mung bean vermicelli (dry weight; soaked)
2 caps winter mushrooms (soaked)

Seasoning for the filling:
1 tsp salt
2 tsp rice wine
1 tbsp light soya sauce
1 tbsp sesame oil

1 tbsp cooking oil
extra oil for greasing and brushing

1. Pass the canned tomatoes through a fine sieve to reduce them to a purée. Mix the flour, salt, lard and tomato purée together, add about 80 ml (3 fl oz) water and knead into a pliable dough. Cover with a bowl and leave to rest for about 15 minutes.
2. Cut the soaked vermicelli into 1 cm (½ in) lengths. Dice the mushrooms into mung bean-size pieces.
3. Set the wok on a high heat till hot, and put in the oil. Stir-fry the meat and mushrooms till the meat turns white. Mix in the seasoning, and finally the vermicelli. Transfer to a dish and leave to cool completely. Divide into 20 portions.
4. Roll the rested dough into a cylinder and cut into 20 pieces. Take

one piece and shape with your fingers into a round about 8 cm (3 in)
across. Put a portion of the meat mixture in the centre. Bring in
three sides to meet in the middle and pinch the edges together to
seal completely, forming a pyramid shape. Make the rest in the
same manner.
5. Steam the dumplings in a greased and preheated steaming basket or
steamer over a high heat for about 7 to 8 minutes. Remove the
basket from the heat, and brush each dumpling lightly with some
oil. Take out with a spatula and put on a greased plate.

The raw pastry is apricot-coloured, but it turns to coral after cooking. It
has a tomato flavour, and the vermicelli gives it an interesting crunchy
texture.

MOON CAKES

On the 15th day of the 8th lunar month (roughly our September) the
Chinese celebrate the August Moon Festival, when it is believed that the
moon is at its brightest and biggest. In ancient times the emperor used to
make a ritual spring offering to the sun, and an autumn one after the
harvest to the moon. The August Moon Festival evolved from this
tradition, and continues to this day. Apart from a feast, there is a
celebration of the moon in the evening.

Moon cakes were not originally part of the festival. They are believed to
have been invented towards the end of the Yuan dynasty (1279–1368).
The Yuan were an alien ruling house. A well-known legend relates that
the moon cake was designed to carry a secret message urging the
slaughter of the Mongol soldiers billeted in Chinese households by the
Yuan emperors. By the Qing era (1644–1912), the imperial palace offering
included a nine-joint lotus root, which is a rarity; and a lotus-flower
pumpkin, that is a whole pumpkin sliced from the bottom towards the
stalk into equal segments but still joined together at the stalk end, and
opened out like the petals of a lotus flower. The joined petals served as a
symbol of reunion and harmony, as the occasion is also known as
Tuanyuanjie or Reunion Festival. The Qing imperial moon cake was
enormous, several feet in diameter. The emperor would lead the offering
ceremony with joss sticks, followed by the empress and the entourage of
concubines. The high point of the evening was an entertainment and
viewing of the moon, held in the imperial pleasure boats.

For the ordinary people, today as in the past, a table is set with fruits, nuts, pumpkin seeds, moon cakes and tea. It is placed on the verandah, where one is more accessible to the moon, as the Chinese saying goes. The family relaxes and waits for the moon to rise; myths and tales are related and poems recited or improvised. When the moon has risen, the food is first offered to her; then pumpkin seeds are cracked, pomelos cut and peeled, and moon cakes are served with fragrant tea. The favourite myth that is told is that of the woman who swallowed her husband's hidden elixir and found herself turned into an immortal goddess, Chang'e; she then flew to the moon. An ancient version adds that she later turned into a toad on the moon to atone for her presumption. But poets in later dynasties sang the eulogy of Chang'e, describing her beauty and sympathizing with her eternal isolation on the moon.

The Chinese people have a strong feeling for the moon, which is thought to be capable of conveying one's innermost emotions and thoughts. The bright moon is said to convey one's lovesickness to one's lover over a thousand *li* (metaphorically miles) away. When on the other hand one gazes at the bright moon, one inevitably thinks of one's homeland, as is said in a famous line by Li Bai (Li Po) circa 705–762, the great Tang poet famed for his love of the moon. He was at one time a member of a coterie called the 'Six Tramps of the Bamboo Brook' (his residence) and at a later time he was one of the Daoist coterie called the 'Eight Immortals of the Wine Cup'. He was drowned one moonlit night whilst leaning over the boat in an attempt to embrace the moon in the river.

For more sober Chinese, love of the moon is reflected in a dramatic and noisy rescue operation. When *Tiangou*, the dog of heaven, apparently tries to swallow the moon during a lunar eclipse, whole villages or towns indulge in a cacophonous banging of pots and pans, or anything that will produce a clashing noise, louder and louder in a great crescendo until the dog in his fright releases the moon from his jaws. Country folk still hold that, if left unchallenged, the dog of heaven would swallow the moon.

Cantonese moon cakes (Guangdong)

For the pastry:
450 g (1 lb) strong plain white flour
230 ml (8 fl oz) pineapple syrup (see below)
110 ml (4 fl oz) groundnut oil or other vegetable oil
½ tsp lye water

For the pineapple syrup:
230 g (8 oz) granulated sugar
170 ml (6 fl oz) water
110 ml (4 fl oz) pineapple juice
1 tbsp lemon juice

For the filling:
900 g (2 lb) red bean paste or lotus seed paste

For the glaze:
2 egg yolks (lightly beaten with a pinch of salt)
flour for dusting

1 moon cake mould

1. Prepare the syrup at least 3 days or up to 2 weeks beforehand, so that it has time to mature. Dissolve the sugar in the water and boil for about 10 minutes. Add the pineapple juice and lemon juice. Continue to boil for about 30 minutes on a medium heat. When froth appears, be sure to lower the heat or it will boil over. Leave to cool, cover and store in a cool, dry place.
2. Prepare the red bean paste (*see page* 237). Make sure the paste for the moon cake is not too soft, or it will affect the pastry when baked. Also lard should be used for the fat in the proportion of 1 part lard to 4 parts red bean purée; otherwise the filling would be too crumbly. Divide the red bean paste into 15 equal portions, and shape them into balls.
3. Make the pastry. Sift the flour onto a flat surface. Make a well in the centre and pour in the syrup, oil and lye water. Use your hand to draw in the flour, and mix into a pliable dough. (It looks and feels like a kneaded marzipan.) Cover with a bowl and leave for at least an hour before use; otherwise the pastry would stick to the mould.
4. Preheat the oven to 200°C (400°F, gas 6). Grease two baking sheets. Divide the rested pastry into 15 equal portions. Shape one portion with your fingers into a round about 8 cm (3 in) across and put a portion of the red bean paste on it. Gather the edges together, pinch to seal, and shape into a ball. Dust the cake mould with some flour. Press the ball into the floured mould, gathered-side-up. Press to print the pattern on to the pastry. Turn the mould over and gently tap it to release the cake on to the greased baking sheet. Make another 14 in the same way.
5. Bake the cakes for about 15 minutes or till pale golden. Take them out and brush with the beaten egg yolk. Return them to the oven and bake till golden brown, about another 10 minutes.

Flaky moon cakes – Suzhou style

For the oil pastry:

230 g (8 oz) strong plain white flour
110 g (4 oz) lard or white vegetable fat

For the water pastry:

280 g (10 oz) strong plain white flour
60 g (2 oz) lard or white vegetable fat
30 g (1 oz) granulated sugar
½ tsp salt
140 ml (5 fl oz) cold water

For the filling:

550 g (1¼ lb) red bean paste

20 squares greaseproof paper, 5 × 5 cm (2 × 2 in)
a little red colouring

1. Divide the red bean paste into 20 equal portions, and shape them into balls.
2. Make the oil pastry. Sift the flour on to a flat surface. Rub the lard into the flour with your fingers (or this may be done in a food processor) and then mix into a dough. Do not overwork it. Divide into 20 equal parts, cover with an upturned bowl and rest them for at least 30 minutes.
3. Make the water pastry. Sift the flour with the salt on to a flat surface. Make a well in the centre, and put in the lard, sugar and water. Mix with your hands into a pliable dough. Divide into 20 equal parts, cover with an upturned bowl and rest them for at least 30 minutes.
4. Flatten each piece of the rested water pastry with your palm into a round and wrap in it a piece of the oil pastry. There are now 20 balls.
5. Place one ball of the wrapped pastry on a flat surface, and use a rolling pin to flatten it into a strip about 10 cm (4 in) long. With your hand, roll it up into a cylinder. Stand it upright and press it gently with the heel of your palm to flatten it. Roll it out again to about 10 cm (4 in) long, and roll up into a cylinder. Again stand it upright and press it down into a flat disc.
6. Use the rolling pin to enlarge the flattened disc to about 8 cm (3 in) across. Place a portion of the red bean paste in the middle, gather up the edges and pinch them together to seal. Place it, gathered side down, on a greaseproof square. With the rolling pin, press the top

lightly to flatten the cake to about 6 cm (2½ in) diameter. Make the rest of the cakes in the same manner.

7. Hold 3 chopsticks together, dip them in the red colouring and press the tips gently on the top of each cake to make a decorative motif.
8. Preheat the oven to 200°C (400°F, gas 6). Bake for about 15 to 20 minutes till they become crisp and flaky, but are still pale and cream-coloured. Cool them on a cake rack and store in an airtight container. They will keep for about 10 days.

RICE

Eight Treasures rice

For the rice pudding:
230 g (8 oz) glutinous rice
30 g (1 oz) lard
60 g (2 oz) granulated sugar

For the mixed fruits and nuts:
12 glacé cherries
60 g (2 oz) crystallized winter melon
60 g (2 oz) crystallized angelica
30 g (1 oz) crystallized peel
60 g (2 oz) chestnuts
30 g (1 oz) walnuts
1 tbsp pine kernels
4 honey dates
110 g (4 oz) red bean paste

For the syrup:
60 g (2 oz) granulated sugar
60 ml (2 fl oz) water

lard for greasing

1. Rinse the rice, and boil it as you would long-grain rice. Mix in the lard and sugar when it is still hot. Set aside.
2. Cut each glacé cherry into half and put on a plate. Slice the winter melon into oblong slivers and put them in a pile next to the halved cherries. Slice the angelica in pieces the same size as those of the melon and put on the same plate.

3. Boil the chestnuts for 10 minutes, remove any bits of red skin, and chop. Pour boiling water on the walnuts, skin them with a cocktail stick, beginning from the flat side, and chop. Rinse the pine kernels. Pour hot water on the honey dates to soften them, stone and chop. Chop the peel. Mix all the nuts and dates together with the rice and set aside.

4. Grease a pudding basin with lard, making sure it is well covered. Arrange the halved cherries to cover the whole of the base, cut side up. Line the sides of the basin completely with the oblong slivers of the angelica so that the lower ends just touch the cherries. Arrange the winter melon slivers above the angelica on the sides of the basin. Chop any leftover cherries, melon and angelica and add them to the rice mixture. Mix well.

5. Half fill the basin with the rice mixture. Press it slightly to level it. Spread the red bean paste on it, leaving a 1 cm (½ in) border all round. Put the rest of the rice mixture on top. Spread to cover the basin completely, pressing in lightly to firm it. Cover the top with cling film and secure with a rubber band. (Up to this stage, the pudding may be prepared in advance and refrigerated overnight.)

6. Steam in a pot on a medium heat for 45 minutes to 1 hour or longer. After the first hour turn down the heat to a simmer; it is impossible to overcook this pudding. Turn it out on to a dish.

7. Dissolve the sugar in the water, bring to the boil and pour over the pudding.

One never gets tired of this pudding, as the ingredients may be varied every time. The richness depends on the amount and number of fruits and nuts used. A really plain and simple one may contain only rice, red dates and red bean paste; in fact these were originally the only ingredients. The present ornate form of Eight Treasures rice was said to have been evolved in the imperial kitchen; it has since become a classic dessert for festive occasions. The number 8 is auspicious. It is associated with the eight trigrams or *bagua*, arranged in an octagonal shape. These symbols were invented by the father of the first king of the Zhou dynasty (1027–256 BC), and have traditionally played a great part in divination. In later times, and now, the design is both decorative and protective; it often appears in porcelain, on doors and pendants. (*See illustration.*) One may say the number has a similar force in China to the number 7 in the West. There are references to eight kinds of vegetables eaten by the emperor at certain times of the year, before which no commoner should eat them. And there were 8 delicacies on which the emperor was supposed to dine (*see page* 99). For the Buddhists the Eight Treasures are the eight organs of Buddha: the heart, gall bladder, spleen, lungs, liver, stomach, kidneys

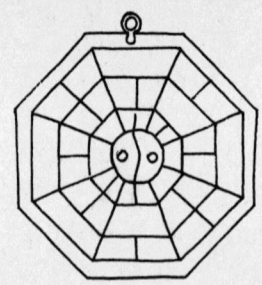

A decorative bagua *pendant*

and guts. But for the Daoists they represent the emblems of the Eight Immortals of Daoism: the sword, fan, basket of flowers, lotus flowers, flute, gourd, castanets and another musical instrument.

Hainan chicken rice (Guangdong)

1 plump chicken, about 1.8 kg (4 lb)
1 slice ginger (bruised)
1 stalk spring onion (whole)
2 tsp salt

For the pilaf:
450 g (1 lb) rice
2 cloves garlic (minced)
1 slice ginger (minced)
1 stalk spring onion (minced)
2 tbsp raw chicken fat (chopped) or vegetable oil
850 ml (1½ pt) chicken stock from the cooking liquor

For the soup:
coriander leaves (whole)
60 g (2 oz) salted mustard greens (shredded)
generous 1 l (2 pt) chicken stock

For the dip:
5 cm (2 in) piece galangal lesser (ginger)
2 whole fresh chillies
2 cloves garlic
1 tsp salt
3 tbsp vinegar
2 tbsp rendered chicken fat or vegetable oil

1. Bring 2.5 l (4 pints) of water to the boil over a high heat with the ginger, spring onion and salt. Put in the chicken, breast up. Bring to the boil again, skim, reduce the heat to medium, cover and boil gently for 10 minutes. If boiling too fast, reduce the heat. Turn the chicken over, cover and boil gently for another 10 minutes. Turn off the heat, but leave the pot covered on the stove for another 25 to 30 minutes for the chicken to cook through.
2. Transfer the chicken to a colander and reserve the cooking liquor. Rinse the skin with cold water to prevent further cooking and shrinking. Leave to cool completely at room temperature.
3. Rinse the rice in several changes of cold water and drain in a fine sieve. Set a thick-bottomed pot on a medium heat and cook the chicken fat till the oil runs out. Stir-fry the spring onion, ginger and garlic till fragrant and pale golden. Stir-fry the rice till it begins to crackle. Pour in 850 ml (1½ pt) of the reserved liquor, and stir to mix well. Cover and bring to the boil over a high heat. Reduce the heat to low and cook for about 15 minutes, then turn off the heat but leave the pot on the stove for another 5 minutes, or until required, for the rice to swell further.
4. Meanwhile, scrape the galangal and pound finely. Rinse in cold water till only the hair-fine fibres are left. Squeeze dry and put in a little bowl. Chop and pound the chillies, removing the seeds to reduce the fierceness, and when well broken up add the garlic and salt. Pound to a purée. Scoop out with a spoon and add to the galangal fibre. Mix in the vinegar. Render the chicken fat, or heat up the vegetable oil if used, and add to the chilli mixture. Mix well and put into individual saucers.
5. Chop the cooled chicken into bite-size pieces, and arrange neatly on a large serving plate.
6. Bring the rest of the stock to the boil. Skim off any excess fat. Put in the shredded salted mustard greens, bring to the boil again, skim, and pour into a soup tureen. Sprinkle with the coriander leaves. Scoop the rice into a large bowl.
7. Take the chicken, soup, dip saucers and rice to the table. Each diner is served with a bowl of rice, a bowl of soup and a saucer of the chilli dip. This amount serves 4 to 6 people, depending on their appetite.

If preferred, individual saucers of light soya sauce may be added as a dip. The soup is eaten at the same time as the rice and chicken, but it may be eaten as a first course in the Western style. This simple, yet delicious and complete meal is eaten every festival day by the people of Hainan, the tropical island off the south coast of China. Traditionally a plump, tender young hen just beggining to lay eggs is preferred. For a big family a capon around 2.3 to 2.7 kg (5 to 7 lb) is best.

Labazhou – Seven Treasures porridge

For the porridge:
170 g (6 oz) glutinous rice
30 g (1 oz) walnuts
60 g (2 oz) shelled dried chestnuts or 110 g (4 oz) fresh chestnuts
15 g (½ oz) pine kernels
30 g (1 oz) crystallized lotus seeds
3.5 l (6 pt) water

For the flavouring:
10 red dates (soaked and stoned)
10 almonds (blanched and chopped)
1 dried persimmon (soaked and chopped)
30 g (1 oz) crystallized winter melon (chopped)
30 g (1 oz) sultanas
granulated sugar to taste

1. Pour boiling water on the walnuts, and leave for 2 minutes. Skin, starting from the flat side, with a cocktail stick, and rinse. Boil the chestnuts briefly and remove any bits of red skin.
2. Rinse the rice and bring to the boil with the walnuts, chestnuts, pine kernels and lotus seeds in the water. Reduce the heat to medium and cook till the rice grains burst, stirring occasionally to prevent sticking.
3. Add all the fruits for the flavouring to the cooked rice. Bring to the boil. Sugar to taste. Ladle into 6 individual bowls and serve hot.

Seven Treasures porridge or *labazhou* is a ceremonial food eaten as a snack on the 8th day of the 12th lunar month, which is known as *laba* day. On this day cakes, fruits and nuts are offered to one's ancestors. This is the penultimate feast before the Spring Festival, the last one being the 24th of the 12th lunar month, the festival of the kitchen god. Way back in Zhou times (1027–256 BC), there was a tradition of hunting (*la*) wild animals for offerings in the 12th lunar month. As a result the 12th lunar month became known as *la* month, and the 8th of that month *laba*. In those days the Spring Festival actually began on the *laba* day; it was also called the Minor New Year. For in China from that day onwards the days begin to lengthen. This mixed fruit and grain porridge is eaten to ensure a good harvest of the five grains in the New Year. For the Chinese Buddhists the *laba* festival has a very different meaning. It is the Festival of Enlightenment, for, as legend has it, Buddha was enlightened on that day, following a meal of similar porridge cooked by a shepherdess who found him semi-conscious by the wayside. Hence it is the tradition for Buddhist temples to serve *labazhou* to monks and visitors on that day.

The earliest *labazhou* was cooked with simpler ingredients: glutinous rice and red aduki beans. Gradually more ingredients were introduced until there were seven kinds of mixed fruits, nuts and grains; hence the names 'Seven Treasures porridge' (*Qibaozhou*) or 'Five Flavours Porridge' (*Wuweizhou*). Some recipes contain a mixture of millet, glutinous millet, glutinous rice, long-grain rice, chestnuts, water chestnuts and red dates, which are then flavoured with chopped walnuts, almonds, peanuts, watermelon seeds, hazelnuts and sultanas. In fact there is a cornucopia of ingredients: favourites include a mixture of husked *kaoliang* (sorghum), maize, barley, madonna lily bulbs, lotus seeds, mung beans, and even longans, all flavoured with crystallized fruits. In north-west China a savoury version is prepared with lamb. In Shanxi province it is usual to cook a version with eight kinds of vegetables, which is then poured over cooked noodles and known as *labamian*, or *laba* noodles. Inevitably, in humid Sichuan the *laba* noodles are also spiced with hot chillis. In Harbin in the cold northwest there are *laba* leeks, and in Beijing it is usual to eat *labazhou* chilled.

Stir-fried savoury Eight Treasures rice

450 g (1 lb) glutinous rice

For the meat and vegetable mixture:
1 tbsp dried shrimps (soaked)
30 g (1 oz) dried cuttlefish (briefly soaked and shredded)
170 g (6 oz) boiled belly pork or charsiu (diced pea-sized)
4 caps winter mushrooms (soaked and diced pea-sized)
1 tbsp dried black wood ears (soaked and diced pea-sized)
60 g (2 oz) cooked ham or smoked back bacon (diced pea-sized)
60 g (2 oz) cooked garden peas
1 tbsp pine kernels
30 g (1 oz) fried peanuts

Marinade for the belly pork:
1 tbsp light soya sauce
2 tsp rice wine
pepper to taste

Seasoning for the rice:
1 tbsp light soya sauce
1 tsp salt
2 tsp granulated sugar
pepper to taste

Garnish:
2 tbsp coriander leaves or parsley (chopped)

4 tbsp cooking oil

1. Rinse the glutinous rice, and soak for at least 3 hours or overnight. Drain and scald in boiling water for 1 minute, then drain well in a fine sieve.
2. Marinate the belly pork, if used, for about 15 minutes. (For *charsiu see page* 35.)
3. Set the wok on a high heat till hot, and put in 1 tbsp oil. Stir-fry the shrimps and cuttlefish and when fragrant and crackling, add the pork, mushroom and wood ears. Stir-fry for about 2 minutes. Add the ham, garden peas and pine kernels. Stir-fry for another minute, and when thoroughly fried and fragrant, mix in the peanuts and dish up.
4. Return the wok to a medium heat; there is no need to rinse it. Put in the rest of the oil. Stir-fry the rice, sprinkle with cold water and cover for 1 minute, then lift the cover and stir-fry to mix well. Repeat this process about 4 or 5 times or till the grains are cooked through, when they become soft and break easily. If a softer rice is preferred, repeat the process. Mix in the seasoning for the rice and adjust.
5. Stir in the cooked meat and vegetable mixture. Mix well and dish up. Garnish with chopped coriander leaves.

On the birth of a child this savoury Eight Treasures Rice is eaten in celebration by the family, and usually a small bowl is sent round to neighbours and friends to announce the new arrival. This custom is prevalent in rural Guangdong and Fujian.

FIRE POTS

The fire pot or 'steamboat' is used to cook raw sliced meat, fish, seafood, vegetables or noodles in a strong, well-flavoured stock. The special pot with its built-in stove is a warming presence on the dining table, so that this is a popular winter meal, especially at festive times. A dinner with a steamboat on the eve of the New Year is called *weilu*, 'surrounding the stove', a symbol of family reunion and harmony. The ingredients and accompanying dips may differ from area to area.

Historical records show that various kinds of pots similar to the fire pot were used in China as early as the Eastern Han period (AD 25–220). Recently a mural has been found in Inner Mongolia which depicts three people sitting on the floor with a kind of fire pot, in front of which is a small table with wine cups, and at the side a container full of chunks of lamb. This mural shows that fire-pot cooking may well have been usual for more than a thousand years in north-eastern China. We certainly know that the Manchu inhabitants of this area brought their steamboat cooking into China following their conquest, and that wild game steamboat eating became a fashion in the Qing time (1644–1912). Pheasant and lamb were among the favoured ingredients. Steamboats are known to have been a festive favourite in the imperial palace.

One of the Qing emperors, Qianlong (1736–1796), was very fond of steamboat cooking, so that during his six tours of the Jiangnan, the provinces south of the Yangzi, he was always greeted with steamboat banquets. This circumstance did much to assist the spread of steamboat eating throughout the country. It is recorded that at the coronation celebration of the Qing emperor, Renzongrui, in January 1796, a great banquet was held in the imperial palace in Beijing, to which eminent people from all over the country were invited. At this banquet more than 1,500 fire pots were used, besides the normal range of delicacies from land and sea. It is considered the biggest steamboat banquet ever held in the history of China or anywhere else.

In the old days the classic ingredients were wild game with herbs such as ginseng, and including such items as deer's tendons, pheasant and grouse, augmented by pork, lamb, beef, fish, chicken, duck, prawns and other seafood. Now the steamboat is used everywhere in festive cooking: in the north-east there are the 'white meat steamboat' and 'mixed meat steamboat'; in Beijing the 'lamb fire pot'; in Shanghai the 'chrysanthemum fire pot'; in Guangdong the *'tapinglu'* (translated literally as 'surrounding the stove'); and in Sichuan the 'hairy tripe fire pot' and many others. However, the best steamboat is deemed to come from the north-east, the homeland of the Manchurian tribes. Their pot is large and takes a great quantity of ingredients, so providing a hefty meal. The 'white meat steamboat' is rather unusual in that the pork is par-cooked and cut into square chunks and then boiled and allowed to freeze solid in its juice; then it is thinly sliced into shavings of white meat. The remaining cooking liquor is brought to the boil in the steamboat and the meat shavings added. Other ingredients such as preserved or pickled vegetables, mung bean vermicelli, *doufu*, soaked dried shrimps, oysters and mushrooms are added.

Assorted fire pot (Hunan)

110 g (4 oz) lean pork loin
110 g (4 oz) fresh white fish (skinned and boned)
1 fresh pig's kidney
110 g (4 oz) skinned and boned chicken breast
12 fish balls
80 g (3 oz) bamboo shoots
4 large caps winter mushrooms (soaked)
110 g (4 oz) bocai or spinach leaves
110 g (4 oz) Chinese celery cabbage leaves
110 g (4 oz) chrysanthemum leaves or lettuce leaves

Marinade for the fish and meat:
1 tbsp light soya sauce
2 tsp rice wine
2 tbsp stock

For the soup:
generous 1 l (2 pt) strong chicken stock
1 tbsp light soya sauce
1 tsp salt
pepper to taste
2 tsp rendered chicken fat

For the dip:
chilli sauce

1 tbsp lard or cooking oil

1. Cut the pig's kidney in half lengthwise and core thoroughly. Rinse, and cut into thin, bite-sized slices. Slice the pork, chicken and fish into thin, bite-size pieces. Lay them neatly in 4 separate small plates. Sprinkle them all with the marinade.
2. Rinse the spinach, lettuce and cabbage leaves well, shake dry and put in 3 separate plates. Cut the cabbage if too long. Cut each fish ball into two. Slice the mushrooms and bamboo shoots into juliennes.
3. Set the wok on a high heat, put in the lard and briefly stir-fry the

bamboo shoots, winter mushrooms and the fish balls, then add the stock. Bring to the boil and season. Finally, stir in the rendered chicken fat. Pour into the fire pot. Put burning charcoal in the stove of the firepot.

4. Take the fire pot to the table and place on a heatproof mat. Place the 4 plates of raw sliced fish and meat and the 3 plates of vegetables and chilli sauce in little individual saucers round the fire-pot.

5. To eat, each diner puts a piece of fish or meat in a little brass wire mesh strainer and lowers it into the soup. When cooked it is taken out and eaten with the dip. Cook and eat the vegetables in the same way. The soup is drunk in between.

For the fish balls *see page* 232. Ready-made ones are available. The ingredients may be varied according to your taste, and the fire pot replenished from the stockpot if required.

Fish ball fire pot (Hunan)

16 fish balls
110 g (4 oz) pork loin
110 g (4 oz) bamboo shoots
4 large caps winter mushrooms
80 g (3 oz) mung bean vermicelli
140 g (5 oz) Chinese celery cabbage

For the soup:
generous 1 l (2 pt) strong chicken stock or pork stock
1 tsp salt
1 tbsp light soya sauce
pepper to taste

1 tbsp melted lard or vegetable oil

For the dips:
chilli sauce
light soya sauce

1. Pour boiling water on the vermicelli. Leave for 5 minutes, drain, rinse in cold water and drain again thoroughly. Cut into 12 cm (5 in) lengths with a pair of sharp kitchen scissors. Cut the pork, bamboo shoots, winter mushrooms and cabbage into julienne strips. For fish balls *see page* 232. Rinse them in boiling water.

2. Put the vermicelli in the fire pot. Place the cabbage on top. Put the

fish balls on the cabbage. Lay the bamboo shoots, mushrooms and pork on the fish balls. Sprinkle with the melted lard.

3. Bring the stock to the boil, season and pour into the fire pot. Put burning charcoal inside the stove of the fire pot. Take it to the table and place on a heatproof mat. (The charcoal should keep the soup simmering.) Serve the chilli and soya sauce in small individual saucers.

4. When the pork is cooked, lift it out and serve with the bamboo shoots and mushrooms, followed by the fish balls, cabbage and finally the vermicelli.

Always have extra stock in reserve so that the fire pot may be replenished when necessary. For more fire pot recipes, please see *The Chinese Kitchen* by the same author (Weidenfeld and Nicolson, London, 1986).

Qiaoguo – Fruit of Skill

Qiaoguo, literally 'fruit of skill', is a pastry snack traditionally eaten on *qixi*, the evening of the 7th day of the 7th lunar month, when every year the weaver goddess, the cowherd boy and their children are reunited across the Milky Way. This festival is particularly popular in Guangzhou. During the evening young girls are dressed up to look as pretty as goddesses and fruits, nuts, *qiaoguo* and tea are laid out on a table under the trellis. Each girl is given seven threads and seven needles and the one who threads most needles in the shortest time under the moonlight will become the most skilful in needlecraft. The weaver goddess is the genius of weaving and needlework, and anyone who aspires to excel in these skills besieges her for inspiration and perfection. This begging is called *qiqiao*.

A fascinating legend relates the origin of this celebration. One poor orphan cowherd boy was banished by his cruel sister-in-law to rear nine cows in the wilderness, with the instruction never to return until there were ten in the herd. In the wild an old man appeared to the disconsolate boy, and told him to rescue a sick ox near the foot of a hill. The ox recovered after several days and told the boy he was the grey ox god, banished from heaven for having brought the five grains to earth. The cowherd boy returned home with his tenth animal. Naturally his sister-in-law was displeased, and so they divided the family property. The cowherd boy received only an old cart and the grey ox. When he moved into a hut of his own, the ox spat out a bean that grew into a rambling bush and the cowherd boy built a trellis for it to climb on. The ox told the boy, 'If you hide under the trellis at night you will be able to see the goddesses in heaven. And the one who secretly returns your gaze for seven continuous nights wishes to marry you. Then I shall drive you up there in the cart to bring her here.' On the 7th day of the 7th month a magpie delivered a message from the weaver goddess to the ox to meet her, and she arrived on earth with her loom and silkworms and they were happily married. (The magpie is thus a bird of good tidings in the Chinese tradition.) In three years they had a boy and a girl, called 'Gold Brother' and 'Jade Sister'.

But this happy state of affairs did not last long. One day the ox told the cowherd boy that the queen of heaven was after his head for having taken her daughter to earth and they would be her next target, but that if they ate his flesh after he died they would turn into a god and a goddess. This they did. On the 7th day of the next 7 month, the queen of heaven abducted her daughter back to heaven. The cowherd boy grabbed his children, one in each hand, and followed in pursuit. Suddenly the queen of heaven drew a line below her feet with a gold hairpin, and immediately created a galaxy that separated them forever. The weeping of the children and the cowherd boy beside the galaxy touched the heart of the king of heaven, who permitted the family to meet once a year on the eve of the 7th day of the 7th lunar month. Hence the bright star next to the Milky Way is the weaver goddess and the three new stars on the other side are her family. It is believed that every year on that evening anyone who stays under a trellis will be able to see a string of magpies forming a heavenly ladder, and the cowherd boy and his children ascending the Milky Way for the annual reunion.

450 g (1 lb) strong plain white flour
1 tsp salt
110 g (4 oz) icing sugar
30 g (1 oz) black sesame seeds
110 g (4 oz) bean curd (sieved)
1 egg (lightly beaten)

generous 1 l (2 pt) cooking oil
extra flour for dusting

1. Sift the flour and salt on to a flat surface, and make a well in the centre. Put the sugar, sesame seeds, sieved bean curd and egg with 60 ml (2 fl oz) water in the well. Use your hand to mix these into a pliable dough. Cover with an upturned bowl or basin and leave to rest for about 30 minutes.
2. Cut the rested dough in half and roll each on a well-floured surface into a paper-thin pastry. Dust well with more flour, and cut with a sharp knife into strips about 4 cm (1½ in) wide and 8 cm (3 in) long.

Make 2 cuts about 5 cm (2 in) long along the length of each strip, about 1 cm (½ in) apart. Insert one end of the strip through one of the slits and pull through (*see illustrations*). Do this to all the strips.
3. Deep-fry in hot oil till golden and crisp. Take out with a brass wire mesh strainer and drain well on kitchen paper. When cooled, store in an airtight container.

Folk Cuisine

BREAKFASTS, LUNCHES AND SNACKS

The most usual Chinese breakfast consists of rice porridge: rice cooked in plenty of water till gluey, rather like Scottish oat porridge. Plain rice porridge is often eaten with boiled salted eggs; salted fish, fried or steamed; salted or pickled vegetables; cooked or raw *doufu* with soya sauce; *youtiao* or *youzhagui*, a deep-fried twisted dough stick; or dried meat squares. Sometimes slices of meat, meat balls, or fish are dropped into the boiling porridge, which is then served with shredded onions, ginger and soya sauce. Though not heavy it is very satisfying. However, breakfasts vary according to areas and occupations. In towns and cities, deep-fried twisted dough sticks, steamed bread buns, noodles, dumplings and cakes are preferred, although rice porridge may also be eaten. It is a matter of choice and availability. Everywhere in urban areas restaurants, markets and stalls cater for breakfasters, unlike in the countryside where farmers eat a rice or grain porridge breakfast prepared at home.

Lunches, as well as dinners, are normally a grain dish; rice or wheat, millet or *kaoliang* (sorghum) eaten with vegetables, fish and/or meat with a soup.

Apart from breakfast, lunch and dinner, the Chinese also love to indulge in snacks, known as *dianxin* (timsum in Cantonese). *Dianxin* means literally 'dotting the heart'; they are expected to be tasty, to stay the pangs of hunger, and to bring pleasure to the heart, a crucial organ in Chinese ideas of bodily health. *Dianxin* is always something to be savoured and enjoyed, never mere fuel food or a belly-filler. The Chinese enjoy eating small meals and often take three snacks a day: one in the morning around 10 am, one in the afternoon around 3–4 pm, and one any time after 8 or 9 pm. Chinese dinners usually occur between 5 and 6 pm. Everywhere there are shops and stalls selling snacks: sweet and savoury cakes, pastries, dumplings, pasta, noodles, steamed buns and so on. It should be noted that most snacks may be eaten for breakfast, which is also known as *zaodian* or 'early dotting the heart'. But snacks or *dianxin* are not served at meal times, except at banquets, when they take the form of delicate pastries and cakes.

BISCUITS AND PASTRIES

Almond shortbread Suzhou style (Jiangsu)

280 g (10 oz) self-raising flour (or plain flour with 1 tsp baking powder)
1 tsp bicarbonate of soda
80 g (3 oz) ground almonds
140 g (5 oz) icing sugar (or ground granulated sugar)
140 g (5 oz) lard or white vegetable fat
1 egg

For the topping:
20 whole almonds

1. Preheat the oven to 180°C (350°F, gas 4). Grease 2 baking sheets.
2. Sift the flour and bicarbonate of soda (and baking powder if plain flour is used) together. Mix in the ground almonds.
3. Beat the lard and sugar till fluffy, then beat in the egg (this may be done in a food processor). Stir in the flour and almond mixture and mix well. It will be slightly dry, but do not overwork.
4. Take a portion about 30 g (1 oz) in weight and squeeze into a ball in your hand. Place it on the greased baking sheet. Press it down with the heel of your hand to flatten it to about 7 cm (2½ in) across so that the edges crack slightly. Press an almond firmly into the middle so that it sinks well in otherwise it will pop out on cooking. Make the rest of the mixture into rounds in this way. Space them out well on the sheet, as they will expand by about 2.5 cm (1 in) during cooking.
5. Bake for about 15 to 20 minutes or till pale golden. Transfer with a

wok spatula to a cake rack, and cool. Store in an airtight tin. They will keep for several weeks.

This shortbread is delicious and crumbly. The cracked, irregular edges give it a rustic look.

Blind man's biscuits (Guangdong)

230 g (8 oz) mung bean flour
230 g (8 oz) rice flour
340 g (12 oz) icing sugar
110 g (4 oz) sesame seeds
60 g (2 oz) roasted peanuts
110 g (4 oz) lard or white vegetable fat
2 eggs (lightly beaten)
2 tsp baking powder
140 ml (5 fl oz) cold water

rice flour for dusting

wooden biscuit mould

1. Dry-fry (without oil) the rice flour, mung bean flour and sesame seeds separately till pale yellow and fragrant. Crush or grind the peanuts and sesame seeds separately; they should not be too fine but slightly gritty.
2. Cream the sugar and lard till soft, and gradually stir in the eggs. Add the sesame seeds, peanuts and cold water. Sift the toasted rice flour with the baking powder into the nuts and eggs mixture. Add the mung bean flour. Mix all into a firm dough, which should look like marzipan.
3. Press a walnut-size piece of dough into each hole in a wooden mould dusted with cornflour, or improvise with a *petits fours* tin. Turn over and gently tap the mould to release the biscuits on to a baking sheet. Arrange them neatly in rows with a palette knife.
4. Bake in a preheated moderate oven at about 180°C (350°F, gas 4) till a pale golden colour, about 15 minutes. Transfer to a wire rack with a palette knife and cool. Store in an airtight container.

This Cantonese biscuit is said to have been invented by a blind man. This amount makes about 80 *petits fours*-size biscuits. They may be shaped into 2.5 cm (1 in) balls and flattened lightly, if no mould is available.

Flaky red bean pasties

For the oil pastry:
110 g (4 oz) strong plain white flour
60 g (2 oz) lard or white vegetable fat

For the water pastry:
140 g (5 oz) strong plain white flour
45 g (1½ oz) lard or white vegetable fat
30 g (1 oz) sugar
½ tsp salt
70 g (2½ fl oz) water

For the filling:
280 g (10 oz) red bean paste
850 ml (1½ pt) cooking oil

1. Divide the red bean paste into 20 equal portions, and shape into balls.
2. Make the oil pastry. Sift the flour and rub in the lard (this may be done in a food processor). Mix into a dough, but do not overwork. Shape into a ball, cover with an upturned bowl and leave to rest for at least 30 minutes.
3. Make the water pastry. Sift the flour with the salt. Make a well in the centre, and put in the lard, sugar and water. Mix into a pliable dough with your hands. Cover with an upturned bowl and rest it for at least 30 minutes.
4. Use the rolling pin to flatten the rested water pastry into a round large enough to wrap up the oil pastry ball. Place the oil pastry on the rolled-out water pastry and wrap up into a ball. Flatten the ball and roll into an oblong. Fold both ends towards the centre, so that you have a three-layered oblong. Repeat the rolling and folding once. Roll the folded pastry into an oblong again, and roll up into a cylinder of about 5 cm (2 in) diameter (*See illustrations.*) Cut the cylinder into 40 slices with a sharp knife.
5. With the rolling pin, roll two slices separately into rounds of 6 cm (2½ in) diameter. Put a ball of the red bean paste on one of the rounds, cover it with the other. Pinch the edges well to seal. Make another 19 in the same manner.
6. Deep-fry in hot oil till golden, and drain well on kitchen paper.

If preferred, the pasties may be baked in the oven at 190° to 200°C (375° to 400°F, gas 5 to 6) for about 18 to 20 minutes. They keep well in a tin for about a week.

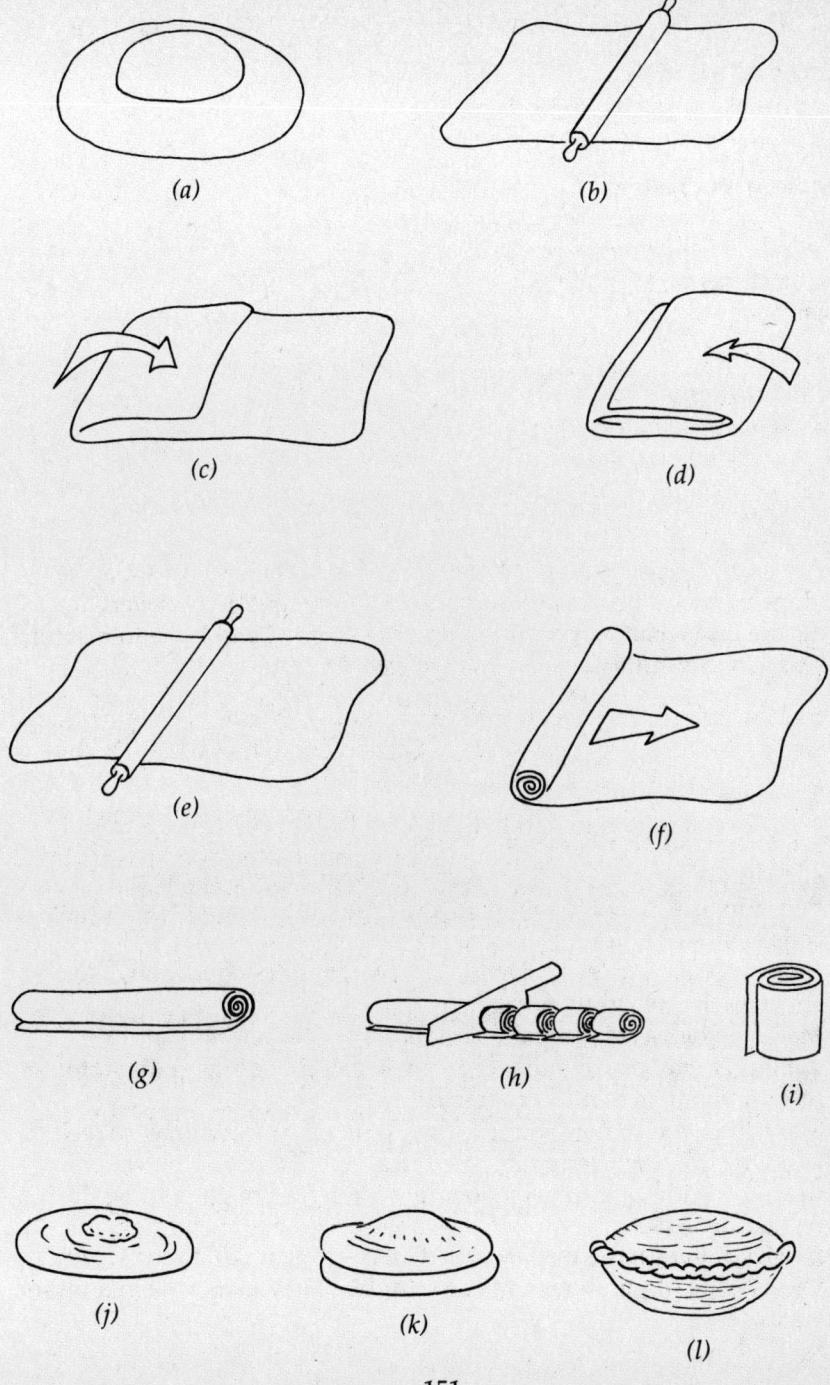

(a)

(b)

(c)

(d)

(e)

(f)

(g)

(h)

(i)

(j)

(k)

(l)

Laobobing – old wives' cakes (Guangdong)

For the oil pastry:
200 g (7 oz) strong plain white flour
110 g (4 oz) lard

For the water pastry:
230 g (8 oz) strong plain flour
80 g (3 oz) lard
60 g (2 oz) sugar
110 ml (4 fl oz) water

For the filling:
350 g (12 oz) crystallized winter melon
110 g (4 oz) sesame seeds
140 g (5 oz) granulated sugar
140 g (5 oz) glutinous rice flour
1 tbsp vegetable oil
400 ml (¾ pt) water
60 g (2 oz) potato flour with a little water

24 squares greaseproof paper, 5 × 5 cm (2 × 2 in)
1 egg lightly beaten with a pinch of salt for glazing

1. Put the crystallized melon through a mincer or hand-dice into pea-size pieces. Dry-fry the sesame seeds and crush them. Dry-fry the glutinous rice flour till lightly coloured.
2. Put all the ingredients for the filling, except for the potato flour, in a saucepan and bring to the boil on a medium heat, stirring to prevent sticking. When the rice flour turns transparent, stir in the potato flour mixture. Cook for a while, and when the mixture takes on the consistency of a firm paste take off the heat. Scrape into a plate and leave to cool completely. Divide the paste into 24 equal parts, and shape each one lightly into a ball.
3. Make the oil pastry. Rub the lard into the flour and mix into a dough. Do not overhandle. Leave in a cool part of the refrigerator to rest for about 30 minutes or longer.
4. Make the water pastry. Put the flour on a flat surface, make a well in the centre. Put the sugar, lard and 30 ml (1 fl oz) of the water in the well. With your fingers work into a pliable dough, adding the rest of the water gradually. Leave in a cool part of the refrigerator for about 30 minutes or longer.
5. Shape each of the pastries into a cylinder, and cut each into 24 equal pieces.

6. Take a portion of the water pastry, and shape into a round with your fingers. Put a piece of the oil pastry in it and wrap up into a ball. Flatten it with a rolling pin into a strip about 10 to 12 cm (4 to 5 in) long. Roll the strip up into a cylinder. Stand it upright and flatten it with the heel of your hand. Roll again into a strip as before. Fold one-third of the strip over towards the middle, then the other third, forming three layers.
7. With the rolling pin, lightly roll the layered pastry into a round about 12 to 14 cm (5 to 5½ in) across. Put a portion of the filling in the centre, gather the edges together and pinch to close. Place it, gathered-side-down, on a greaseproof square. Press it lightly with the rolling pin into a round about 9 cm (3½ in) across. Make another 23 in the same way.
8. Cut a slit about 2.5 cm (1 in) long in the centre of each cake with a sharp paring knife. Brush the top with the beaten egg. Bake in a preheated oven at 190°C (375°F, gas 5) for about 20 minutes.

In Chouzhou, it is the custom for the bridegroom to offer this cake to his relations and friends. In China before the Communist Revolution of 1949 it was not uncommon among the peasantry for arranged marriages to be made between a girl of sixteen and an infant boy of one or two. The economic reason was that the wife brought up her husband; as a result certain men very often found their wives old, hence old wives' cakes. The wedding ceremony usually took place when the boy came of age.

This cake is beautifully golden and shiny with a crisp, flaky, multi-layered and paper-thin pastry – the result of the rolling and layering of two pastries. Although the proportion of fat to flour is considerably less than that of a Western puff or flaky pastry, it is just as flaky and tasty. These cakes keep well for about a week.

NOODLES

Historical records show that noodles have been eaten in China since the Han period (202 BC–AD 220). Not only are noodles a favourite Chinese food, particularly in the north where they are a mainstay in the diet, but they are also a symbol of longevity and happiness, and invariably appear in meals for birthday and wedding celebrations as 'long life noodles' and 'happiness noodles'. In Shandong province, there is still a custom when a newborn child reaches the age of 100 days for friends and relations to be invited to a noodle feast called the 'Hundred Year Celebration'. In other parts of China husbands and wives share a bowl of 'happiness noodles' on their wedding night. Chinese noodles may be roughly divided into eight main categories according to their ingredients and the method of making them. They may be fresh or dried.

Egg noodles: these have a high proportion of eggs to flour, about 5 eggs to 450 g (1 lb) of flour.

Family noodles: made with flour, salt and water.

Green noodles: family noodles with *bocai* (spinach) juice added.

Hand-pulled noodles: a plain dough without the addition of eggs or lye water is hand-pulled to the thickness of coat-hanger wire without the aid of any tool. Fresh commercially-made ones are available in Britain. This is a northern speciality. Kaifen, an ancient imperial city in Shanxi province, is famous for its hair-fine, hand-pulled noodles known as 'dragon's whiskers'. One speciality here is a sweet-and-sour fish veiled in deep-fried 'dragon's whiskers', giving a contrasting texture to the succulent fish. It is claimed that in Kaifen, 550 g (1¼ lb) of hand-pulled noodles is more than 200 *li* (100 km, 60 miles) long, enough to go round the city wall twenty-seven times.

Knife-shaved noodles: the dough is pared with a knife into 'shavings', more like a pasta.

Lye-water noodles: about 2 tsp lye water is added to 450 g (1 lb) flour. They may be made with or without eggs. After boiling, the noodles are rinsed in hot water to remove excess lye water before tossing in oil.

Silver thread noodles: plain flour noodles cut hair-fine and usually dried. Very fast-cooking, they are a speciality of Fujian province, where they are eaten for breakfast.

Yufu noodles: egg noodles boiled and then deep-fried crisp before being braised.

It is not difficult to make noodles by hand.

To make egg noodles: sift 450 g (1 lb) strong white unbleached plain flour with 1 tsp salt on to a flat surface. Make a well in the centre, and break in 5 eggs. Using your hand, break the eggs to blend, and draw in the flour gradually, adding a little cold water, gradually, until you have a pliable dough. Knead till it is shiny and stops sticking to the work surface or your hands. Cover with a bowl or a damp tea towel, and leave to rest for at least

30 minutes or up to 1 hour. Cut the dough into two portions, if the amount is large. Roll each out on a floured board into a thin sheet. (Dusting with cornflour would make the noodles more *al dente*.) Fold into a cylinder and cut into strips. The thickness of the strips depends entirely on personal taste. Loosen the round of strips by dusting with more cornflour, and divide them into 4 to 6 individual portions ready for boiling or steaming. Do not leave too long, particularly if the room is warm, or they will stick together and may start to ferment. If the noodles have to be made well in advance, the best thing is to boil or steam them immediately, rinse in cold water and toss in oil. Cool, and keep in a closed container in the refrigerator. They will keep well for a couple of days. Other varieties of noodles are made in the same manner.

To boil fresh noodles: bring a large pot (or wok) of water to a rolling boil. Loosen a portion of the noodles, shake off excess flour and drop in the water. Use a pair of long chopsticks to separate them so as to stop them sticking together or to the bottom of the pot. When they float, add some cold water as this stops the boiling and allows the noodles to cook right through without overcooking. When the water comes back to the boil, take the noodles out with a brass wire mesh strainer. Dip them in a bowl of hot water to remove excess starch or lye water, drain well and toss in some oil. They are now ready to be served or cooked as directed in the recipe. Repeat the process with another portion.

To steam fresh noodles: place the noodles loosely on a greased steaming basket or steamer and steam over a high heat for about 8 minutes. When cooked, take out, rinse in cold water, drain and toss in some oil. Lye-water noodles are better boiled in order to remove excess lye water.

Dried, machine-made noodles are available in many varieties and are very convenient when time is at a premium; but fresh hand-made noodles are unbeatable in taste and are still preferred by the Chinese. However, excellent fresh, commercially-made noodles are available from Chinese shops in Britain. In the following recipes, unless specifically stated, any type of noodle, fresh or dried, may be used.

Across-the-Bridge noodles (Yunnan)

4 portions rice sticks or fresh noodles
2 tbsp sesame oil

For the meat platter:
170 g (6 oz) boned boiled chicken
170 g (6 oz) boned boiled or roasted duck

110 g (4 oz) pig's liver
1 pig's kidney (optional)
170 g (6 oz) lean pork
170 g (6 oz) squid (body only)
1 tsp five-spice salt
1 tsp Sichuan pepper salt

For the vegetable platter:
110 g (4 oz) bocai *or other greens in season (blanched)*
1 cucumber
60 g (2 oz) coriander leaves *or parsley (cut into 8 cm, 3 in lengths)*

Spicy dip mixture in 4 little individual bowls:
1 tbsp cooking oil
½ tsp Sichuan peppercorns
2 tbsp soya sauce
1 tbsp sugar
2 tbsp sweet salted bean paste *or sesame paste*
2 tbsp chilli oil
2 stalks spring onion (chopped)
2 slices ginger (minced)

Sweet and sour dip mixture in 4 little individual bowls:
2 tbsp soya sauce
1 tbsp granulated sugar
2 tbsp sesame oil
1 tbsp white wine vinegar

For the soup:
8 pigeon's or quail's eggs
generous 1 l (2 pt) strong clear chicken or pork stock
2 tbsp lard or vegetable oil
salt and pepper to taste

1. Rub the chicken with the Sichuan pepper salt and the duck meat with the five-spice salt, and leave to stand for about 2 hours. Cut into julienne strips and arrange neatly in 2 piles in a large platter.
2. Clean and rinse the squid, and scald briefly in boiling water. Refresh in cold water and cut into juliennes. Core the kidney, cut into thin slices and scald in boiling water. Drain as soon as they begin to curl up. Refresh immediately in cold water to prevent further cooking and toughening. Drain well. Boil the liver till par-cooked and slice into bite-size pieces. Slice the pork thinly and scald in boiling water till cooked. Cut into juliennes. Add the squid,

kidney, liver and pork juliennes in neat individual piles to the chicken and duck platter.

3. Rinse and deseed the cucumber, and cut into juliennes. Arrange the three vegetables in another platter.

4. Heat 1 tbsp oil and on a low heat, cook ½ tsp Sichuan peppercorns till they turn dark red. Take out. Mix together with the ingredients for the spicy dip, and divide into 4 small individual dip bowls. Do the same with the sweet and sour dip, and put in 4 individual bowls.

5. Boil the rice sticks or noodles in water till just cooked. Refresh in cold water and toss in the sesame oil. Put in 4 individual bowls. There is no need to keep them warm. (Steps 1 to 5 may be done in advance.)

6. Just before serving, have ready 4 large individual soup bowls. Break two pigeon's or quail's eggs into each soup bowl, add 2 tsp lard or oil and salt and pepper to taste. Bring the stock to the boil. Ladle the boiling stock on to the eggs in each bowl, and take to the table immediately with the meat and vegetable platters, boiled rice sticks and sauces. Each diner has 2 saucers of sauces, and 1 bowl each of noodles and of hot soup.

7. To eat, each diner takes some of the meat and drops it into his soup bowl to heat through, before dipping in the sauces and eating. Then the vegetables and noodles or rice sticks are added to the soup.

Rice sticks made from rice flour are a speciality of Yunnan, where dried or fresh ones are available. For this particular dish the coarser type (about the size of spaghetti) is normally used, but if unavailable the finer kind, or even thick wheat noodles, dried or fresh, may be used. 'Across-the-Bridge' noodles is rather like a fire pot, except that the stock is not actually boiling. In Yunnan the soup is served scorchingly hot (a layer of oil on the sufrace of the soup seals in the heat) so that the meat is cooked through at table by the diner. The list of ingredients may look daunting at first sight, but in actual fact it is an easy and simple meal to prepare, as almost everything may be done in advance. The cooked chicken or duck may be saved from other meals. The choice of meat and vegetables may be varied to your taste or seasonal or regional availability. In Yunnan boiled bean curd skins, soaked wood ears, shredded soaked kelp, boiled and shredded bamboo shoots and raw Chinese chives are some of the favourite vegetables used. The pig's kidney must be absolutely fresh to be cooked in this way.

This meal is said to have been invented by the wife of a scholar who, for want of peace and quiet, studied on an island in preparation for the imperial examinations. His wife daily crossed the bridge to deliver his meals, but they tended to be spoilt by the delay between cooking and eating. To amend the situation she invented this noodle dish. Incidentally, in home cooking the soup may be left out, in which case it is eaten as a salad noodle.

Cantonese won ton noodle soup (Guangdong)

For the won ton skin and noodles:
450 g (1 lb) strong white unbleached plain flour
5 eggs
2 tsp lye water mixed with 2 tbsp cold water
cornflour for dusting

For the won ton filling:
170 g (6 oz) minced pork
60 g (2 oz) peeled uncooked prawns (minced)
1 egg yolk
1 tsp sugar
1 tsp salt
2 tsp sesame oil
1 tsp cornflour with a little water
pepper to taste

For the soup:
generous 1 l (2 pt) clear strong chicken and pork stock
30 g (1 oz) dried bream (grilled)
15 g (½ oz) rock sugar (crushed)
pepper to taste
2 stalks spring onion (chopped)

For the topping:
170 g (6 oz) charsiu (barbecued pork; thinly sliced)
170 g (6 oz) seasonal greens (bokchoi, bocai, lettuce)

1. Make the noodles, (*see page* 154). Save 110 g (4 oz) of the noodle dough for the *won ton* skins.
2. Simmer the stock with the grilled dried bream and rock sugar for 30 minutes. Strain through muslin or a fine sieve, and set aside.
3. Make the *won ton* skin: roll out the noodle dough on a flat surface dusted with cornflour into a 1.5 mm (¹⁄₁₆ in) thick sheet. Use a sharp knife or razor blade to cut in to 9 cm (3½ in) squares. The thinner the skin the better the *won ton* will be. If not required immediately, wrap in cling film and keep in the refrigerator.

4. Mix together the ingredients for the filling, adding the sesame oil and the cornflour mixture last.
5. Fill a square with ½ tsp of the meat mixture. Fold it over into a triangle. Fold the base of the triangle upwards, enclosing the filling, making a fold about 2 cm (½ in) wide, with the rest of the apex showing behind it. Moisten the two opposite ends at the base and bring them together and stick. (*See illustrations page* 116.) Make all in the same way.
6. Boil the noodles (*see page* 155) and the *won ton* in the same way. Place a portion of noodles and *won ton* in each individual bowl. Top with the sliced *charsiu* and greens. Sprinkle with pepper to taste.
7. Bring the soup to the boil and ladle into individual bowls. Sprinkle with the chopped spring onions and serve beside the *won ton* and noodles. Eat the noodles and the soup at the same time.

If preferred, the *won ton* and noodles may be served without the soup. The dried bream and particularly the rock sugar, are essential for an authentic taste. Ready-made fresh lye-water noodles and *won ton* skins are available. For *charsiu see page* 35.

Cantonese yufumien – braised crabmeat noodles (Guangdong)

450 g (1 lb) fresh noodles

For the topping:
110 g (4 oz) dressed crab meat (white)
6 large caps winter mushrooms (soaked)
110 g (4 oz) tinned straw mushrooms
110 g (4 oz) mung bean sprouts
1 stalk leek or 2 stalks spring onion whites

Seasoning for the topping:
2 cloves garlic (minced)
1 stalk spring onion (chopped)
1 tbsp oyster sauce
2 tsp light soya sauce
2 tsp dark soya sauce
1 tsp salt
pepper to taste

400 ml (¾ pt) chicken stock
1 tsp cornflour with a little water

1 tbsp sesame oil
850 ml (1½ pt) cooking oil

1. Boil the noodles (*see page* 155). Drain well, and deep-fry in hot oil in a brass wire mesh strainer till crispy. Drain well. Scald the deep-fried noodles in hot water to make them less greasy. Refresh in cold water and drain well.
2. Braise the scalded noodles on a medium heat in 280 ml (½ pt) of the stock till the liquid is absorbed. Remove to a heated serving dish and keep hot.
3. Set the wok on a medium heat, and when hot put in 2 tbsp cooking oil, the garlic and spring onion. Stir-fry till fragrant, then add in the two kinds of mushrooms and the bean sprouts. Stir-fry briefly, and pour in the remaining stock. Bring to the boil, stir in the crab meat and the rest of the seasoning. Thicken with the cornflour mixture. Finally stir in the leek and sesame oil. Pour over the braised noodles.

This is a well-known Cantonese noodle dish for a snack or lunch. If dried noodles are used, boil them in the normal way before deep-frying. If preferred, for a family meal the deep-frying may be left out.

Dandanmian – Sichuan spicy noodles

4 portions fresh noodles

For the topping:
1 leek (chopped) or 3 cloves garlic (minced)
2 stalks spring onions (chopped)
2 slices ginger (minced)
2 tbsp Sichuan chilli paste
230 g (8 oz) peeled cooked shrimps

For the sauce:
2 tsp chilli powder or to taste
4 tbsp dark soya sauce
½ tsp salt
1 tbsp granulated sugar
2 tbsp sesame paste (thinned with a little water)
1 tsp ground Sichuan peppercorns
3 cloves garlic (minced)
60 ml (2 fl oz) Zhenjiang vinegar (dark vinegar)

30 ml (1 fl oz) sesame oil

1. Set the wok on a high heat till hot. Put in the sesame oil and stir-fry the spring onions, ginger and leeks till golden. Add the Sichuan chilli paste and when the oil turns red, stir in the shrimps. Stir-fry for ½ minute, dish up and set aside.
2. In a mixing bowl, mix together all the ingredients for the sauce. Stir in the cooked shrimp mixture, and set aside.
3. Boil the noodles in batches (*see page 155*), and place in 4 bowls. Cover each bowl with a quarter of the topping and serve.

This sweet, sour and spicy noodle dish is a speciality from the provincial capital of Sichuan, Chengtu. The Sichuan chilli paste may be substituted by a mixture of salted soya bean paste and chilli powder.

Lahmian – family hand-pulled noodles

For the noodles:
450 g (1 lb) strong white unbleached plain flour
1 tsp salt
280 ml (½ pt) cold water

For the topping:
230 g (8 oz) minced pork or beef

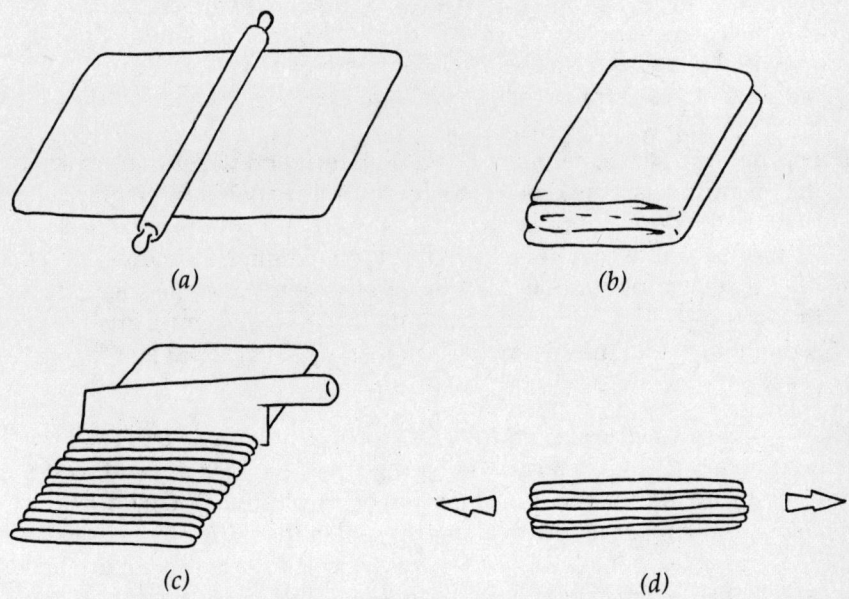

(a)

(b)

(c)

(d)

Seasoning for the topping:
2 stalks spring onions (chopped)
2 tbsp salted soya bean paste
2 tbsp dark soya sauce
1 tbsp rice wine
1 tbsp sugar
140 ml (5 fl oz) stock or water
1 tbsp sesame oil

2 tbsp cooking oil plus extra for tossing

1. Place the flour with the salt on a flat surface. Add the water a little at a time, and work into a pliable dough. (You may need more or less water than the amount given.) Knead till smooth and shiny. Cover with a bowl and leave to rest for at least 30 minutes.
2. Roll the rested dough on a floured board into a cylinder about 30 cm (12 in) long. Use a rolling pin to flatten it into a piece about 23 cm (9 in) wide and 0.6 cm (¼ in) thick. Cover with a damp tea towel to prevent the surface from hardening. Leave to rest for another 15 minutes.
3. Bring a pot of water to a fast boil. Fold up the rested sheet of dough lengthwise several times and cut into 1 cm (⅜ in) wide strips. Cut and cook immediately: cut the amount required for one portion, take up the cut strips by both ends and give them a pull to stretch both ways evenly so that you have a regular width all along the lengths of the noodles. (*See illustrations.*) Drop the pulled noodles into the boiling water and cook in the normal way. Take out with a brass wire mesh strainer, drain well and toss in a little oil. Put in a bowl and top with the meat sauce.
4. For the meat sauce, set the wok on high heat and when hot put in the oil and the spring onion. Stir-fry the spring onion till fragrant, add the pork and continue till it turns white. Mix in the bean paste, soya sauce and wine. Reduce the heat to medium if too fierce. Cook till the meat and sauce begins to separate, then stir in the sugar and finally the stock. Continue cooking till the meat and sauce are separated. Stir in the sesame oil and dish up. This sauce may be prepared well in advance.

These noodles are *al dente* and full of flavour. Ready-made fresh *lahmian* are available in Chinese shops. Choose the ones that look dry and white, not grey-brown and sticky. Take them out of the plastic bag as soon as you can, spread them out on a dish and keep cool in the refrigerator. Cook as soon as possible, as if allowed to dry for too long they become hardened and will need a much longer cooking time, about 10 minutes. If not required for one or two days, boil them, refresh in cold water, toss in oil, cool and keep refrigerated. Before further cooking scald in boiling water to heat through.

Neegumian – nun's noodle (Guangxi)

450 g (1 lb) fresh noodles
1 tbsp sesame oil for tossing

For the topping:
110 g (4 oz) deep-fried wheat gluten (sliced)
15 g (½ oz) black wood ears (soaked)
110 g (4 oz) canned straw mushrooms (sliced)
110 g (4 oz) bamboo shoots (sliced)
60 g (2 oz) jinzhencai *(lily flowers; soaked and picked over)*
110 g (4 oz) greens in season (blanched)

For the seasoning:
1 tbsp light soya sauce
2 tbsp sesame oil
salt and pepper to taste

Garnish:
110 g (4 oz) vegetarian ham (sliced)
2 tbsp deep-fried peanuts
2 tbsp coriander leaves (chopped)

1.4 l (2½ pt) vegetarian stock
2 tbsp groundnut oil

1. For vegetarian ham *see page 27*. For wheat gluten *see page 240*.
2. Boil the noodles (*see page 155*). Drain and simmer in some well-seasoned vegetarian stock to cover till the stock is well absorbed by the noodles. Drain, and toss in the sesame oil. Put into 4 individual bowls and keep warm.
3. Set the wok on a high heat and when hot, put in the groundnut oil. Stir-fry all the vegetables except the greens for a few minutes. Add the wheat gluten and stir-fry briefly. Pour in the stock. Bring to the boil and simmer for about 15 minutes. Add the greens and heat through. Season with soya sauce, salt and pepper, adjust and stir in the sesame oil. Divide equally among the noodle bowls. Arrange a few slices of vegetarian ham on one side of each bowl, and some coriander leaves on the other side. Scatter on some peanuts and serve.

This noodle dish is named after the *neegu* or nun who used to serve supremely good vegetarian noodles to visitors to a nunnery in Guilin – where the tradition continues to this day.

Salad noodles (Sichuan)

4 portions noodles

For the topping:
110 g (4 oz) cooked chicken (shredded)
110 g (4 oz) peeled cooked shrimps
2 eggs
110 g (4 oz) mung bean sprouts
1 tbsp young ginger (shredded)

For the dressing:
2 tbsp sesame paste or peanut butter
3 tbsp sesame oil
1 tbsp chilli oil (or to taste)
2 tbsp white wine vinegar
2 tbsp light soya sauce
1 tbsp sugar

vegetable oil for tossing the noodles

1. Boil the noodles in individual portions (*see page* 155). Cool in cold water, drain well and toss in a little vegetable oil. Set aside in individual bowls or plates.
2. Pick the tails from the mung bean sprouts. Rinse and scald in boiling water for ½ minute, drain and leave in cold water to keep them crisp.
3. Thin the sesame paste with a little water and mix with the rest of the ingredients for the dressing. Make an omelette with the 2 eggs and shred finely. Drain the sprouts well. Put the topping ingredients in separate bowls or dishes.
4. Take the noodles, the toppings, and the salad dressing to the table. Just before eating, top each bowl of noodles with the shredded chicken, omelette, shrimps, mung bean sprouts and ginger. Pour a quarter of the dressing into each bowl. Mix well and eat.

This is a popular summer noodle dish from Sichuan. Shredded cooked ham, cucumbers, carrots, lettuce, are some of the many suitable ingredients.

Sichuan Zhajiangmian – noodles with meat sauce

4 portions fresh fine noodles

For the meat topping:
230 g (8 oz) minced pork or beef
2 tsp rice wine
½ tsp salt
1 tbsp sweet salted soya bean paste

For the soup:
550 ml (1 pt) chicken or pork stock
30 g (1 oz) Sichuan preserved vegetable (zhacai; finely chopped)
4 stalks spring onion (chopped)
2 tbsp dark soya sauce
3 tbsp sesame paste
1 tbsp white wine vinegar
1 tbsp chilli oil
1 tbsp sesame oil

Garnish:
230 g (8 oz) bocai *(blanched)*

2 tbsp cooking oil

1. Stir-fry the pork in the oil till it turns white, the water evaporates and the oil begins to run out. Stir in the seasoning, and stir-fry for a few minutes till the meat is cooked and dark. Take out and set aside.
2. Boil individual portions of the noodles separately (*see page* 155), and place in individual bowls. Divide the *bocai* into 4 portions and place one in each bowl over the noodles on one side. Top each bowl with a quarter of the meat sauce.
3. Bring the stock to the boil, and add in all the seasonings for the soup. Bring to the boil again and ladle some into each bowl of noodles from the side.

This hot and sour noodle dish is a traditional Sichuan speciality.

PANCAKES

Onion oil cakes (Beijing)

230 g (8 oz) strong plain white flour
80 g (3 oz) cooked ham or smoked back bacon (finely diced)
4 stalks spring onion or 1 medium onion (finely chopped)
½ tsp salt
pepper to taste

1 tbsp cooking oil
flour for dusting
1 tbsp sesame oil for brushing

1. Mix the flour together with the salt and pepper on a flat surface. Mix in 110 ml (4 fl oz) cold water, and knead into a pliable dough. Cover with an upturned bowl and leave to rest for 15 minutes.
2. Mix together the diced ham and spring onion.
3. Roll out the rested dough into a 0.6 cm (¼ in) thick oblong. Brush lightly all over with the sesame oil. Sprinkle with the onion and ham mixture, covering the whole pastry. Roll up into a cylinder. Cut into 24 equal parts.
4. Stand a pastry round, cut-side-up, on a floured, flat surface. Flatten it with the heel of your hand, and then roll it into a thin circle of about 11 to 12 cm (4½ to 5 in) in diameter, with a rolling pin. This is the onion oil cake. Spread each one out as it is made.
5. Set a thick, flat-bottomed frying pan or an iron griddle on a low heat. Grease it with 1 tsp oil. Cook the cakes till both sides are golden with bubbles and spots. Brush one side lightly with sesame oil and take out.

These are delicious eaten hot. To reheat, wrap them in foil and bake in a hot oven for about 15 minutes. They are most suitable for a barbecue party in the garden, where the guests could cook or even roll out their own cakes. They are also easily portable for picnics. If preferred, the brushing with oil may be left out, but the cakes would be drier and slightly reminiscent of an Indian *nan*.

Pancake parcel (Beijing)

For the pancake batter:
110 g (4 oz) strong white bread flour
1 egg
30 g (1 oz) granulated sugar
pinch salt
170 g (6 fl oz) water

For the filling:
230 g (8 oz) red bean paste

vegetable oil for cooking

1. Make the batter. Put the flour, sugar and salt in a mixing bowl. Make a well in the centre. Break the egg into the well. Beat it with a wooden spoon and gradually pour in the water a little at a time, drawing in the flour from the sides. Continue till all the water is used up. Beat the batter till it is smooth, and leave in the refrigerator to rest for about 30 minutes.
2. Divide the bean paste into 6 equal portions.
3. Set the wok on a medium heat and grease it with a little oil. Reduce the heat to low, pour in one-sixth of the batter, and swirl the wok round to spread the batter into a circle about 18 cm (7 in) in diameter. While the pancake is still wet, put a portion of the red bean paste in the middle and spread it into an oblong about 8 × 5 cm (3 × 2 in). Fold two opposite sides of the pancake over the paste, then fold in both ends, pressing them down lightly to seal. When the underside is golden, turn the parcel over. If it gets too dry, trickle in a little oil. Cook till both sides are golden and take out. Make another 5 in the same way.

The red bean paste and pancake make a delicious combination. The Mandarin word *ban-ji* is a transliteration of 'pancake'.

Pumpkin pancake

For the batter:
230 g (8 oz) pumpkin purée
110 g (4 oz) strong plain white flour
1 egg
½ tsp salt
110 ml (4 fl oz) water

60 ml (2 oz) granulated sugar

cooking oil

1. Make a pancake batter with the flour, egg, salt and water. Stir in the sugar and pumpkin purée. The batter is slightly thicker than a normal one.
2. Put 1 tbsp oil in a saucer, fold a piece of kitchen paper into a square, saturate it with the oil and leave it in the saucer. Set a thick-bottomed omelette pan or griddle on a medium heat and when hot, grease it with the oiled paper.
3. Reduce the heat, pour in 2 fl oz of the batter and spread it out with the back of the spoon in a circular motion. Cook on a low heat, as the pumpkin burns easily, till the surface is dry. Flip it over and cook till it puffs up and both sides are golden. Cook the rest in the same way.

This pancake from the countryside is red-gold and tasty. If preferred it may be spiced with cloves, cinnamon and ginger.

Savoury pumpkin pancake (Beijing)

For the batter:
230 g (8 oz) pumpkin
110 g (4 oz) flour
1 tsp salt
2 eggs
1 stalk spring onion (chopped)
110 ml (4 fl oz) water

For the dip:
1 tbsp vinegar
1 tbsp sesame oil
1 clove garlic (minced)

2 tbsp cooking oil

1. Peel the pumpkin and discard the seeds. Grate the flesh finely.
2. Make a batter with the flour, egg and water. Stir in the grated pumpkin, spring onion and salt.
3. Set a thick, flat-bottomed frying pan on a medium heat. Put in a little oil to cover the base of the pan completely. Pour in a ladleful of the pumpkin batter. Swirl the pan round to spread the batter to about 0.6 cm (¼ in) thick. Cook till it is dry. Trickle a few drops of

oil down the sides of the pan. Cook till both sides are golden. Make another 3 in the same way.

4. Mix the vinegar with the sesame oil and garlic. Serve the pumpkin pancake with this as a dip.

In Beijing this is regarded as an economical, time-saving and trouble-saving family fast food. The pumpkin is a vegetable that stores well and thus its eating season is extended considerably.

Shrimp and chive pancakes (Beijing)

For the batter:
110 g (4 oz) strong plain white flour
1 tsp baking powder
½ tsp salt
1 egg
140 g (5 fl oz) cold water
1 tsp granulated sugar
1 tsp shrimp paste (optional)
2 tsp vegetable oil
pepper to taste

For the filling:
80 g (3 oz) peeled cooked shrimps (chopped)
80 g (3 oz) Chinese chives or English chives (chopped)
30 g (1 oz) carrot (boiled and chopped)

cooking oil for greasing

1. Make the batter. Sift the flour, salt and baking powder into a mixing bowl. Make a well in the centre. Break in the egg, and add the sugar, shrimp paste and water. With a wooden spoon, gradually draw in the flour. When well mixed, stir in the oil and pepper. Set aside to rest for about 15 minutes.
2. Mix the chopped peeled shrimps, chives and cooked carrots into the batter.
3. Set a thick omelette pan or a griddle on a medium heat, and grease it with a little oil. Pour a quarter of the batter mixture into the pan, forming a circle of about 12 to 15 cm (5 to 6 in) diameter. When the pancake is set and holes appear, turn it over. Cook till both sides are golden and take out. Make another 3 in the same way.

This is a simple and tasty fast food for a snack, lunch or supper. The filling may be varied with bacon, ham, parsley, celery, leeks, or *charsiu* (*see* page 35).

PASTA

'Cat's ears' (Zhejiang)

For the dough:
250 g (9 oz) strong plain white flour
170 ml (6 fl oz) water
½ tsp lye water (optional)
1 tsp salt

For the soup:
110 g (4 oz) boned chicken (diced into pea-sized pieces)
60 g (2 oz) cooked ham (diced into pea-sized pieces)
170 g (6 oz) raw prawn meat or peeled cooked shrimps
110 g (4 oz) bocai or lettuce (cut into 8 cm, 3 in lengths; blanched)
850 ml (1½ pt) chicken stock or water

For the seasoning:
1 stalk spring onion (minced)
1 slice ginger (minced)
1 tsp salt
1 tbsp rice wine
pepper to taste

cornflour for dusting
1 tbsp cooking oil
1 tbsp rendered chicken fat

1. Sift the flour with the salt on to a flat surface. Make a well in the centre, mix the lye water with a little of the water and pour into the well. With your hand, draw in the flour, gradually mixing and adding water a little at a time until all the water and flour are used up and a pliable dough is formed. Divide the dough into 2 equal portions. Roll each into a cylinder of about 2 cm (¾ in) diameter, and cut into slices about 0.6 cm (¼ in) thick. Roll them in some cornflour.
2. Turn a stiff wire sieve upside down. Place a piece of the cut dough upright on the back of the sieve, and with the ball of your thumb press down and out, so that a soft cat's-ear shape is formed. Pick it up and drop it on to some cornflour. Continue till all the dough is used up. (*See illustrations.*)

3. Bring a pot of water to the boil. Drop the 'cat's ears' into the boiling water in batches. When they float, pick them out with a brass wire mesh strainer and drain them in a colander.

4. Set the wok on a high heat, put in the cooking oil and stir-fry the spring onion and ginger till fragrant. Stir-fry the chicken till it turns white. Pour in the stock and add the seasoning. Bring to the boil and add the 'cat's ears'. Bring to the boil again and add the ham, prawns and *bocai*. When it comes back to the boil and the prawns turn pink, stir in the chicken fat. Pour into a soup tureen and serve.

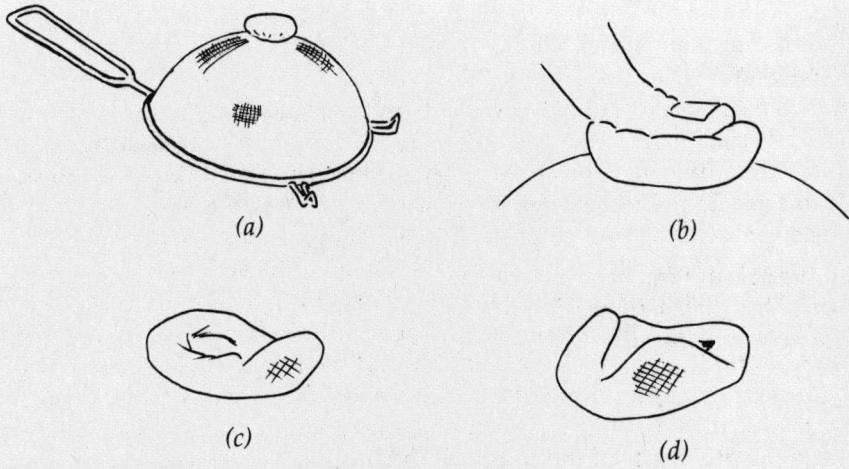

(a)

(b)

(c)

(d)

If a softer texture is preferred, leave out the lye water which makes the 'cat's ears' *al dente*. If peeled cooked shrimps are used, put them in only after dishing up. This is a Zhejiang speciality, a snack served by street hawkers.

'Mice tails' – Dabu rice pasta (Guangdong)

450 g (1 lb) rice flour

For the topping:
2 cloves garlic
350 g (12 oz) minced lean pork or beef
3 tbsp fish sauce (or light soya sauce)
140 ml (5 fl oz) stock or water
2 stalks spring onion (chopped)

pepper to taste

2 tbsp cooking oil
extra rice flour
generous 1 l (2 pt) clear stock (optional)
lard or cooking oil for tossing

1. You will need a Chinese solid metal strainer with holes of about 0.6 cm (¼ in) diameter. This is actually a substitute for the real appliance, which is not available here. (*See illustrations.*)
2. Prepare the topping: set the wok on a high heat and put in the oil. When the oil is hot, stir-fry the garlic till fragrant and a pale golden. Add the mince and stir-fry till it loses its pink colour. Pour in the fish sauce and stock. When it comes back to the boil, transfer to a bowl and set aside.
3. Make the pasta. Put half the rice flour in a saucepan and add 550 ml (1 pt) cold water. Mix well and cook on a medium heat, stirring all the time, till a firm paste is formed. Take off the heat. Mix the rest of the rice flour with enough water to make a firm dough. Mix this raw dough with the cooked paste with a wooden spoon. When cool enough to handle with your hands, knead until smooth.
4. Have a saucepan of water boiling on a medium heat. Break off a piece of dough the size of an egg, and put it in the metal strainer. Hold the strainer over the boiling water. Use the back of a spoon to press the dough through the holes, then scrape the spoon towards you. Strings of white spaghetti-like pasta or 'mice tails' will appear on the other side of the strainer. As the spoon scrapes over each hole, the 'mice tails' will break off and fall into the water below. They vary from 5 to 10 cm (2 to 4 in) long. The longer you press without scraping the longer the tails will be. When cooked they float to the surface. Stop every now and again to fish them out with a brass wire mesh strainer, dip them in a basin of cold water and drop them gently into a colander.
5. Just before serving, put a teaspoon of lard in each individual bowl. Heat individual portions separately in a brass wire mesh strainer dipped in boiling water. Shake dry and put in the bowl. There is no need to mix. Cover each bowl with a portion of the meat topping, scatter the chopped spring onions on top and sprinkle with pepper. Bring the stock to the boil, and pour a ladleful into each bowl down the side. Stir to mix well before eating. If preferred, it may be served without the stock.

The pasta may be made in advance, or the night before. It keeps well in the refrigerator for several days. It may stick together, but will separate

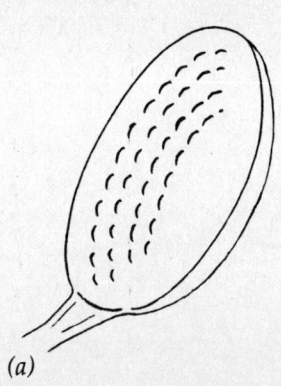

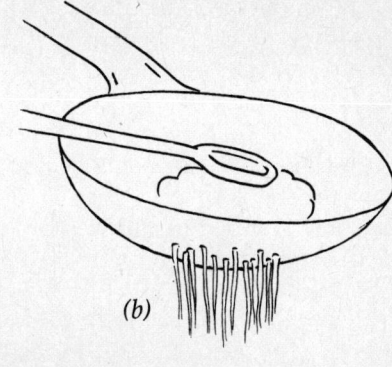

(a)

(b)

when dipped in boiling water. However, handle it gently. Bought Western beef mince is not suitable, as it contains beef fat which would totally change the taste and flavour. This is a classic dish from the Dabu clan of the Hakka people in Guangdong province, and is enjoyed by the rural farmers as well as town dwellers. Street stalls serve it as a fast-food lunch or snack. For the family it is a popular weekend lunch, the making of which sometimes involves the whole family as the pasta is normally made from whole rice grains, which have to be soaked overnight, hand-milled with water in a stone grinder and pressed dry. The above is a reasonable short cut.

Taro pasta (Guangdong)

For the pasta:
450 g (1 lb) taro
350–450 g (12 oz–1 lb) potato flour
1 tsp salt

For the sauce:
1 clove garlic (minced)
1 slice ginger (minced)
230 g (8 oz) minced pork
2 tbsp dried shrimps (soaked and pounded)
1 tbsp dried wood ears (soaked and shredded)
6 caps winter mushrooms (soaked and shredded)
2 eggs (lightly beaten)
400 ml (¾ pt) stock or water

1 tbsp fish sauce
1 stalk spring onion (chopped)
pepper to taste

cooking oil

1. Peel, rinse and slice the taro. Boil it in some water with the salt till cooked, about 10 to 15 minutes. Mash it into a purée with a potato masher. Transfer to a flat surface, and while still warm, gradually mix in the potato flour to form a pliable dough. Knead till smooth.
2. Have ready a large pot of boiling water. Break the dough into greengage-size pieces, roll each into a ball, and press it in the middle with your thumb, making a dent. Drop them into the water as you make them. When they float, fish them out with a brass wire mesh strainer and leave them in a bowl of cold water to cool. When all are done, drain them well in a colander and toss in some oil. Up to this stage they may be made in advance and kept refrigerated.
3. Make the sauce. Set the wok on a high heat till hot. Put in 2 tbsp oil and stir-fry the garlic and ginger till fragrant. Stir-fry the pork till it turns white; add the shrimps and when fragrant, stir in the mushrooms and wood ears. Stir-fry till the wood ears make exploding noises, then tip in the stock and fish sauce. When it comes to the boil, add the pasta. Bring to the boil again and cook for 1 minute to heat through and for the flavour to blend. Stir in the eggs and dish up. Sprinkle with the chopped spring onion and pepper.

This is a traditional dish from the Dabu clan in rural Guangdong, normally eaten on festive occasions. The proportion of flour to taro varies according to the variety of taro used. More flour makes a more *al dente* pasta.

PORRIDGE

Boat people's porridge (Guangdong)

For the porridge:
110 g (4 oz) long grain rice
3.5 l (6 pt) water
2 dried scallops (optional)

For the accompaniments:

2 deep-fried twisted dough sticks
110 g (4 oz) fried or roasted peanuts
60 g (2 oz) mung bean or rice vermicelli
110 g (4 oz) salted jellyfish (soaked and shredded)
110 g (4 oz) fresh cuttlefish or squid (shredded)
110 g (4 oz) shelled uncooked prawns
110 g (4 oz) white fish meat (monkfish, haddock or cod; sliced)

Garnish:

1 tbsp young ginger (finely shredded)
1 tbsp spring onion white (finely shredded)
2 tbsp coriander leaves or parsley (cut into 2.5 cm, 1 in lengths)

For the seasoning:

light soya sauce
sesame oil
rice wine
salt

850 ml (1½ pt) cooking oil

1. Rinse the rice and bring to the boil with the dried scallops in 3.5 l (6 pints) water. Cook, uncovered, on a medium heat, stirring occasionally.
2. Meanwhile, snip the dough sticks (*see page* 185) with kitchen scissors into 1 cm (½ in) pieces and put in a dish.
3. Pound the peanuts coarsely and put in a dish.
4. Season the soaked jellyfish (*see page* 234) with some sesame oil and soya sauce to taste. If too salty, the soya sauce may be left out.
5. Marinate the sliced fish, shredded cuttlefish and shelled prawns separately with some salt and a little rice wine for about 10 minutes. Deep-fry them separately till cooked, and put each in a separate dish.
6. Deep-fry the vermicelli and put in a dish.
7. Put the shredded ginger, spring onion white and coriander leaves in separate dishes.
8. Cook the rice till the grains disintegrate, and pour the porridge into a soup tureen, cover and take to the table immediately with the 10 little accompanying dishes. Place the porridge in the middle of the table surrounded by the dishes.
9. To serve, empty all the accompanying dishes except the garnish into the hot porridge. Mix well and ladle into individual bowls. Top each

with the shredded ginger, spring onion white and coriander leaves. This amount serves 4 to 6.

This is the famous boat people's porridge or *tingzizhou* served on board the junks cruising along the Pearl River in Guangzhou (Canton). It is the custom for passengers to be served a light meal during the journey.

Cantonese kaichook – chicken congee (Guangdong)

140 g (5 oz) long grain rice
1 slice ginger (minced)
1 stalk spring onion (minced)
3.5 l (6 pt) strong chicken stock.

For the seasoning:
1 tbsp light soya sauce
1 tsp salt
pepper to taste

For the topping:
230 g (8 oz) boiled chicken
1 tbsp spring onion (finely shredded)
1 tbsp ginger (finely shredded)

1 tbsp cooking oil

1. For the boiled chicken and stock *see* 'Hainan chicken rice', *page* 136.
2. Rinse the rice and drain well in a sieve. Heat the oil in a large, thick-based pot over a medium heat, and cook the ginger and spring onion till fragrant. Stir-fry the rice till it begins to crackle. Pour in the stock. Bring to the boil over a high heat, and stir well to prevent sticking. Continue cooking, uncovered, on a medium heat, stirring occasionally till the rice grains burst and the porridge becomes gluey. Towards the end, reduce the heat to a bare simmer.
3. Meanwhile, skin and bone the meat. Lightly beat it with the back of a chopper to loosen the fibres and tear it into fine shreds.
4. Season the porridge with the soya sauce and salt. Ladle into 4–6 individual bowls. Sprinkle with the shredded chicken meat, ginger, spring onion and pepper, and serve hot.

Known as 'chicken congee' in the West, this is a most popular snack in Guangzhou (Canton). It may be served as a breakfast, snack, lunch or supper. In the old days this porridge was cooked with the broken rice grains from the mills. A strong chicken stock is vital for a full and authentic taste.

Oyster porridge (Fujian)

12 shelled oysters (fresh or frozen)
110 g (4 oz) par-boiled belly pork
110 g (4 oz) glutinous rice or long grain rice
2.8 l (5 pt) water

For the seasoning:
2 tbsp light soya sauce
1 tsp salt
pepper to taste

For the shallot oil:
4 shallots (chopped)
2 tbsp vegetable oil

Garnish:
80 g (3 oz) tender leeks or spring onion white (finely shredded)

1. Defrost the oysters thoroughly if frozen. Slice the pork thinly.
2. Set the wok on a high heat till hot, put in the oil and stir-fry the shallots until pale gold. Take them out with the oil and set aside in a little bowl. Put the shredded leeks in a separate little bowl.
3. Rinse the rice well and bring to the boil with the water. Stir well to prevent sticking. Add the pork and oysters. Cook uncovered, on a medium heat, stirring occasionally, till the grains burst. Season and ladle into 4 individual bowls. Garnish with the shredded leeks.
4. To eat, sprinkle with the shallots and oil to taste.

This delicious porridge is from Xiamen (Amoy).

Pork porridge (Fujian)

170 g (6 oz) glutinous rice or long grain rice
170 g (6 oz) skinless belly pork (parboiled and diced into peanut-size pieces)
1 tbsp dried shrimps (soaked)
60 g (2 oz) peanuts (blanched)
4 caps winter mushrooms (soaked and diced into peanut-size pieces)
3.5 l (6 pt) water

Marinade for the pork:
1 tbsp fish sauce
2 stalks spring onion (chopped)
2 tbsp rice wine

For the seasoning:
1 tbsp fish sauce
1 tbsp sesame oil
2 tbsp rice wine
pepper to taste

1 tbsp cooking oil
2 tsp cornflour with a little water

1. Rinse the rice and bring to the boil in 3.5 l (6 pt) water over a high heat. Stir well to prevent sticking. Reduce the heat to medium. Add the soaked shrimps with their soaking water, mushrooms and peanuts. Leave to boil uncovered, stirring occasionally, till cooked, when the rice grains burst and the peanuts have become tender.
2. Marinate the pork for about 10 minutes. Set the wok on a high heat, put in the oil and stir-fry the marinated pork till cooked. Take out and set aside.
3. When the rice porridge is cooked, thicken with the cornflour mixture. Reduce the heat to low, and add in the cooked pork and all the seasoning. When it comes back to the boil, ladle into individual bowls and serve. This amount gives 6 helpings.

Raw fish porridge (Guangdong)

For the porridge:
110 g (4 oz) rice
2.3 l (4 pt) stock or water

For the marinated raw fish:
230 g (8 oz) fresh white fish (skinned and boned)
1 tbsp rice wine
2 tbsp light soya sauce
1 tsp salt
1 tsp pepper (or to taste)

For the seasoning:
1 tbsp lard
2 tbsp ginger (minced)
1 tbsp spring onion green (chopped)

Garnish:
1 tbsp spring onion white (shredded)
1 tbsp tender young ginger (shredded)

1. Rinse the rice and boil in the stock or water till the grains burst.
2. Slice the skinned and boned fish paper-thin and marinate for 30 minutes. Divide into 4 portions.
3. Line 4 individual bowls with 1 portion each of the marinated fish slices: one slice at the bottom of the bowl and some slices up the sides all round so that the bowl is covered. Put 1 tsp each of the minced ginger, spring onion greens and lard in the bottom of the bowl on the fish.
4. To serve, ladle the boiling porridge into each bowl. Sprinkle with shredded spring onion whites, ginger and some more pepper. Let the fish poach in the boiling porridge till cooked, about a couple of minutes, and then eat.

This is a firm favourite with the Chouzhou (Teochiew) people in Guangdong. The fish has to be really fresh, as it is barely cooked.

SAVOURY SNACKS

Beef cheongfan – mock pig's intestines with beef (Guangdong)

For the skin:
230 g (8 oz) rice flour
110 g (4 oz) potato flour or wheat starch
500 ml (18 fl oz) water
1 tbsp groundnut or vegetable oil
1 tsp salt

For the beef stuffing:
450 g (1 lb) tender lean beef (topside or aitchbone)
1 tsp salt
1 tsp granulated sugar
1 tbsp sesame oil
pepper to taste

2 tsp cornflour with a little water to mix

For serving:
2 oz sesame seeds (toasted)
dark soya sauce
groundnut oil

extra oil for greasing the tins

1. Remove any fat or gristle from the beef and slice thinly. Mix with the seasoning and lastly the sesame oil. Steam in the wok over a high heat for about 8 minutes or till cooked.
2. Mix the two flours with the water into a batter. Stir in the groundnut oil and the salt.
3. Put a 20 cm (8 in) tin to steam over fast-boiling water in a wok, and when heated take it out and brush all over with some oil. Give the batter a thorough stir and pour 140 ml (5 fl oz) of it into the tin. Swirl it round to distribute the batter evenly, covering the base completely. Steam over a high heat for about 3 minutes. When bubbles appear it is done.
4. Take out (placing another tin in the wok to preheat), and pile the cooked beef in a row in the centre of the skin. Loosen the skin all round with a spatula. Gently pull one side over the beef and then the opposite one, making a roll. Lift out with a spatula on to a serving plate. Make another 5 in the same way. Sprinkle with the toasted sesame seeds and a little groundnut oil and soya.

The filling may be varied with *charsiu* (*see page* 35), or cooked shelled prawns.

Cantonese five-spice doughnuts (Guangdong)

For the dough:
450 g (1 lb) strong plain white flour
20 g (¾ oz) fresh yeast or 1½ tsp dried yeast
110 g (4 oz) granulated sugar
30 g (1 oz) lard or white vegetable fat
280 ml (½ pt) tepid water

For the filling:
2 tsp five-spice powder
3 tbsp red fermented bean curd (mashed)
1 tsp salt

Extra flour for dusting

1. Make a basic steam bun dough with 350 g (12 oz) of the flour, the yeast, 1 tsp of the sugar and the tepid water, and leave to rise till doubled in size before mixing in the remaining flour and the lard (*see page* 195).
2. Mix together the ingredients for the filling and set aside.
3. Roll the dough into a rectangle about 1 cm (½ in) thick. Cover it completely with the five-spice mixture. Roll up like a Swiss roll, and leave to prove for about 45 minutes in a warm place, covered.
4. Cut the risen dough into 18 slices each about 2.5 cm (1 in) thick. Stand the slices, cut-side-up, on a floured surface and sprinkle with more flour. Flatten them lightly with your palm.
5. Deep-fry them in hot oil over a low heat till they float, and continue cooking till golden. Take out and drain well on kitchen paper.

These doughnuts are spicy, sweet and savoury, quite delicious. Hawkers sell them for breakfast in Cantonese towns. In Cantonese they are called *humjienpeng*, meaning 'savoury fried cake'.

Cantonese nomaikai – glutinous chicken and rice parcels (Guangdong)

450 g (1 lb) glutinous rice

Seasoning for the rice:
½ tsp salt
2 tsp granulated sugar
1 tbsp light soya sauce
1 tbsp lard or cooking oil
2 tsp sesame oil

For the filling:
230 g (8 oz) boned chicken (diced)
110 g (4 oz) pork with some fat (diced)
60 g (2 oz) smoked back bacon (diced)
4 caps winter mushrooms (soaked and diced)
60 g (2 oz) boiled chestnuts

Seasoning for the filling:
1 slice ginger
1 clove garlic
½ tsp salt
1 tbsp oyster sauce
1 tbsp rice wine

2 tsp granulated sugar
1 tsp five-spice powder
2 tbsp sesame oil

2 large dried lotus leaves

1. Rinse and steam the glutinous rice in the wok or a lined steaming basket till cooked, about 40 minutes. Spray with some cold water halfway through cooking. When cooked, take out and mix in the seasoning for the rice. Set aside.
2. Soak the lotus leaves in warm water for about 20 minutes. Drain and pat dry with kitchen paper.
3. Set the wok on a medium heat, and put in the sesame oil. When it is hot, stir-fry the ginger and garlic till fragrant. Add the chicken and pork, and stir-fry till they turn white. Add the bacon, mushrooms and chestnuts. Stir-fry briefly. Stir in the wine, oyster sauce, sugar, salt and five-spice powder. Mix well and add water to cover. Cover and cook till the juice is reduced and sticky.
4. Spread one prepared lotus leaf on a flat surface. Spread half the cooked and seasoned rice on it. Put in half the cooked chicken mixture. Fold the rice over the chicken mixture to enclose it. Wrap up the lotus leaf envelope-wise into a parcel. Place it on a plate, folded-side-down. Make another parcel in the same manner.
5. Steam both together on a plate in the wok or steaming basket for about 45 minutes over a medium heat.

The parcels may be prepared in advance. As all the ingredients are precooked, the steaming is to blend the flavour. In fact, the flavour improves with further steaming. *Nomaikai* is eaten as a snack or breakfast, or as part of the repertoire of Cantonese *timsum*. To reheat, steam for about 20 minutes. Dried lotus leaves imported from China are available here. If stored in a plastic bag in a cool, dry place, they keep almost indefinitely.

Cantonese shaomai (Guangdong)

For the skin:
230 g (8 oz) flour
1 tsp lye water in 3 tbsp cold water
1 egg (lightly beaten)
1 tsp salt

For the filling:
450 g (1 lb) shoulder of pork (minced)

110 g (4 oz) uncooked shelled prawns (minced)
4 caps winter mushrooms (soaked and finely diced)
2 tsp rice wine
1 tsp salt
2 tsp granulated sugar
1 tbsp sesame oil
pepper to taste
1 tsp cornflour with a little water

extra potato flour or cornflour for dusting

1. Mix the minced prawns and pork together with the rest of the filling ingredients.
2. To make the skin, sift the flour together with the salt on to a flat surface. Make a well in the centre, and put in the egg and the lye-water mixture. Use your hand to mix in the egg and lye water and draw in the flour from the sides. Mix into a stiff dough. Knead till smooth. Roll into a cylinder and cut into 48 pieces. Roll each piece on a lightly floured surface into a circle about 6 cm (2½ in) in diameter. You may roll 4 pieces at once: flatten them first, dust with some flour, stack them floured sides together and roll to the required size. Separate them immediately.
3. Form a ring with your left thumb and index finger. Place a piece of the skin over the ring. Put a portion of the filling in the middle of the skin. Close your fingers and shape the filling within the wrapper into a cylindrical shape, with the wrapper pleating naturally all round. Level the top of the filling with a spatula or knife. (*See illustrations.*)
4. Steam them in a greased and preheated steaming basket or steamer, well spaced apart, for about 6 minutes over a high heat, or till cooked.

Ready-made *won ton* skins may be used, but first trim the corners to make a circle.

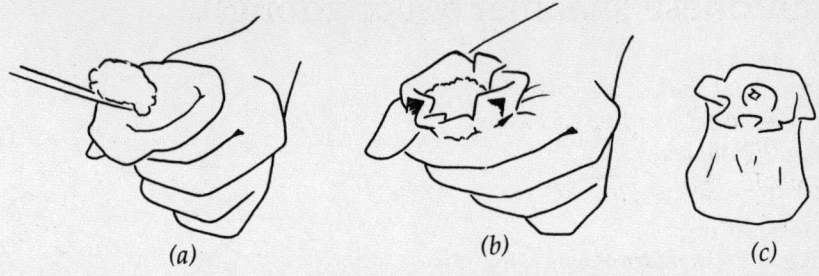

(a)   (b)   (c)

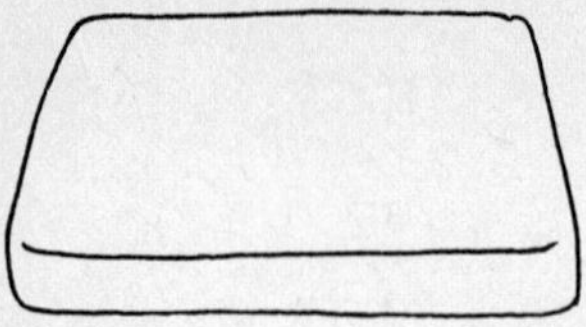

(a)

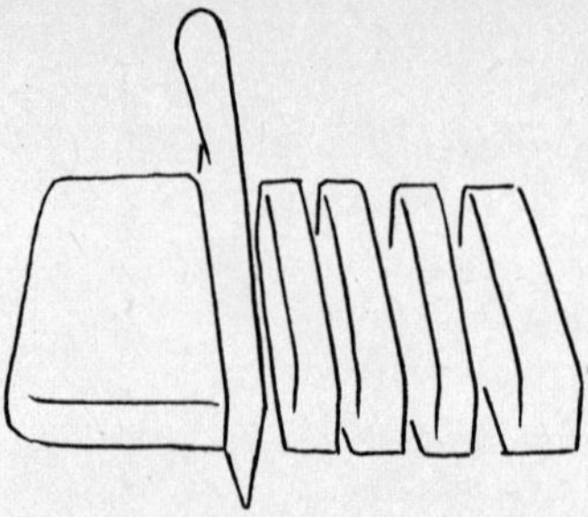

(b)

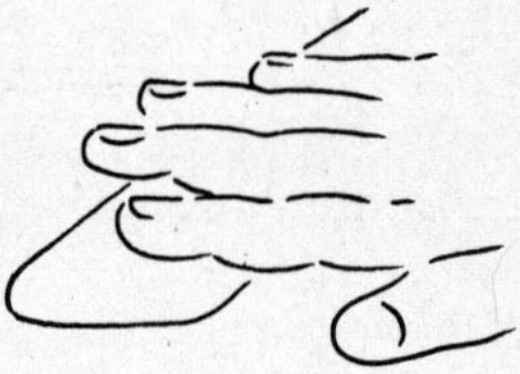

(c)

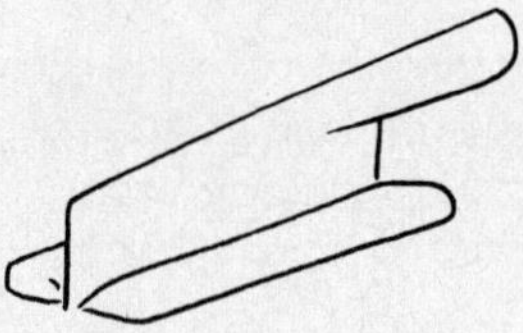

(d)

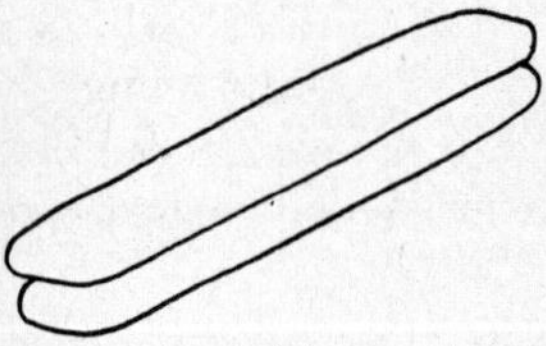

(e)

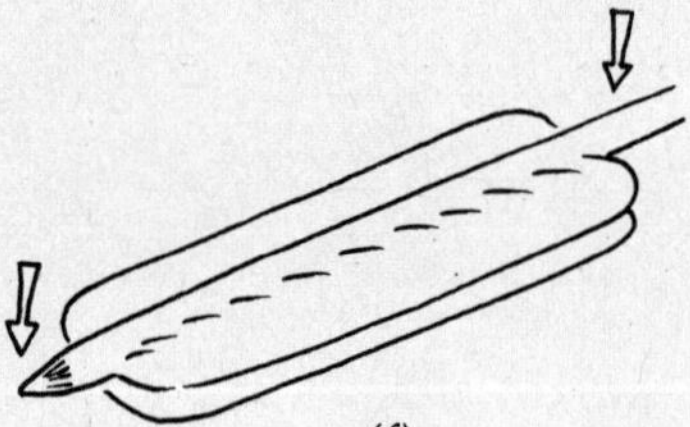

(f)

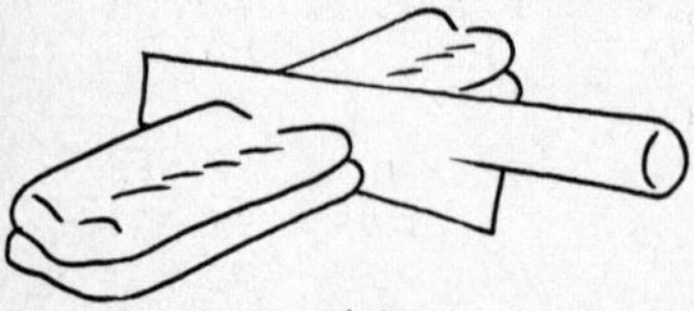

(g)

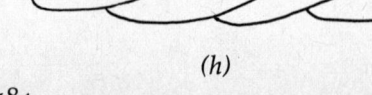

(h)

Deep-fried twisted dough sticks (Fujian)

For the yeasted dough:
450 g (1 lb) strong plain white flour
2 tsp salt
1 tsp bicarbonate of soda
20 g (¾ oz) fresh yeast or 1½ tsp dried yeast
280 ml (½ pt) tepid water
1 tsp granulated sugar

generous 1 l (2 pt) peanut oil or vegetable oil
flour for dusting

1. Dissolve the yeast and sugar in the tepid water and leave till froth appears. Sift the flour with the salt and bicarbonate on to a flat surface, and make a well in the centre. Pour in the frothy yeast mixture and mix into a pliable dough. Cover and leave in a warm place to rise till trebled in size.
2. Knock down the dough and cut into 2 parts. Do not knead. Use your hands to shape the dough on a floured surface into an oblong. With a rolling pin, flatten it out to about 12 cm (5 in) wide and 1 cm (½ in) thick. With a hay-cutting motion, i.e. with your right hand holding the handle, and your left hand the back of the blade, cut the dough into 2.5 cm (1 in) wide strips. Sprinkle with more flour.
3. Preheat the oil to 190°C (375°F) on a deep-frying thermometer. Take a strip and press gently with 4 fingers to flatten to about 5 cm (2 in) wide and 18 cm (7 in) long. Cut into 2 equal parts lengthwise with a hay-cutting motion. Lift one piece up by both ends and place it on top of the other. With a chopstick, press down the middle along the length on the top one so that a dent is formed in the centre and the two strips are joined together. Cut it across into 2 equal parts. (*See illustrations page 184.*)
4. Pick up one of the double dough sticks by both ends, twist it 2 or 3 times and pull to stretch it to about 20 cm (8 in) long. Drop it into the hot oil. Turn it over and over with a pair of long chopsticks. Cook till it puffs up, looking like a plait, golden and crisp. Take out and drain well on kitchen paper. Continue in the same way with the rest of the dough. This amount makes 24 to 26 dough sticks, each about 18 cm to 20 cm (7 to 8 in) long.

Usually the cooking is undertaken by two people, one of whom prepares the dough and places it in the hot oil while the other attends to the frying. In China and among the Chinese communities of South-East Asia hawkers cook this snack in the early morning on street corners for takeaway breakfasts or eating on the spot. The recipe given here comes from Fujian province, although deep-fried twisted dough sticks are especially popular in North China, Beijing itself being credited with the finest ones. It boasts one version shaped like a Western doughnut, but so crisp that it shatters to pieces when dropped.

Legend has it that deep-fried twisted dough sticks are effigies of a treacherous Southern Song official, Oingui, and his wife. In the twelfth century this man was responsible for a serious defeat at the hands of the northern nomads. His devious policies ended with the partition of China, the provinces to the north of the Yangzi river valley passing out of Chinese control. The Chinese name for this deep-fried twisted dough stick, *youzhagui*, means deep-fried devils, a homonym to deep fried Gui, the traitor, for in ancient China one method of capital punishment involved the frying of traitors in oil.

These delicious and crispy doughnut sticks go very well with creamy hot soup or rice porridge. They may be served whole with the soup or snipped into rings and scattered over it just before serving.

Fish skin dumplings (Zhejiang)

For the skin:
350 g (12 oz) white fish (skinned and boned weight)
1 tsp salt
110 g (4 oz) potato flour

For the filling:
110 g (4 oz) minced pork
3 peeled water chestnuts (finely diced)
2 caps winter mushrooms (soaked and finely diced)
1 tbsp dried shrimps (soaked and finely diced)
1 stalk spring onion (chopped)
2 tsp rice wine
1 tbsp light soya sauce
1 tsp granulated sugar
1 tsp salt
pepper to taste

850 ml (1½ pt) strong chicken or pork stock
white wine vinegar
lard

Garnish:

1 stalk spring onion (chopped)

1. Mix together all the ingredients for the filling and shape into 30 equal-sized balls. Set aside on a plate, spaced apart.
2. Mince the fish finely with the salt till it becomes sticky (this may be done in the food processor). Take out and make into 30 equal-sized fish balls: squeeze a portion of the fish mixture in your left hand so that a ball comes out between your left thumb and index finger. Pick out the ball with a spoon and leave it on a plate.
3. Put the potato flour on a flat surface. Take a fish ball and cover it completely with the flour. Press it gently into a flat disc with the heel of your hand. With your fingers, dipped in more flour if sticky, gently shape it into a round of about 6 cm (2½ in) diameter, slightly thinner at the edges than the middle. Spread a portion of the meat mixture in the centre. Fold over the fish skin into a semicircle. Pinch the edges to seal. Gently press the filling to flatten, and fold the semicircle in the middle and pinch the ends together. Gently open out the edges so that it looks like a trumpet. (*See illustrations.*)
4. When all are done, put them in a greased dish (or sandwich cake tin) and steam in a steaming basket, steamer or wok over a high heat for 5 minutes, or till cooked, when they become semi-transparent and firm.
5. Bring the stock to the boil. Place the required number of dumplings in individual bowls with 2 tsp each of vinegar and lard. Ladle the boiling stock on to the dumplings and sprinkle with the spring onion.

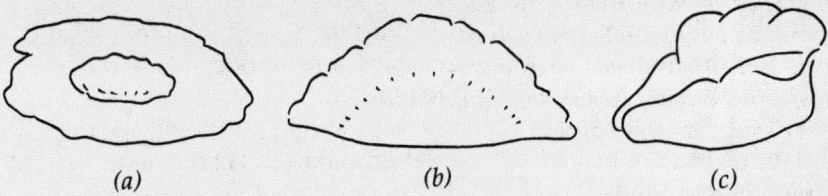

(a)   (b)   (c)

These are very attractive white dumplings with the many coloured filling faintly visible beneath the almost transparent skin, and they float in the soup like lilies. The texture is surprisingly *al dente* and there is no fishy taste at all. This is a traditional snack along the coastal areas of Zhejiang.

Glutinous rice sausages (Guangdong)

For the casing:
450 g (1 lb) pig's intestines (2 packets)

For the filling:
350 g (12 oz) glutinous rice
4 oz black-eyed beans
60 g (2 oz) dried shrimps (soaked)
60 g (2 oz) minced pork or smoked back bacon

Seasoning for the filling:
1 tsp salt
2 tsp five-spice powder
1 tbsp granulated sugar
1 tbsp sesame oil
2 tbsp light soya sauce
pepper to taste

Seasoning for the oil:
4 shallots (minced)
1 clove garlic (minced)

1 tbsp cooking oil
trussing string

1. Rinse the rice and beans, and soak separately for at least 1 hour.
2. Prepare the pig's intestines (*see page* 236), but leave them raw.
3. Set the wok on a medium heat, put in the oil and stir-fry the shallots and garlic till fragrant and golden. Add the shrimps and pork, and stir-fry till the meat turns white. Stir in the seasoning, mix well and add in the rice. Stir-fry till the rice begins to crackle, mix in the beans, transfer to a dish and leave to cool.
4. Cut off the larger end of each intestine so that the casing is more regular; reserve the cuttings for other cooking. (There are six altogether from two packets.) Tie up one end of the casing with trussing strings. Take a handful of the rice mixture, squeeze into a cylinder shape and push into the casing. Fill four-fifths full, and tie up the other end. Roughly tie the filled casing into sections of 18 to 20 cm (7 to 8 in) long; they shrink considerably on cooking. Shake off any stuffing sticking to the outside. Continue in the same way with the rest.
5. Use a fine skewer or cocktail stick to prick each sausage in several places to prevent bursting. Place a tea plate at the bottom of a large

pot, to prevent sticking, and lay the sausages on it. Cover with plenty of water and bring to the boil over a high heat. Reduce the heat to medium, and boil the sausages for about 1 hour or till cooked.

6. Drain, cool slightly and cut into rounds before eating.

Normally small intestines are used for this, but they are not easily available here. These sausages look slightly dark because of the seasonings. They are delicious and filling, a rustic speciality of the Hakka people of Guangdong. Whenever a pig is slaughtered, strings of rice sausages are prepared and hung up in the kitchen. Steam to reheat.

Stir-fried bean sprouts and rice sticks (Fujian)

230 g (8 oz) rice sticks
230 g (8 oz) mung bean sprouts
170 g (6 oz) Chinese chives (cut into 2.5 cm, 1 in lengths)

For the seasoning:
1 tbsp cooking oil
2 tbsp light soya sauce
1 tbsp caramel

For the sauce:
4 cloves garlic (minced)
2 tbsp toasted sesame seeds (crushed)
2 tbsp sugar
1 tbsp chilli sauce (or to taste)
1 tbsp vinegar

2 tbsp cooking oil

1. Tail the bean sprouts, rinse well and drain. Scald them briefly in boiling water, drain and refresh in cold water. Boil the rice sticks in water till *al dente*. Drain and toss in the seasoning. Mix it with the scalded bean sprouts.
2. Mix together all the ingredients for the sauce.
3. Set the wok on a high heat and when hot, put in the oil. Stir-fry the rice sticks and bean sprout mixture with the chives till cooked, about 3 minutes. Put in 4 individual dishes.
4. Serve the rice sticks and the sauce separately. To eat, sprinkle the rice sticks with the sauce to taste, and mix well.

This is a very simple but well-known snack from Xiamen (Amoy).

Taro savouries (Fujian)

For the taro skin:
340 g (12 oz) taro
220 g (8 oz) plain flour
30 g (1 oz) sugar
1 tsp baking powder

For the filling:
170 g (6 oz) minced pork
60 g (2 oz) peeled uncooked prawns (chopped)
4 caps winter mushrooms (soaked and finely diced)
5 water chestnuts (chopped)
1 tbsp light soya sauce
2 stalks spring onion whites (chopped)

flour for dusting
generous 1 l (2 pt) cooking oil

1. Mix together all the ingredients for the filling. Set the wok on a high heat, put in 1 tbsp oil and stir-fry the filling mixture till cooked. Leave to cool and divide into 30 portions.
2. Peel, rinse and cut the taro into juliennes. Steam in a wok till cooked. Take out and mash. Sift in the flour, together with the sugar and baking powder. Mix into a firm dough. Add more flour if necessary. Knead till smooth. The dough will be slightly lumpy with bits of taro. Break into 30 equal parts and leave them on a well-floured surface.
3. Preheat the oil to hot. Take a portion of the taro skin. Dip your fingers in some flour and shape it into a round of about 7 cm (2½ in) across. Put in a portion of the filling mixture and wrap up into a ball. Press lightly to flatten and drop into the hot oil. Continue in the same way with the rest.
4. Cook till they are puffed up and golden. Take out with a brass wire mesh strainer and drain well on kitchen paper.

This delicious savoury is best eaten hot. The purple, fragrant 'areca-nut' variety of taro is best for this.

Teochiew taro rice (Guangdong)

450 g (1 lb) taro (diced into pea-sized pieces)
450 g (1 lb) long grain rice

1 tbsp dried shrimps (soaked and diced)
170 g (6 oz) fatty pork (diced into pea-sized pieces)
4 caps winter mushrooms (soaked and diced)
110 g (2 oz) bamboo shoots (diced into pea-sized pieces)
110 g (2 oz) carrots (diced into pea-sized pieces)
110 g (2 oz) garden peas

For the seasoning:
4 shallots (chopped)
1 clove garlic (minced)
2 tsp rice wine
1 tbsp light soya sauce
1 tsp salt
pepper to taste

850 ml (1½ pt) cooking oil

1. Rinse the rice and drain in a fine sieve.
2. Deep-fry the diced taro till golden. Drain well on kitchen paper.
3. Set the wok on a high heat, and when hot put in 2 tbsp oil. Stir-fry the shallots and garlic till fragrant. Add the pork and stir-fry till the fat runs out. Sprinkle with the wine. Add the shrimps and stir-fry till fragrant. Put in the carrots, bamboo shoots and mushrooms. Continue stir-frying till fragrant. Add the rice, and stir-fry till it is well mixed and makes a crackling noise. Pour in 700 ml (1¼ pt) hot water. Add the peas, salt and soya sauce. Mix well, cover.
4. When it comes to the boil, put in the fried taro; lay it over the rice, but do not stir. Cover, reduce the heat to low, and cook for about 10 to 15 minutes, until the liquid is absorbed and the rice cooked through. Mix well and dish up into individual bowls.

This is a rural delicacy, a meal in itself, normally served as a lunch. If preferred, shredded dried squid or cuttlefish may be added with the shrimps.

Yangzhou fried rice (Jiangsu)

For the fried rice:
230 g (8 oz) long grain rice
3 eggs (lightly beaten)
1 tsp salt
1 stalk spring onion

For the topping:
80 g (3 oz) lean pork (shredded)
110 g (4 oz) peeled uncooked prawns
30 g (1 oz) cooked ham or smoked back bacon (diced into pea-sized pieces)
60 g (2 oz) cooked chicken (diced into pea-sized pieces)
2 large caps winter mushrooms (soaked and diced into pea-sized pieces)
60 g (2 oz) bamboo shoots (diced pea size)
60g (2 oz) cooked garden peas

Seasoning for the topping:
½ tsp salt
1 tbsp light soya sauce
1 stalk spring onion (chopped)

2 tbsp lard or vegetable oil

1. Rinse the rice and boil till cooked (*see page* 237).
2. Set the wok on a high heat and when hot put in 1 tbsp lard. Reduce the heat to medium and stir in the beaten eggs. When it is still wet, add in the cooked rice. Immediately stir-fry till well mixed. Sprinkle with salt. If it gets too dry, sprinkle with a little water, not oil which would make it greasy. Add the spring onion and stir-fry briefly. Dish up on to a platter.
3. Reheat the wok, and when hot put in the rest of the lard. Stir-fry the pork till it loses its pink colour. Add the prawns and stir-fry till they turn pink. Stir in all the rest of the ingredients for the topping, and continue stir-frying till well heated through and fragrant, about 2 to 3 minutes. Sprinkle with the seasoning, mix well and cover the rice with the topping.

This is simple to cook, and may be served as a fast-cooking all-in-one dish for a lunch, or as a colourful rice dish with interesting and tasty morsels for the buffet table.

Yangzhou shaomai (Jiangsu)

For the skin:
230 g (8 oz) strong plain white flour
60 ml (2 fl oz) boiling water
30 ml (1 fl oz) cold water

For the filling:
230 g (8 oz) glutinous rice
110 g (4 oz) pork

1 stalk spring onion (minced)
1 slice ginger (minced)
1 tsp granulated sugar
1 tsp salt
1 tbsp light soya sauce
2 tsp rice wine
80 ml (3 fl oz) stock
30 g (1 oz) lard

For the dips:
chilli sauce
soya sauce

1 tbsp cooking oil

1. Rinse the glutinous rice, and soak for about 4 to 5 hours. Drain and steam in the wok, or a steaming basket lined with a piece of muslin, over a high heat for about 25 to 30 minutes, or till cooked. Take out and leave to cool.
2. Dice the pork into rice-size pieces.
3. Set the wok on a medium heat till hot, and put in the oil. Stir-fry the pork till it turns white and the oil runs out. Add the spring onion and ginger and stir-fry till fragrant. Stir in the rest of the seasoning, except the lard. Bring to the boil and add in the rice. Mix well and, when the liquor is completely absorbed by the rice, stir in the lard. Take out and leave to cool.
4. Put the flour in a bowl, stir in the boiling water and mix till the flour is flaky, like snowflakes. Add the cold water, mix well and knead into a smooth dough. Shape into a cylinder and cut into pieces of about 10 g (⅓ oz) each.
5. Take a piece of the dough and, with a rolling pin, form it into a circle of about 7 to 8 cm (2½ to 3 in) in diameter. Form a ring with your left thumb and index finger. Place the circle over it. Put a portion of the rice mixture in the centre. Close your fingers so that the skin gathers round the filling in pleats. Squeeze the middle of the cylinder to pack the filling, forming an indented waist. (*See illustration* for Cantonese Shaomai, *page* 183). Tap the dumpling to flatten its base, and level the top with your index finger. Continue with the rest of the skins and filling in the same way.
6. Arrange the dumplings slightly apart in a lightly greased steaming basket, and steam over a high heat for about 10 minutes or till cooked. Serve with the chilli sauce and soya sauce.

These glittering and semi-transparent dumplings are a local speciality of

Yangzhou, south of the Yangtze river. To reheat, steam them over a high heat for about 4 minutes.

BAOZI AND MANTOU – STEAMED BUNS

Steamed bread buns, (*baozi* and *mantou*) are said to have evolved from ancient sacrificial foods. It is thought that the prehistoric inhabitants of China offered the heads of captives to their gods in order to ensure plentiful harvests. However, with the arrival of civilized times, huge buns were substituted for human heads. They were made in stages by covering a cooked bun with more dough, re-steaming it and adding successive layers till it reached the required size. In the period, after 1700 BC, these buns were used in the rites of ancestor worship and consumed by the descendants after the ceremony. Even now, there exists in Jiaodong in Shandong province a New Year steamed bun (without stuffing) about 2 to 3 kg (4½ to 6 lb) in weight. As time went on smaller buns appeared, some of them with a meat filling.

Nowadays two kinds of steamed bread buns exist: the first, with a seasoned meat stuffing, is called *baozi*; the second, without, is called *mantou*. Served as the main filling part of a meal in Beijing and the North, *mantou* is usually eaten with meat and vegetables instead of rice. Sometimes unfilled dough is shaped into 'lotus leaf', 'silver thread' or 'spiral' buns. These buns may also be served as a snack on their own.

Baozi is popular in both the northern and southern provinces. It may be eaten for breakfast, as a snack, for lunch, at a picnic, or when travelling. It is one of the Chinese equivalents of the hamburger, a self-contained and convenience food that is both delicious and satisfying. Some *baozi* are sweet, with red bean paste or lotus seed paste for filling. Savoury ones may be filled with seasoned pork, lamb, beef, duck or chicken, sometimes with boiled eggs added. The variety is immense. The Cantonese *charsiu bao*, filled with barbequed pork, is well-known in the West. Western bread dough when steamed would not give the same result, as there is a slight difference in the final stages of preparation (*see below*) though the ingredients are similar.

Chinese steamed bun dough is traditionally leavened with a sour dough which is started with potato water and a sprinkling of a cereal wine. The dough starter is then fed with equal amounts of water and flour every day for 3 to 4 days before it is ready. To perpetuate the yeast culture, a little starter is saved and fed with flour and water. The remaining starter is then mixed with flour in the ratio of 7 to 3 (with some water) to make a pliable dough, and it is left to rise till doubled in size. It is then mixed with sugar and a little diluted lye water to counteract the acidity and slow down fermentation. The resulting steamed buns are quite different from the steamed Western bread dough and are delicious, fluffy and sweet. This method can be rather frustrating for beginners as it is liable to go wrong. This is partly because a Western flour and yeast culture does not require the addition of lye water. The following recipe, however, is a tried and proven one using fresh or dried yeast. The proportion of yeast, water and flour is the same as in a Western bread dough except for the sugar which is added with about a quarter of the flour from the total amount in the final kneading.

Basic steamed buns dough

1.1 kg (2 lb) strong white unbleached plain flour
½ tsp salt
20 g (¾ oz) fresh yeast or 1½ tsp dried yeast
30 g (1 oz) lard
60 g (2 oz) granulated sugar
425 ml (¾ pt) tepid water

1. Dissolve the yeast with 1 tsp of the sugar in the tepid water (half boiling and half cold). Leave till froth appears on the surface.
2. Sift 700 g (1½ lb) of the flour with the salt on to a flat surface, and make a well in the centre. Pour the frothy yeast mixture into the well. Use your hand to draw in the flour and mix into a pliable dough. Knead lightly till smooth and shiny. Place in a mixing bowl, cover with cling film and leave in a warm place till doubled in size.
3. Mix the rest of the sugar, lard and flour into the risen dough with another 2 tbsp water. Knead till smooth, and leave to rise again for 30 minutes or longer, or till it springs back when touched. Cut it into 2 equal parts; if the cut surface is covered in air holes – it is ready. Use the dough as directed in the recipe.

When the amount of flour in a recipe varies from that given above, always save about a quarter of the total for the second rising. The tepid water used in the first rising is based on the proportion of 150 ml to 250 g flour, or ¼ pt to ½ lb. In the second rising the amount of water added is about 2 to 4 tbsp, depending on the softness of the dough; in some recipes 1 egg and some milk are used instead.

Goubuli baoji – Dog-Won't-Care steamed buns (Tianjin)

For the yeast dough:
680 g (1½ lb) strong plain white flour
½ tsp salt
280 ml (½ pt) tepid water
20 g (¾ oz) fresh yeast or 1½ tsp dried yeast
30 g (1 oz) lard or white vegetable fat
60 g (2 oz) granulated sugar

For the filling:
550 g (1¼ lb) minced pork (¼ fat)
4 tbsp light soya sauce
4 tbsp dark soya sauce
110 ml (4 fl oz) stock or water
1 tsp granulated sugar
2 tbsp sesame oil
4 stalks spring onion (chopped)
1 slice ginger (minced)
1 tsp cornflour with a little water

20 squares greaseproof paper, 5 × 5 cm (2 × 2 in)

1. Make the basic steamed bun dough using 450 g (1 lb) of the flour, salt, yeast, 1 tsp of the sugar and 280 ml (½ pt) tepid water. Leave to rise before mixing in the rest of the ingredients (*see page* 195).
2. Meanwhile mix the pork and soya sauces, stirring in one direction till the mixture is sticky and the sauces are completely absorbed by the meat. Add in the stock, a little at a time, in the same way. Finally mix in the sugar, sesame oil, spring onion, ginger and cornflour mixture. Divide into 20 portions and set aside.
3. Cut the twice-risen dough into equal parts, and roll each into a cylinder. Cut each into 10 equal parts. Dust them well with flour to prevent them from sticking together.
4. Take one piece of the dough and with your fingers shape into a round about 6 cm (2½ in) across. Put a portion of the meat mixture in the centre. Gather the edges by pleating all round, and pinch them together to close. Place it pleated side up on a greaseproof square. Leave to prove for about 15 to 20 minutes.
5. Steam the buns in batches, spaced apart, in a preheated steaming basket or steamer lined with a folded piece of muslin, over a high heat for 8 minutes. Take out and cool on a rack if not required immediately.

The traditional meat-filled steamed buns of Tianjin have this name because the cook who made the best Tianjin steamed buns in town in his time was nicknamed 'Dog-Won't-Care'. In the old days and even now, Chinese parents like to give unworthy nicknames to their male offspring to deceive the envious gods who might take them away.

Sichuan baoji – steamed buns

For the yeast dough:
900 g (2 lb) strong plain white flour
½ tsp salt
20 g (¾ oz) fresh yeast or 1½ tsp dried yeast
¾ pt tepid water
60 g (2 oz) granulated sugar
30 g (1 oz) lard or white vegetable fat

For the filling
550 ml (1¼ lb) minced pork
80 g (3 oz) dongcai (preserved vegetable; optional)
80 g (3 oz) Sichuan preserved vegetable (zhacai)
80 g (3 oz) bamboo shoots

Seasoning for the filling:
1 stalk spring onion (chopped)
1 slice ginger (minced)
2 tsp light soya sauce
2 tsp rice wine
30 g (1 oz) granulated sugar
1 tsp cornflour with a little water
60 g (2 fl oz) stock or water

1 tbsp cooking oil
30 squares greaseproof paper, 5 × 5 cm (2 × 2 in)

1. Make the basic steamed bun dough (*see page* 195), and leave to rise.
2. Rinse the *dongcai* and *zhacai* to remove excess salt and chilli powder. Dice the three vegetables into dice-sized pieces.
3. Set the wok on a high heat till hot, and put in the cooking oil. Stir-fry the spring onion and ginger till fragrant. Add the pork, and stir-fry till it turns white, the water evaporates and the oil runs out. Stir in the rice wine and soya sauce. Add in the three diced vegetables and the sugar. Mix well and tip in the stock. Thicken with the cornflour mixture. Transfer to a dish and set aside to cool.

4. Cut the risen and rested dough into 2 equal parts. Roll each into a cylinder, and cut each into 15 equal parts. Dust with flour to prevent them from sticking together.
5. Take one piece of the dough, and flatten into a round of about 8 cm (3 in) diameter with your fingers. Put about 2 tsp of the filling in the centre. Gather the edges into pleats and pinch together. Place it, pinched side up, on a greaseproof square. Make the remainder in the same way. Let them rest for about 15 minutes.
6. Steam them in batches in a preheated steaming basket or steamer, spaced out, on a folded piece of muslin, for about 10 minutes. Take out, and cool on a rack if not required immediately.

These buns are sweet, salty and slightly spicy.

Yangroubao – steamed lamb buns

For the yeast dough:
680 g (1½ lb) strong plain white flour
½ tsp salt
20 g (¾ oz) fresh yeast or 1½ tsp dried yeast
280 ml (½ pt) tepid water
60 g (2 oz) granulated sugar
1 tbsp milk
1 egg

For the filling:
350 g (12 oz) lean lamb (from a leg)
1 tsp salt
1 tbsp Sichuan pepper water
1 tbsp light soya sauce
1 slice ginger (minced)
1 stalk spring onion (minced)
1 tbsp sesame oil
2 tsp salted soya bean paste
230 g (8 oz) Chinese celery cabbage (finely chopped)
3 tsp cornflour with a little water

20 squares greaseproof paper, 5 × 5 cm (2 × 2 in)

1. Make the basic steam bun dough, using 450 g (1 lb) of the flour, salt, yeast, 1 tsp of the sugar and 280 ml (½ pt) tepid water. Leave to rise before mixing in the rest of the ingredients. (*See page 195.*)
2. Remove every visible trace of fat from the lamb, then mince it. Mix the lamb with the salt and Sichuan pepper water. Add the soya

sauce. Stir in one direction till the mixture becomes sticky. Add the ginger, spring onion, sesame oil and salted bean paste. Squeeze the chopped cabbage lightly to remove excess water, and mix into the meat mixture. Finally stir in the cornflour mixture. Divide into 20 equal portions.

3. Gently knead the twice risen dough and shape into a cylinder. Cut into 20 equal parts.

4. Use your fingers to shape one piece into a disc of about 10 cm (4 in) in diameter, with the edges slightly thinner than the middle. Fill the centre with a portion of the meat mixture. Gather the edges together and pinch to close. Place it on a greaseproof square, pinched-side-up. Make another 19 in the same way.

5. Preheat a steamer or steaming basket lined with a folded piece of muslin, over a high heat. Start steaming when a batch of 6 to 8 buns is ready, depending on the size of your steaming basket. Space them apart in the steamer, and steam for about 15 minutes over a high heat. Meanwhile, make the next batch.

These steamed lamb buns come from the Muslim community in China, which numbers over 30 million.

SWEET SNACKS

Gold Coin taro cakes (Guangdong)

For the pastry:
350 g (12 oz) taro
170 g (6 oz) glutinous rice flour

For the filling:
230 g (8 oz) red bean paste

For the syrup:
110 g (4 oz) granulated sugar
110 ml (4 fl oz) water

2 tbsp cooking oil

1. Divide the red bean paste into 30 portions, and shape into balls.
2. Scrub and boil the taro till cooked (test by piercing with a skewer, which should easily go through). Let it cool slightly, and peel.

3. Break up the peeled taro and knead in the rice flour to make a pliable dough. Roll into a cylinder, and cut into 30 equal pieces.
4. Shape a piece of the dough into a round about 6 cm (2½ in) across, thinner at the edges than the middle. Put a bean paste ball in the centre, gather the edges and pinch them together. Roll into a ball. Put it on a plate and press lightly to flatten into a 'gold coin'. Continue with the rest in the same way.
5. When all are made, set a thick, flat-bottomed frying pan on a medium heat. Grease well with some oil. Arrange some of the 'gold coins' spaced apart in the pan. Cook on a low heat till both sides are golden and puffed up. Transfer them to a dish. Cook the rest in the same way.
6. When the 'gold coins' are cooked, dissolve the sugar in the water and boil till it turns red but is not smoking, which will make it bitter. Pour the syrup over the 'gold coins'.

If preferred, the syrup may be left out as these cakes are delicious enough to eat as they are. They are eaten as a dessert or a snack.

Hainan coconut cake (Guangdong)

For the dough:
340 g (12 oz) glutinous rice flour
30 g (1 oz) wheat starch
60 g (2 oz) granulated sugar

For the filling:
230 g (8 oz) mung bean paste
80 g (3 oz) freshly grated or desiccated coconut

For the coating:
60 g (2 oz) grated or desiccated coconut

20 pieces dried or fresh bamboo leaves
20 wooden cocktail sticks

1. Mix the coconut and the mung bean paste together, divide into 20 equal portions and shape into balls.
2. Boil the bamboo leaves in plenty of water till the colour changes. Rinse in cold water. Trim each into an oval shape about 20 cm (8 in) long. Large leaves may be cut into 2. Soak in water till required.
3. Sift the wheat starch to remove any lumps. Pour 230 ml (8 fl oz) of boiling water on to the wheat starch and stir immediately to mix well. Cook briefly on a low heat, stirring all the time.

4. Mix the glutinous rice flour with cold water, a little at a time, till you have a firm dough. Work the cooled, cooked paste into the rice dough, and knead in the sugar till smooth. Divide into 20 pieces.

5. Drain the bamboo leaves and wipe dry. Take a piece of the dough, and use your fingers to shape it into a round about 5 cm (2 in) across. Put a portion of the bean paste in the middle and wrap up. Roll it in the coconut to coat completely. Place it in the centre of a bamboo leaf. Fold one end over to meet the other and secure with a wooden cocktail stick. Make another 19 in the same way. (*See illustrations.*)

6. Steam over a high heat in a preheated steaming basket for about 10 minutes or till cooked.

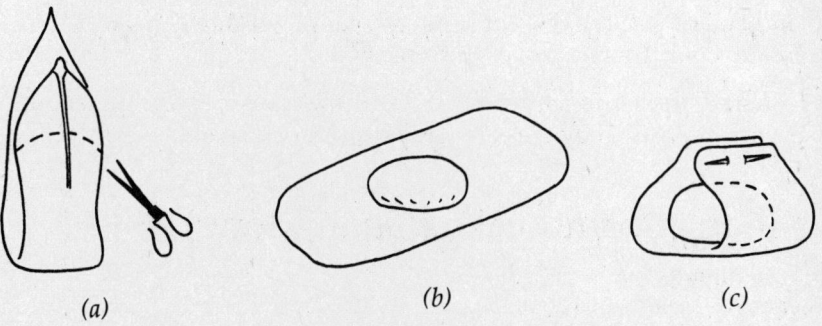

(a)   (b)   (c)

Banana leaves are preferred in tropical Hainan, but bamboo leaves in other areas of China. These cakes may be eaten hot or cold. Store in the refrigerator in an airtight container. They will keep for about a week refrigerated. Resteam to restore their softness.

Hokkien mung bean rice cakes (Fujian)

450 g (1 lb) glutinous rice flour
110 g (4 oz) granulated sugar

For the filling:
340 g (12 oz) mung bean paste

banana leaves or spinach leaves,
cut into 16 rounds, 8 cm (3 in) diameter

1. Mix the glutinous rice flour with cold water into a pliable dough. Take out one-fifth of the dough, and cook in boiling water till it

floats. Knead the cooked dough into the raw dough with the sugar till smooth. Shape into a cylinder, and break into 16 pieces.
2. Divide the mung bean paste into 16 portions, and shape into balls.
3. Shape a piece of the dough into a round about 8 cm (3 in) across. Place a mung bean ball in the centre. Gather the edges together and pinch to seal. Press lightly to flatten and place, sealed side down, on a piece of banana leaf. Make the rest in the same way.
4. Steam them, spaced out, in a preheated steaming basket over a high heat for about 10 minutes or till cooked.

This sweet rice cake may be kept for a week in a sealed container in the refrigerator. Steam to reheat.

Malagau – steamed sponge (Guangdong)

230 g (8 oz) self-raising flour
230 g (8 oz) soft brown sugar
5 eggs plus 1 yolk
80 ml (3 fl oz) milk
2 tsp baking powder
1 tsp bicarbonate of soda with 2 tsp cold water
1 tbsp dark soya sauce
1 tbsp vegetable oil (optional)

1. Mix together the flour and sugar. Make a well in the centre.
2. Break the eggs into the well. Whisk them till creamy, and then draw in the flour and continue whisking till smooth and thick. Finally whisk in the milk a little at a time. When the milk is well blended, gradually whisk in the oil. Finally whisk in the soya sauce. Keep the bowl in a *warm* place.
3. Put a steamer on to boil to preheat it. Grease a 20 cm (8 in) cake tin or steaming basket and line with greaseproof paper.
4. Whisk the baking powder, then the bicarbonate of soda with the water, into the cake mixture. (Mix the soda with the water only immediately before use.)
5. Pour into the greased and lined tin. Line the steamer with a folded piece of muslin to absorb any excess moisture. Place the cake tin or basket on the folded cloth. Cover and steam over a high heat for about 25 minutes. Test with a skewer. If it comes out clean, the cake is cooked.

The cooking time is based on the use of a cake tin with a non-removeable base and perforated with holes, or a Chinese steaming basket. For an ordinary Western cake tin increase the time to about 50 minutes. When cooked, the cake should have a wrinkled surface, and when cut it should be riddled with airholes. This simple but delicious cake is from Guangzhou (Canton). *Malagau* is Cantonese for Malay cake because it has a beautiful dark tan colour, rather like the complexion of a Malay. Nowadays there are many variations, some of which are completely white.

Ruyijuan – 'lucky' roll

280 g (10 oz) glutinous rice
30 g (1 oz) granulated sugar

For the filling:
170 g (6 oz) red bean paste

For the coating:
60 g (2 oz) white sesame seeds (toasted and crushed)

1. Rinse the rice, and soak for at least 1 hour.
2. Drain the rice, and steam in a steaming basket or steamer lined with a piece of muslin for about 35 to 40 minutes over a high heat, or till cooked. About halfway through cooking, lift the cover and spray the rice with some cold water. This makes the rice swell better.
3. Transfer the rice to a bowl, and mix in the sugar. Leave till cool enough to handle. Put the rice in a new freezer food bag, and knead till it becomes a cohesive dough with some rice grains still visible.
4. Sprinkle a flat surface with the sesame seeds. Transfer the rice dough on to the seeds. Shape into a cylinder of about 5 cm (2 in) diameter, covered in sesame seeds. Put it in a piece of cling film. Grease a rolling pin lightly, and roll the dough into an oblong about 30 × 20 cm (12 × 8 in). Spread the red bean paste all over the top to cover it completely. Roll up one end towards the centre and then the opposite end, meeting in the middle like a double Swiss roll. Press lightly so that the two rolls stick together. Cut into rounds about 2.5 cm (1 in) thick. Arrange the rounds on a plate, cut-side-up. (*See illustrations page 204.*) Serve at room temperature.

This is a popular summer sweet or snack. *Ruyi* is an S-shaped ornament usually made of jade, a symbol of good luck. *Ruyi* also means 'as one wishes', which is a happy state of being, hence fortunate and lucky.

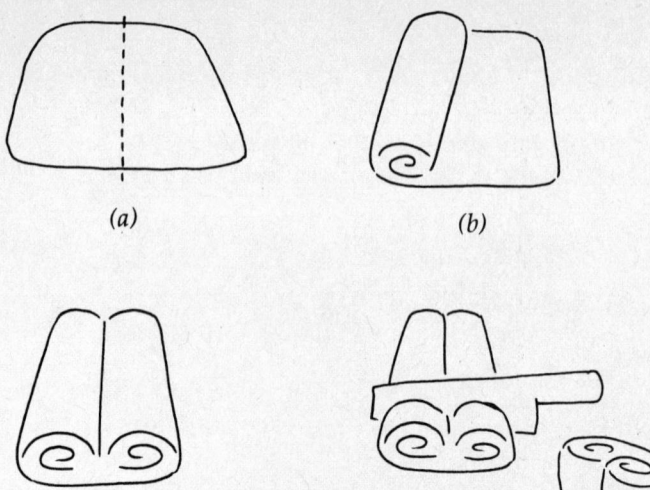

(a)

(b)

(c)

(d)

Shallot cake (Fujian)

For the sponge:
140 g (5 oz) self-raising flour
140 g (5 oz) granulated sugar
5 eggs

For the topping:
5 shallots
2 tbsp groundnut or vegetable oil

1. Peel and chop the shallots. Set the wok on a medium heat till hot, and put in the oil. Stir-fry the shallots till they just turn brown; do not allow them to turn black or they will be bitter. Take out and drain on kitchen paper. Reserve the oil for other cooking.
2. Grease an 18 cm (7 in) cake tin.
3. Beat the eggs and sugar over a saucepan of hot water (or with an electric beater without the hot water) till creamy-white and thick. Sift in the flour and fold it in with a plastic spatula. Pour the sponge mixture into the greased tin. Sprinkle with the shallots, and steam in a steaming basket or steamer over a high heat for 30 minutes or till cooked.

The red variety of shallot is a favourite flavouring ingredient in both sweet and savoury dishes in south China.

Steamed ham sponge

For the sponge:
170 g (6 oz) self-raising flour
170 g (6 oz) granulated sugar
6 eggs

For the topping:
30 g (1 oz) cooked Chinese ham (minced)

1. Grease and line an 18 or 20 cm (7 or 8 in) cake tin.
2. Preheat a steaming basket or steamer by putting the water on to boil.
3. Whisk the eggs and sugar over a saucepan of hot (not boiling) water (or it may be done with an electric whisk without the hot water) till creamy-white and thick.
4. Sift the flour into the egg mixture and gently fold it in with a palette knife. Pour into the prepared tin. Sprinkle with the minced ham.
5. Steam in the preheated basket or steamer for about 20 minutes or till cooked.

A mixture of sweet and savoury is a favourite Chinese taste. Chinese ham is quite similar in flavour to the Western smoked back bacon, which may be substituted here, after being grilled.

Sweet potato cakes (Guangxi)

450 g (1 lb) sweet potato
450 g (1 lb) glutinous rice flour
110 g (4 oz) granulated sugar

cooking oil

1. Peel, rinse and slice the sweet potatoes. Boil in 140 ml (5 fl oz) water till cooked. Reduce it to a purée with a potato masher. Mix in the sugar and rice flour. Knead into a firm dough. If too wet, add more rice flour.
2. Break the dough into 24 equal pieces, and roll into balls the size of an egg. Press lightly into flattened cakes.
3. Set a thick, flat-bottomed frying pan on a medium heat, and when hot put in a 1 tbsp oil. Reduce the heat to low and arrange several cakes in the pan. Cook very slowly till one side is golden. Turn over and cook the other side. When both sides are done, about 6

minutes, take out. During the cooking trickle in a little more oil if necessary.

These simple and delicious cakes, soft and resilient at the same time, glow like a ripe persimmon. They are a special kind of New Year cakes from Qinzhou district in Guangxi. Here it is the custom for the womenfolk to prepare these cakes on the third day of the Spring Festival to entertain visitors. They keep well for about a week, if refrigerated. To refresh, either pan-fry on a low heat or put in a hot oven for a few minutes.

SWEETS AND TITBITS

Crystallized kumquat peel

450 g (1 lb) kumquats
280 g (10 oz) granulated sugar

1. Rinse the kumquats. Remove any stalks or leaves. Cut them open, and pull out the flesh together with the seeds. (Save the insides for a beautifully golden and tasty marmalade.)
2. Put the peel in a small pot with just enough water to cover. Bring to the boil and simmer till tender, about 20 minutes. Add half the sugar. Dissolve the sugar and simmer for another minute. Leave to soak in the syrup overnight.
3. Strain the syrup into a saucepan. Add the rest of the sugar. Dissolve on a low heat and bring to the boil. Cook the syrup till bubbles appear all over. Pour in the soaked, cooked peel. Mix well, and take off the heat. Leave to cool in the syrup.
4. Use a pair of chopsticks to pick up the peel and put it on a wire rack to dry out. When dried, it will be covered with a coating of white sugar crystals. Store in an airtight container. It will keep indefinitely if fully dried.

The word *kumquat* in Cantonese, or *jinju* in Mandarin means 'golden tangerine'. Like the Seville, Valencia and navel oranges, the kumquat is a native of south China. It is a citrus fruit, the size and shape of a quail's egg with a thin golden skin, crisp, sharp flesh and tiny seeds. It may be eaten whole raw, but it is best crystallized, for the peel lacks the bitter taste of Seville oranges yet possesses a stronger fragrance and taste after preserving. As it is a very tender fruit, it is quick to prepare. In China it is also preserved whole in sugar and spices and eaten as a confection. One variety, *Fortunella margarita*, is now imported into Britain, mainly from Sicily. Cleaned peels from both Seville and sweet oranges may be prepared in the same way.

Peanut brittle

110 g (4 oz) raw peanuts
280 g (10 oz) granulated sugar
½ tsp salt

cooking oil for greasing

1. Rinse the peanuts, drain and dry. Put the peanuts in a baking tin in one layer and roast in a moderately hot oven, about 190°C (375°F, gas 5) for about 8 minutes. Take out and shake the tin so that they brown evenly. Return it to the oven and roast for another 5 minutes, or till just cooked. Take out, let cool, rub off the red skins and discard them.
2. Line a 20 cm (8 in) sandwich cake tin with foil and grease it lightly.
3. Put the sugar with 4 tbsp cold water in a thick-bottomed saucepan. Mix well and cook on a low heat to dissolve the sugar, stirring all the while. When the sugar has dissolved, raise the heat to medium and cook till the sugar syrup turns a reddish-gold colour – but not black or smoking, which would make it bitter. Immediately add the prepared peanuts, mix well and pour into the greased and lined tin. Level out evenly to fill the tin in a single layer.
4. While still warm and soft, cut it up in the tin, lengthwise into strips about 1 cm (½ in) wide. Take out the strips and chop into 5 cm (2 in) long fingers.

If preferred, it may be cut into squares. Peanut brittle and sesame snaps (*see* next recipe) are used in both sweet and savoury cooking, and eaten as a confection. These sweets, when wrapped in little red packages, are used to announce an engagement among friends and relations.

Sesame snaps

230 g (8 oz) white sesame seeds
350 g (12 oz) granulated sugar
30 g (1 oz) maltose
½ tsp salt

cooking oil for greasing
1 sheet greaseproof paper, 28 × 20 cm (11 × 8 in)

1. Pick through the sesame seeds and discard any grit. Rinse in a fine sieve and drain well. Dry-fry (without oil) in the wok till they start to make a crackling noise. Take out.
2. Line a Swiss roll tin about 28 × 20 cm (11 × 8 in) with foil, and lightly grease the foil with some oil.
3. Put the sugar, maltose and salt in a thick saucepan with 4 tbsp water. Stir over a low heat to dissolve the sugar. Add the sesame seeds, and continue to cook over a medium heat till the syrup begins to turn red but is not smoking, which will make it bitter.
4. Pour immediately into the lined and greased tin. You will find that it solidifies very quickly, almost immediately. Place a piece of oiled greaseproof paper over the sesame mixture. Then, with a rolling pin, press down the greaseproof paper firmly to even out the mixture.
5. Remove the foil and paper from the sesame slab while it is still warm and pliable. Cut it into 1 cm (½ in) wide strips with a hay-cutting motion – with your right hand holding the handle of the knife and your left hand on the back of the blade. Take the strips out of the tin and chop them into 5 cm (2 in) long fingers.

The cutting must be done while the mixture is still warm and pliable or it will be too hard to cut. This amount makes about 550 g (1¼ lb). If a less sweet snap with more sesame is preferred, reduce the sugar to 230 g (8 oz).

Spiced peanuts

230 g (8 oz) raw peanuts (blanched)

For the seasoning:
2 pods star anise
2 tsp Sichuan peppercorns
1 tbsp salt

1. Bring 400 ml (¾ pt) of water with the spices and salt to the boil. Cover, and simmer for about 5 minutes. Put in the blanched peanuts, turn off the heat and leave to soak for about 2 hours. Do not soak any longer, or the peanuts will be over-saturated with water and will not crisp well.
2. Drain and discard the spices, and leave in a colander to dry out in an airy place for several hours or overnight.

3. Spread the spiced and dried peanuts in a baking tray, and roast in a moderately hot oven at about 180°C (350°F, gas 4) for about 30 minutes, shaking them once every 5 minutes. When they are golden and crisp, take out and let cool completely. Store in an airtight container. They will keep for about a month.

If preferred, the peanuts may be deep-fried in oil or dry-fried (without oil) in a wok till crisp. One traditional Chinese method is to dry-fry them in hot sand. They are a popular snack with drinks or eaten on their own. They may also be eaten with plain rice porridge for breakfast.

Spiced sunflower seeds

230 g (8 oz) raw sunflower seeds (shelled)

For the seasoning:
2 tsp salt
1 tsp granulated sugar
2.5 cm (1 in) cassia bark
1 pod star anise

1. Put the sunflower seeds with the seasoning into a pot, and add 280 ml (½ pt) cold water. Bring to the boil, lower the heat, cover and simmer for 5 minutes.
2. Drain, and discard the spices. Put the sunflower seeds in a wok, and fry-fry (without oil) over a medium heat till the moisture disappears. Lower the heat, and continue stir-frying till they are lightly coloured.

Ingredients

The following are some ingredients used in the recipes in this book. They are generally available in Britain in Chinese shops, some ethnic shops and delicatessens, and sometimes in supermarkets.

OIL

Lard: used for some dishes, pastries, cakes and puddings. A good quality odourless white vegetable fat may be used instead.

Sesame oil: a favourite for flavouring both savoury and sweet food. It is also used in cooking. In one district in Henan province, the sesame oil is the only one used for cooking, for oil lamps and greasing cartwheels. Sesame oil comes in many grades, some pure and some blended with other oils. Generally, in Chinese shops, the price is a good indicator of the quality. The best sesame oils are the pure ones from China or Hong Kong (but one brand from South-East Asia tastes of cockroach droppings!). A good-quality sesame oil has a beautiful fragrance and a delicate taste. For Chinese cooking do not substitute Greek sesame oil, as this has a stronger taste because it is pressed from raw seeds, while the Chinese sesame oil is made with roasted seeds.

Groundnut oil: preferred for green leafy vegetables and deep-frying, but any odourless, good-quality vegetable oil such as sunflower, corn or rape seed oil will suffice.

Rendered chicken fat: chicken fat only (not skin) either rendered immediately before use or prepared in advance and stored in the refrigerator.

Rendered duck fat: duck fat only (not skin) rendered, or dripping from roast duck.

RICE

Long grain rice: the ordinary rice eaten at meals. There are myriads of varieties, sticky or non-sticky. The amount of water and the cooking time depend on the variety and its age. Generally a sticky type or a newly-harvested rice needs less water than the non-sticky kind or one that has been stored a couple of years. On average the proportion of rice to water is 1 to 1 or 1 to 1½, and the cooking time is about 8 to 10 minutes after the initial boiling. New or sticky rice needs less time to cook than non-sticky or stored.

Glutinous rice: an opaque long grain rice which turns translucent and sticky on cooking and has a sweetish fragrance. It is used for puddings, cakes and as a stuffing for poultry and game.

FLOUR

Wheat flour: strong unbleached plain flour for noodles and pasta, dumplings, pastries and some cakes. A good quality strong plain flour may be used instead.

Rice flour: ground from raw long grain rice is used in pasta, cakes and dumplings. Western rice flour is not suitable, as it is toasted before being ground.

Glutinous rice flour: ground from raw glutinous rice, it is the favourite flour for cakes, puddings and dumplings.

STARCH

Derived from various roots, cereals and legumes, it plays an important part in Chinese cooking. It thickens the liquid in food and gives a velvety texture to a sauce. It binds meat and seafood together, as in fillings and meat balls, and gives them a moist consistency. As a coating it preserves the taste of food by preventing the moisture from escaping when the food is heated, and therefore stops it from becoming dry and tasteless. Coating or marinating food with starch before stir-frying or deep-frying acts as a sealing agent and makes the finished dish look as attractive as it tastes. The starches used in Chinese cooking are potato flour, cornflour, mung bean flour, Chinese water chestnut flour, lotus root flour, broad bean flour and arrowroot. These starches do not have a floury taste and therefore do not need to be cooked in fat as in a *roux*. On cooking they turn clear and translucent, giving a sauce or glaze a glistening look, and they are also a great absorber of liquid. When used to thicken sauces, these starches never separate, nor do they exude water on cooling. By far the

Chinese favourite is potato flour, followed by cornflour and mung bean flour; all possess the qualities of a good binder and emulsifier. In the recipes in this book cornflour is used, as it is cheaper and more easily available here.

Wheat starch: is used in some cake making, and may be home-made as the by-product of gluten (*see* 'Wheat', *page* 240).

SOYA SAUCES

Dark soya sauce: this type has caramel and a little wheat flour added during fermentation, and is thick and dark in colour. Full-bodied and delicious, it is used both in cooking and as a dip at table. Keeps indefinitely.

Light soya sauce: also known as 'white soya sauce', is actually amber coloured like a strong clear tea. It does not contain wheat flour or caramel, and has a clear, delicious soya taste. It is normally used for white meat, in soup and as a dip at table. Keeps indefinitely. Though not easily available here, there are also soya sauces flavoured with mushrooms or with shrimps (not the same as shrimp sauce), which look like fish sauce (*see below*).

OTHER SAUCES FOR A CHANGE

Chilli sauce: contains fresh chillies, vinegar, salt, sugar and sometimes plums to give body. One kind is made from finely ground, seedless chillies and the other from coarsely ground chillies with seeds, very hot. May be used as a seasoning or a dip. Keeps indefinitely.

Fish sauce or gravy: is a concentrate made by fermenting small whole fish with salt. It is light amber-coloured and rather salty. Used like a soya sauce for seasoning and in cooking.

Hoisin sauce: from Guangzhou (Canton), a dark, rich, sweet, salty and mildly spicy paste. It is made from salted soya bean paste with a host of spices, vinegar and sugar. Delicious as a dip, particularly for deep-fried seafood and meat, or as a base for marinade.

Oyster sauce: a thick brown sauce made by boiling oysters in soya sauce and salt and thickened with wheat flour. It gives food a delicious taste and a rich, smooth and velvety texture, without smothering its original taste. Rather salty, it keeps indefinitely in a cool, dry place. Some contain preservatives. Better-quality types are labelled 'extract of oyster'; those called 'oyster flavoured' are nowhere near the real thing.

Plum sauce: main ingredients are plums or apricots with vinegar, salt and sugar. It is a delicious dip for deep-fried food, cold meats or Chinese pancakes, or can be used in a marinade for meat or in a sweet and sour sauce. It may be home-made (*see page* 236). Keeps indefinitely; in fact its flavour improves after a couple of years.

SOME PASTES AND CONDIMENTS

Salted soya beans: whole soya beans fermented with salt, brown in colour, used as a flavouring in the cooking of meat, fish, seafood, *doufu* etc. Keeps indefinitely in an airtight container in a cool, dry place, provided that only a clean, dry spoon is used.

Salted soya bean paste: the same fermented beans ground. It is better prepared at home, as the commercial ones are exceedingly salty.

Hot salted soya bean paste: the above paste mixed with chilli powder, may be mixed at home.

Sichuan chilli paste: a very hot Sichuan speciality made from ground dried whole chilli peppers and salted fermented broad bean paste. Sometimes made with soya beans, which are more easily available. Use only in cooking. Keeps indefinitely. It may be prepared at home by mixing salted soya bean paste with enough chilli powder to taste.

Sweet salted soya bean paste: salted soya bean paste with sugar and sesame oil added. Used in cooking or as a dip at table. It may be prepared at home (*see page* 240.)

Salted black soya beans: fermented with salt, and with soya sauce added. It has a great affinity with fish, meat and bitter gourd. Keeps indefinitely in an airtight container.

Dried salted black soya beans: fermented black soya beans, salted and dried. They have a rather strong and pungent flavour, and must be rinsed and soaked briefly before use. They do not keep very well, so buy in small quantities or store in the freezer.

Red fermented bean curd: American Chinese aptly dub these bean curds 'cheese', as they have a strong, pungent cheesy flavour. They are little brick-red cubes made from pressed and fermented bean curd preserved in wine and spices. They enhance fish, meat and vegetable dishes, giving them a 'mature' taste. They may also be eaten with rice porridge for breakfast. If kept in an airtight container in a cool, dry place, they keep for about a year, provided that clean, dry chopsticks are used to take them out every time. Three brands are available here: one from Zhejiang, one from Beijing and the other from Guangzhou (Canton), with slight differences in taste; the Zhejiang one is the strongest.

Chilli oil: This is a chilli flavoured oil used as a condiment in sauces for cold platter food and salad and in hot soups. It may be prepared at home (*see page* 228.)

Shrimp paste: a thick, pinkish-grey sauce made from shrimps fermented in brine and wine. It is very salty with a strong, pungent flavour, and rather similar to the South-East Asian dried shrimp paste called *blachan*, which comes in a slab. To be used sparingly and in cooking only. Keeps almost indefinitely in a cool, dry place, and if taken out with a dry clean spoon every time.

Sesame paste: there is hardly any difference at all from the Greek *tahini*, which may be used instead. It is used mainly in sauces for cold platter food.

DRIED ALGAE

Agar agar: or *yangcai* in Mandarin. A jelling agent derived from an alga, is commonly used in Oriental cooking from China to South-East Asia and Japan. Agar agar is creamy white in colour and semi-translucent, feels rather like raffia and is very light. A little goes a long way: about 8 g is sufficient for about 1 l liquid (¼ oz for 1½ pt). It congeals in a shorter time than the Western gelatine and at a room temperature of 25°C (80°F). Above all it does not melt easily in warm conditions. Hence its popularity in hot climates and in countries where the refrigerator is not a common household appliance. As it is neutral in colour and flavour, it is used in both sweet and savoury dishes. In Chinese cookery it is also used as a vegetable in salad after soaking in water (*see page* 14.)

Dried hairweed (facai): this is harvested from the semi-desert land in Inner Mongolia but is botanically an alga like seaweed. It looks black and fine like Oriental hair when dried, hence its name, but becomes greenish brown with a crunchy texture when soaked. It is used in soups, braised or steamed dishes, and has a great affinity with pork.

Purple laver (zicai): the name means 'purple vegetable'. It comes in rice-paper thin sheets which are actually dark green in colour. In the West it is better known by its Japanese name, *nori*. It is mainly used as a wrapper or put straight into soup.

DRIED SEAFOOD

Dried bream or brill: a species of bream or brill is dried without any salt. In appearance it is all bones and skin, and seems to have no flesh at all. As a flavouring ingredient: the whole fish, bones, skin and all, is grilled or deep-fried and pounded finely before use.

Dried cuttlefish and squid: both are sun-dried without cooking or salting. They are soaked before cooking, mainly in stir-frying. (*See page* 228.)

Dried scallops: these dark coral coloured cylinders are about 2 cm (¾ in) across, and slightly less in height. When soaked they may be broken into fine shreds which are used to flavour and decorate food.

Dried sea cucumbers: also known as sea slugs or *bêche-de-mer*. They are black and rock-hard. Some are as large as carrots and others as small as your little finger. They swell to about eight times their original volume when soaked in water. (*See page* 238.) Rated a great delicacy in the Chinese food heirarchy, they are wonderfully delicate and gelatinous. They are one of those incomplete foods which have to be cooked with meat, usually pork.

Dried shrimps: these are boiled shrimps, shelled and sun-dried. They are rock-hard and must be soaked before cooking. (*See page* 238.)

Salted jellyfish: leathery-looking, brownish discs about 25 cm (10 in) in diameter. They are heavily salted, and must be rinsed thoroughly, shredded and soaked before using in cold salad dishes. If properly prepared they are not salty, and have a very crunchy texture. (*See page* 234 for preparation, and *page* 25 for further information.)

Prawn crackers: dried transparent slices the size of potato chips before being deep-fried. They are made from shrimps, ground raw and mixed with rice flour and seasoning. When deep-fried in oil they expand to several times their original size and turn an opaque white. They are eaten as a snack like Western potato chips, or may be served with meat or fish dishes in a sauce for a contrast in texture.

PRESERVED VEGETABLES, FRUIT, RICE AND EGGS

Chinese mixed pickle: a colourful assortment of vegetables such as carrots, green peppers, cucumbers, ginger, mustard stalks, hot red chilli peppers, mouli, papaya, etc., pickled in vinegar, sugar and salt. It is delicious: crunchy, sweet, sour and piquant. It may be served with cold meat, fermented eggs, or fried food, and is used in the cooking of sweet and sour dishes. It may be prepared at home (*see page* 235).

Pickled young ginger: this very tender creamy white young ginger is pickled in vinegar, sugar and salt. A natural accompaniment for the fermented eggs, with cold platter meat dishes or in sweet and sour dishes. It may be prepared at home (*see page* 233).

Sichuan preserved vegetable (zhacai):   the knobbly stem of a vegetable, dry-salted with plenty of chilli powder and spices. Rinse before use to remove the excess chilli powder which covers it. Mainly comes in tins. After opening, store in the refrigerator, when it will keep indefinitely. It enhances the flavour of meat. Rather salty, a little goes a long way.

Salted mustard greens: this is the bitter mustard plant preserved in brine, sometimes with wine added. Sour and salty, it has a tangy and piquant fragrance. It may be eaten raw, used in soup or in braised, stir-fried or steamed dishes, or cooked purely as a vegetable. It comes in tins or plastic bags; once opened it should be kept in the refrigerator.

Preserved 'red-in-the-snow' (meikancai):   a species of mustard plant with red turnip-top-like leaves, fermented, preserved in salt and sun-dried. The long preserving process gives it a strong fragrance. It must be soaked and rinsed thoroughly to remove any grit and excess salt. It may be stir-fried, steamed, braised or boiled with meat.

Preserved Chinese celery cabbage (dongcai):   made in Tianjin in north China. The cabbage is chopped confetti-fine and preserved in salt and garlic, and packed in a dark brown terracotta jar. A flavouring ingredient. Rinsing is necessary before sprinkling on to soups or noodles, or steaming with minced meat.

Pickled plums (suanmei):   whole plums pickled in brine. Brownish in colour and soft, they are a flavouring ingredient for meat and fish dishes.

Fermented glutinous rice: glutinous rice mixed with a Chinese wine yeast and fermented alcoholically. It has a very strong alcoholic fragrance, and is used in the flavouring of meat and fish dishes or preserving food such as 'fermented glutinous rice eggs', which are not available in Britain. Fermented glutinous rice is not sold in Britain either, but Chinese shops stock the wine yeast. For the preparation of the fermented glutinous rice *see page* 232.

Salted duck's eggs: traditionally these are duck's eggs preserved in salt covered in a layer of sooty-looking burnt earth, but some are preserved without the earth. When raw the salted egg yolk is a firm bright orange ball and the white is watery. After removing the earth and rinsing, the eggs are boiled for 10 minutes, as they can only be eaten well cooked. When cooked, the yolk is golden and shiny with oil and has an exciting sandy texture (rather like a turtle's egg), delicious but not salty. The white is salty and dishes flavoured with salted eggs need hardly any salting, if at all. For the preparation of salted eggs *see page* 84.

Fermented eggs: these are known as the '100-year-old eggs' in the West, though they are only a few months old. As with the salted eggs, duck's eggs are normally used, as the shells are much stronger than those of hen's eggs. The white is a sparkling amber colour, transparent with white feathery traces like pine needles and slightly rubbery in texture; hence the Chinese name *pitan*, 'leather eggs'. The yolk is the colour of boiled spinach and tastes cheesy. One type, traditionally preserved with a coating of clay-like mixture of limes, ashes, salt and rice husks, does not need cooking. But this kind is not imported nowadays. Instead, a new type without the clay coating is available. This kind must be boiled for about 10 minutes, or 5 minutes if a softer yolk is preferred.

LEGUMES

Mung beans: boiled and eaten as a sweet snack or part of a savoury soup. Sweetened mung bean purée is used as a filling for many cakes, puddings and dumplings. Mung bean flour is also an ingredient in the making of cakes, dumplings and puddings, vermicelli and mung bean skins. The beans are also sprouted as fresh vegetables (*see page* 225).

Peanuts: eaten as a vegetable in soups, braised meat dishes and other vegetables. Roasted, deep-fried, or boiled and sun-dried, peanuts are popular snacks and garnishes for some dishes. They are also made into confectionery such as peanut brittle (*see page* 207).

Red aduki beans: boiled and eaten as a sweet snack or part of a savoury. The sweetened purée is used in the making of cakes, puddings and dumplings (*see page* 237).

Soya beans: apart from being the basis for *doufu* and many other soya products and sauces, they are sprouted as a vegetable (*see page* 225). (*See also below* 'Soya products' and 'Some pastes and condiments' *page* 213.)

SOYA PRODUCTS

Doufu: or bean curd, is soya milk curdled to a solid with burnt gypsum (calcium sulphate). The soft type available here has a high water content, and is cream coloured, with a smooth texture and a mild taste. It may be steamed, boiled, braised, stir-fried or combined with other ingredients. This kind can also be made into firm *doufu* by wrapping it in a piece of muslin and using a weight to remove excess water, *see also pages* 73–4.

Dried bean curd skins: these dried, crisp skins are now packed in single oblong pieces in order to reduce crackings at the folds. They are very brittle and have to be handled carefully. Before using as a wrapper, they should be dipped in hot water very briefly to soften and patted dry. They are broken up to put in soup or vegetarian dishes.

SEASONINGS

Maltose: this amber coloured, sticky sweetener is usually extracted from wheat. It is not as sweet as ordinary sugar, but has a delicious taste and may be eaten as a sweetmeat. For cooking it is used in the making of confectionery, cakes and biscuits as it gives them a beautiful colour, taste and fragrance. As a glaze as in the roasting of meat, e.g. suckling pig, and poultry, including the famous Beijing duck, it gives a crisp finish and beautiful red colouring.

Rock sugar: cane sugar, in amber coloured or white crystal lumps, is less sweet than ordinary sugar and imparts a fragrance to food cooked in it. It must be crushed before use.

Vinegar: the white rice wine vinegar used in Chinese cooking may be replaced by European white wine vinegar.

Zhenjiang vinegar: (labelled 'Chinkiang vinegar' in local Jiangsu dialect): a well-known dark, thick vinegar from Jiangsu province with a low acid content and a lovely fragrance. It is used in the cooking of meat, and as a dip at table.

Worcester sauce: although this is an English sauce it is similar to a seasoning sauce called *jizhi* in Guangzhou (Canton), which is used as a seasoning or as a dip at table when a hot and spicy taste is required. As *jizhi* is not exported, overseas Chinese resort to Worcester sauce.

Wine: the common Chinese wine used in cooking is *shaoxingjiu*, a fortified wine made from the glutinous rice. *Kaoliangjiu*, a spirit made from sorghum (*kaoliang*) is used in some savoury dishes and in the preserving of food. *Meikuilu*, or rose dew, is *kaoliangjiu* flavoured with rose petals and used in the making of cakes and confectionery. In Chinese cooking, rice wine may be substituted with a pale dry sherry. Do not be tempted to replace it with a more full-bodied sherry, as its flavour will overpower and change the taste of the dish.

HERBS AND SPICES

Herbs are used both as a garnish and to impart flavour and fragrance to the food decorated. The Chinese favourites are young green celery leaves, coriander leaves and mint leaves when in season, and the ubiquitous spring onions.

Dried spices used in Chinese cooking are cardamom, ovoid cardamom, cassia bark, liquorice root, dried tangerine peel, cloves, fennel seeds, star anise, Sichuan peppercorns and white peppercorns. Of these, the most frequently used are star anise, dried tangerine peel, Sichuan peppercorns and white peppercorns, *described below*. It would be handy to keep a stock of them.

Dried tangerine peel: hard and very dark brown, it is a flavouring for both sweet and savoury dishes. It is also available in powder form.

Sichuan peppercorns: also known as *fagara*, these resemble black peppercorns but are light (not solid) with a seed inside, and dark reddish brown in colour. Mildly hot with a pleasant aroma, they are used in red-cooked dishes, pickles and salt dips, particularly in Sichuan, Hunan and Yunnan cooking.

Star anise: hard, dark brown pods with 8 pointed petals each containing a seed. A favourite spice in red-cooked dishes, it has a rather similar flavour to the rice-shaped anise seed, but more bitter and pungent. Some recipes call for it in powder form; it is available ready ground.

White peppercorns: these are usually dry-fried (without oil) till fragrant before being finely ground. A very frequently used spice in Guangdong and Fujian cooking.

Dried rose petals: used in the flavouring of sugar, and may also be added directly to the sweets and confectionery (*see also page* 238).

Five-spice powder: a commercially prepared seasoning powder, containing star anise, cloves, cassia bark, fennel seeds and Sichuan peppercorns. In Chinese cuisine it is like the *garam masala* in Indian cooking.

Galangal: or 'galangal lesser', also called 'galangal ginger', a native of South China, this fibrous, bulbous root has a cream coloured, red-tinged skin and a pale creamy flesh with a very strong fragrance. It is used in the cooking of meat and fish dishes in southern China and South-East Asian Chinese cooking.

Garlic: a great deal is used in the seasoning of oil when cooking vegetables. Minced raw garlic is a favourite seasoning for salad dressing and a dip for shellfish.

Ginger: an indispensable ingredient in Chinese cooking, its main function is to deodorize meat and fish. Creamy white, tender young ginger is particularly good when shredded as a garnish for soup and porridge, or sliced and pickled. (*See also page* 43, Sajiang).

Mixed spices for the steeping pot (luliao): the mixture varies from region to region. The Cantonese variant contains nine spices, and is available from Chinese shops in Britain ready mixed. To prepare at home *see page* 16.

Shallot (Allium escalonicum): the red variety is preferred in Chinese cuisine. It is a popular ingredient in Fujian and Guangdong cooking.

PRESERVED MEATS

Chinese ham: this is used mainly as a flavouring for soup and other dishes. Two well-known varieties from China are Jinhua and Yunnan hams. These are also available canned. For cooking purposes, a good substitute is smoked back bacon, which has a similar taste and colour.

Chinese pork sausages: these are waxy-looking thin sausages about 18 to 20 cm (7 to 8 in) long, tied in pairs, and called *lahcang* or waxed sausages. They are reddish with white marbling, sweet and savoury, not unlike some kinds of Italian salami in taste. Made from lean meat and fat, and wind-dried, they must be cooked before eating. They are rarely eaten on their own, and are mainly a flavouring ingredient, used sparingly for a richer taste as in fried rice and other vegetable or meat dishes.
Duck liver sausages: these are similar to pork sausages in appearance, but the red part is darker and they taste less sweet.

DRIED NOODLES, VERMICELLI AND OTHER PASTA

Wheat noodles: these come in many widths and varieties. Some are made with eggs, some are green with spinach juice added, whilst others are yellow with lye water. They must be boiled briefly before further cooking. Fresh noodles may be prepared at home (*see page* 154).

Rice noodles: made from long grain rice, these come in ribbons from 1 to 2 cm (½ to ⅔ in) in width. They are boiled briefly before further cooking. Ready-made fresh ones are available from Chinese shops.

Rice sticks: made from long grain rice, and sold in two thicknesses. They must be boiled briefly before further cooking. To deep-fry, put into hot oil without rinsing. Only the dried form is available.

Mung bean vermicelli: these are hair-fine, transparent and very tough when dry; they must be cut with a sharp pair of kitchen scissors. Soak in boiling water before cooking. They swell a great deal and absorb liquid quickly, and should be added to soup immediately before serving.

Won ton skins: freshly made paper-thin squares used for a filled pasta rather like a kind of ravioli. Made with wheat flour, salt and lye water. They may be kept for about a week in the refrigerator well wrapped up. To prepare at home *see page* 20.

DRIED NUTS AND SEEDS

Almonds: sweet almonds are used in sweet and savoury dishes, cakes, biscuits and puddings and as garnishes for meat and seafood. Bitter almonds are used sparingly to give a subtle flavour to sweet dishes, cakes, puddings, drinks and savoury soups. They are often combined with sweet almonds.

Cashew nuts: similar to Western ones, they are stir-fried with meat, used as a garnish or eaten as a snack.

Chestnuts (dried): similar to Western ones, they are used in sweet and savoury dishes, or roasted and eaten as snacks.

Lotus seeds: these are about 1 cm (½ in) long, oval and ivory-coloured. They are soaked before being boiled in soups and sweets or made into a sweetened paste for filling in cakes and puddings (*see page* 234).

Pine nuts: similar to Western ones, they are used in both sweet and savoury dishes.

Sesame seeds: white sesame seeds are fine and ivory-coloured and slightly smaller than the Mediterranean ones, which may be used instead. They are used in both sweet and savoury dishes. They should be picked through and any grit discarded, then rinsed and dry-fried till fragrant, and used either crushed or whole. The black variety is used mainly in sweets, cakes, biscuits and other confections.

Walnuts: similar to English ones, they feature both in meat dishes and in confectionery.

DRIED FRUITS

Honey dates: these are variously labelled as 'cooking dates', 'palm dates' or even 'coconut dates' in Chinese shops here. They are hard and dark brown, with fine ridges on them and very sharp, narrow, pointed and hard stones inside. Soak in hot water briefly, and the flesh will crumble easily. Very sweet, they are used mainly as an ingredient in sweets, cakes and puddings.

Red dates: these are sun-dried jujubes; they have lacquer-red, shrivelled skins. They are soaked and stoned before cooking with meat or in puddings and cakes. To store, keep in the freezer after picking them over and rinsing, as they ferment easily.

Dried persimmons: round, flattened, leathery-looking, dark reddish-brown fruits covered in white layer of natural fruit sugar. They are mainly used in sweets and puddings, or eaten plain as a snack.

CRYSTALLIZED FRUITS

Crystallized kumquats: these are little golden citrus fruits the size of quail's eggs. They may be eaten as sweets or used in cakes and puddings. To prepare at home *see page* 206. They keep indefinitely.

Crystallized lotus seeds: blanched lotus seeds crystallized in sugar. Best stored in the freezer. May be used in sweets and puddings.

Crystallized winter melon: sold either in transparent white lumps or in fingers covered in crystallized sugar. An ingredient for sweetening meat dishes or in the making of cakes and puddings; it is also eaten as a sweet. Store in the freezer.

Crystallized water chestnuts: small, round and white, covered in sugar crystals. Used in puddings and cakes and, like the other crystallized fruits, eaten as a sweet. Best stored in the freezer, as they ferment quickly.

DRIED FLOWERS AND FUNGI

Dried lily flowers: these are in fact day lilies. They are leathery, about 10 cm (4 in) long, golden-brown and needle-shaped; hence their Chinese name *jinzhencai*, 'golden needles'. They have a distinctive fragrance and a mildly sour taste. Before cooking they must be picked through, the stalks broken off and discarded, and then soaked and rinsed. Buy a little at a time as they do not keep well. Choose ones with a pale golden colour, not brownish ones.

Dried black wood ears: these are black and charred-looking fungi, irregular in shape. When soaked, they swell to six times in volume. They come dried, and must be soaked and rinsed well before use. (*See page* 241.)

Dried silver wood ears: known as 'jelly fungus' in English, they are a cock's comb-like fungus, pale honey-coloured and very light. After soaking they turn white and increase twenty-five times in volume. They have a crunchy texture, but if simmered for a long time they become gelatinous. They appear mainly in soups, either sweet or savoury. (*See page* 239.)

Dried winter mushrooms: these are dark brown, leathery-looking mushrooms with a strong fragrance. They come in dry form only. They have a unique flavour to which there is no substitute. Soak before cooking (*see page* 241).

SOME SPECIAL INGREDIENTS

Dried red fermented rice (hongqu): this is a dry, light, powdery lacquer-red rice produced by fermenting long grain rice with a red mould culture. The best kind should float on water. It is used mainly as a colouring, though also considered a tonic food.

Lye water: a solution of 42% potassium carbonate in 58% water. It is used in some noodles, pastries and cakes and sometimes for blanching or softening dried ingredients.

Rice paper: white round discs of about 20 to 22 cm (8 to 9 in) in diameter, not unlike Western rice paper but thinner.

Wine yeast: this is for home-made Chinese rice wine or fermented glutinous rice. It looks like a ping-pong ball but is smaller, round and smooth, white and light. It should be crushed before use.

FRESH FISH

Some fish used in Chinese cooking and available in Britain are pomfret, grouper, red snapper, sea bass, carp, grass carp and tench. But many kinds of fresh fish are suitable for Chinese cooking, provided that they are really fresh. Whiting, haddock, cod, halibut, turbot, sole, skate, red mullet and grey mullet are all excellent. Monkfish is one of the few fish sold in Britain that can be sliced thinly and stir-fried without falling to bits. Frozen fish must be defrosted thoroughly before cooking in the Chinese way as the time taken for the heat to penetrate is very short.

FRESH VEGETABLES

The following are some Chinese vegetables which appear in recipes in this book. Some are imported, others locally grown.

Angled luffa: a dark green gourd with ridges, about 5 to 8 cm (2 to 3 in) in diameter in the fattest part, and about 30 to 45 cm (12 to 18 in) long. Its Chinese name is *sigua*, 'fibrous gourd', but the pale green meat of the young luffa is very tender and sweet, even the seeds are tender and edible. To cook, shave off the ridges with a peeler and then peel off the rest of the leathery skin as you would with a cucumber. If the gourd is young and tender with the ridges close together and the gourd slender, leave the skin on (after peeling off the ridges) so that it looks stripy. A really delicious and versatile vegetable, it may be stir-fried or cooked in a soup.

Aubergines: these are familiar vegetables in the West. The dark-skinned ones are normally peeled before cooking. The Chinese variety is long and slender, full of fine seeds but tender and sweet. And there is no need to sprinkle salt on them to remove the juice before cooking, as with the aubergines imported from elsewhere. A versatile vegetable, it is cooked in numerous ways. To choose, pick waxy, unblemished ones with the cup-shaped leaf at the stem end still intact and fresh.

Bocai (Spinacia oleracea): is a spinach but sweeter and more tender than the English variety. It may be blanched or stir-fried.

Bokchoi (Chinese cole): looks rather like Swiss chard, except that the white stem is rounded and crisp instead of flat and limp. The white stalks are succulent and the leaves are tender, their taste quite delicious. It is one of the most popular vegetables with the Chinese. In Mandarin it is called *qingcai*, *bokchoi* is Cantonese.

Chinese celery cabbage: this vegetable is familiar in British supermarkets, where it is known as 'Chinese leaves'. In China, its native land, it is variously known as 'Shandong cabbage', 'Tianjin cabbage' and 'Beijing cabbage' and by other names. This vegetable keeps well for a couple of weeks in the refrigerator. Its taste improves if allowed to go limp, after hanging in a cool, dry place, when excess moisture has escaped. It may be eaten raw or cooked.

Chinese chives: both a herb and a vegetable in the Chinese kitchen. They are dark green in colour with strong, flat blades, the flowers are white with a hint of pale purple. They taste sweet and have a strong fragrance and a chewy texture. Quick cooking, they take about 1 minute to stir-fry on a high heat. To prepare, discard any soiled leaves, and break off any soiled ends. Rinse very well, and use both the white and green parts. They may be used as a herb or stir-fried plain, or with bean sprouts as a vegetable; or to complement meat or seafood. Chive buds are also available here. Each succulent green stem has a conical, pale, green-white bud at the tip. They are eaten in the same way as the chives. The tougher ends are broken off before chopping.

Chinese radish (mouli): this large white cylindrical radish has been a common vegetable in England for some time. It has a thin, shiny skin and white, firm juicy flesh. It tastes and smells rather like the little round red salad radish. It may be eaten raw as a salad vegetable, stir-fried, boiled in soup, or pickled. One variety is not edible raw but has a much better taste when cooked; but it is not available in Britain. The delicious leaves from a tender, non-hairy variety (not easily available here), are also eaten as a green vegetable, but not raw.

Chrysanthemum leaves: known as *tongkaucai* in Chinese, they resemble lettuce leaves with rounded lobes. They are pale, powdery green in colour, and have a hint of resinous taste and a herbal flavour. They are mainly eaten raw with cooked meat on festive occasions, or used as a vegetable for the fire pot. On contact with heat they shrink to almost nothing, so they are never cooked. Highly perishable, they should be eaten on the day of purchase.

Fuzzy melon: a small, cylindrical, bright yellow-green mottled melon, covered with soft, fine hair. The flesh is pale green in colour, fine, firm and juicy. After peeling, it is often boiled in soup; or cut into rings, stuffed with meat or fish, and braised.

Papaya: a round, oval or pear-shaped sub-tropical and tropical fruit, often eaten as a vegetable. The under-ripe fruit is cooked in soups or pickled. The hard green fruit turns orange and softens as it ripens. It is best when still firm to the touch when the flesh is thick, smooth, sweet and delicious.

Peashoots: are the tender leaves with tendrils, about 10 to 13 cm (4 to 5 in) long, from garden pea plants or mangetout plants. They are used more like a herb or a garnish when they are put into a hot meat dish or boiling soup. They are tender and fragrant.

Sprouts: germinated from mung beans, they are eaten as a fresh vegetable, either stir-fried or blanched. The Chinese do not eat them raw. They cook very quickly, about 2 minutes stir-fried on a high heat. They have become an increasingly common vegetable in British supermarkets and grocers. Another, less common one, is sprouted from soya beans. These need at least 20 minutes cooking and are never eaten raw.

Sweet potatoes: in the not very remote past this vegetable was the staple food of many rural people in south China. A native of America, this versatile root may be eaten instead of rice or cooked with rice to supplement it, as in 'potato porridge' which is quite pleasant to eat. Sweet potatoes may also be boiled in a savoury soup or as a sweet snack, roasted whole or made into pastries and cakes. There are hundreds of local varieties grown in the world, with white, red or golden flesh. The best varieites are sweet and delicious with a fluffy meat when cooked. It seems that only the red varieties are found here; often they are tasteless and waterlogged. Choose one that is not too heavy for its size, and without blemish.

Taro: known as *wutau* in the Cantonese dialect. A brown, hairy, oval tuber with encircling rings. There are two varieties on sale in Britain. The large 'areca-nut' taro of about 10 to 12 cm (4 to 5 in) in diameter has a stronger fragrance and taste than the smaller, cheaper, egg-sized type. The 'areca-nut' taro has a pale, mottled, purple-coloured flesh similar to that of an areca nut. The smaller kind is white. When peeled, the flesh is slimy, which produces rashes and itching on the hands, due to the presence of oxalate crystals. These may be soothed by rinsing the hands in water mixed with vinegar. For this reason taro is always thoroughly cooked, which takes about 10 to 15 minutes. It may be deep-fried until crisp and eaten as a snack, or braised or steamed with red-cooked pork; or made into taro pastries and cakes.

Water chestnuts: these are the bulbs of an aquatic plant grown in the marshes of south China. The size of walnuts, they are brown, hairy and tough-skinned. Their name in Cantonese, *matai*, means 'horse's hooves', which they resemble in shape. The creamy-white meat is firm, crunchy and slightly sweet. They must be peeled and washed thoroughly before use. In fact, most Chinese would not eat them raw for fear of waterborne parasites. The cleaned flesh is used a great deal in cooking, especially in stuffing. Canned ones retain the texture but not the taste. However, they are more economical, as fresh ones are rather expensive and they deteriorate at an amazing speed, caused by fermentation. If bought really fresh, i.e. when the skin is not shrivelled, they may be peeled and cleaned on the spot and frozen. One reasonable alternative is a brand canned in light syrup, from South-East Asia.

Water spinach (kongsincai):   this is one of the aquatic vegetables grown in southern China. It is related to the morning glory flower, and does not taste like spinach at all. The long, empty stem carries leaves of an arrowhead shape. When cooked they become slightly slimy, rather like the tender shoots of sweet potatoes which belong to the same family. The

Chinese never eat this vegetable raw for fear of waterborne parasites, and it tastes better cooked.

SOME CANNED FOODS

There are a few canned vegetables and fruits which it is useful to keep in the larder.

Vegetables: bamboo shoots, straw mushrooms, oyster mushrooms, mini sweet corn, salted mustard plants and bitter gourd. All these stand up well to canning. They are in clear water and will keep for about a year.

Fruits: longan, litchi and loquat (*pipa*) are canned in light syrup. They are suitable for use in some recipes as a garnish.

For fuller discussion on Chinese ingredients please see *The Chinese Kitchen* by the same author (Weidenfeld & Nicolson, 1986).

Preparation of some Chinese Ingredients

Agar agar: as a gelling agent, rinse and soak in cold water for about 30 minutes till swollen. Then simmer in the amount of liquid specified in the recipe till completely dissolved, stirring continuously to prevent sticking. Strain through a fine sieve and proceed as directed in the recipe. As a salad ingredient, cut into lengths as specified, rinse in warm water and soak in cold water till well swollen. Drain and use as directed.

Chilli oil: Put 30 g (1 oz) chilli powder in a china or enamel container. Heat 140 ml (5 fl oz) of groundnut oil (or any good quality vegetable oil) till bubbles appear, add a slice of bruised ginger and 1 stalk spring onion and cook till the onion is brown. Discard both onion and ginger. Take the oil off the heat and let it cool slightly so that the chilli powder does not get burnt and lose its flavour. Pour the slightly cooled oil on to the chilli powder and stir to mix well. When the oil becomes clear it is ready. Cool completely and bottle. The proportion of oil to chilli is 5 to 1. Keeps for about a year in a cool, dry place.

Cuttlefish or squid: soak dried cuttlefish (or squid) in cold water for 1 to 2 hours. Remove the membranes, rinse and use as directed in the recipe. If the cuttlefish is to be finely shredded and stir-fried there is no need to soak for more than 30 minutes. But sometimes a recipe calls for a well-soaked, tender cuttlefish, in which case 1 tsp of lye water (*see page* 223) is added. Soak for several hours or overnight, till well swollen and spongy to the touch. Over-soaking would dissipate the taste. If not required immediately, cover in cold water and store in the refrigerator. Both cuttlefish and squid increase four-fold in volume after soaking. Score the underside (bone side) diagonally with the knife at a slant of about 45°, and then turn it round and score the other way, forming a criss-cross pattern. Cut in half lengthwise and slice into bite-size pieces. (*See illustrations.*) To shred, cut crosswise into 2.5 cm (1 in) slices and then shred lengthwise finely. When cooked, the pieces curl up into rings. For fresh cuttlefish and squid, use the same slicing technique.

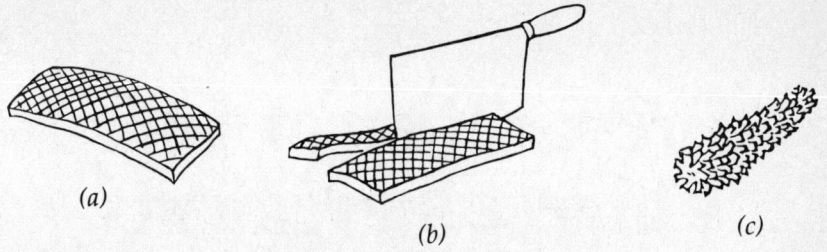

(a)

(b)

(c)

To bone a duck whole: for this choose a meaty bird, a thin one is more liable to break in places where the skin is close to the bones at the back. If frozen, it should be thoroughly defrosted. Begin by removing the neck if still attached. Slit the skin along the back of the neck, then chop the neck bone close to the body and remove. Turn the remaining skin back to as far as it will go – do not force it – and free the meat from the bone with tiny snips, keeping the points of the scissors close to the bones all the time. Snip through the joint where the upper wing meets the body and continue snipping to free the bone, leaving the wing tip unboned. When one upper wing is removed, do the same with the other. Continue to fold back the skin and snip to free the meat from the bones all round. Cut the meat from each upper thigh (oyster) and snip the joint to detach the bone from the drumstick (lower thigh), which is left unboned to avoid it shrinking and losing shape on cooking. Continue to roll back the meat and snip away from the rest of the carcass, keeping close to the bone all the time, and taking care that the points of the scissors are pointing towards the carcass so as not to pierce the skin, particularly along the back where there is hardly any flesh between skin and bone. Snip through the joint where the tail bone joins the backbone of the bird, leaving the tail intact. Rinse the bird inside out and pat dry with kitchen paper. Turn it right side out again, rinse and pat dry. The duck is now ready to be stuffed as directed in the recipe. (*See illustrations.*) Keep the carcass, bones and giblets for stock. Render the fat for cooking leafy vegetables. Through leaving the tail, lower thighs and wing tips intact, the bird when cooked looks deceptively unboned. The whole process takes about 30 minutes for a beginner. Other birds – chicken, pigeon and quails – can be boned in the same way. With quails, after boning the upper wings the meat may be gently pulled back most of the way.

Eggs (fermented): The type covered in clay does not need cooking. Break the clay, remove the shell, rinse, slice and serve. The non-clay type

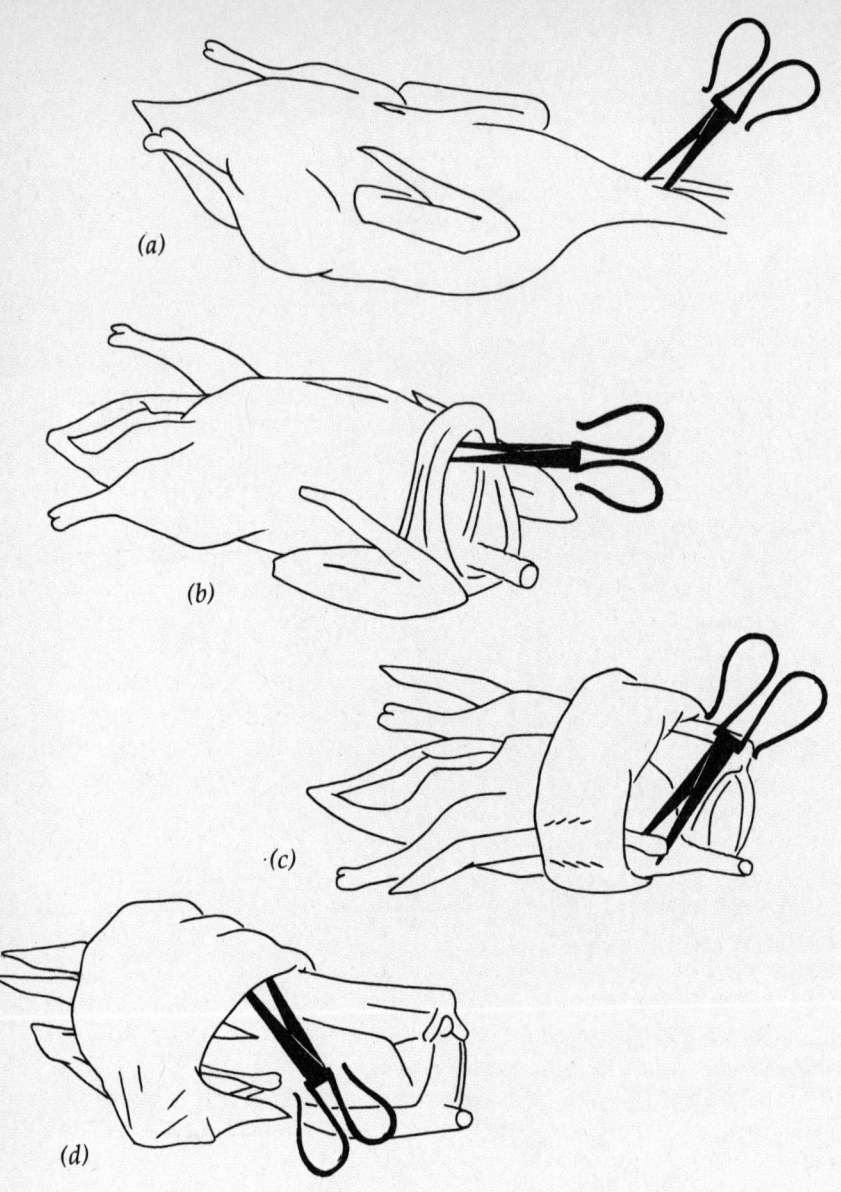

(a)

(b)

(c)

(d)

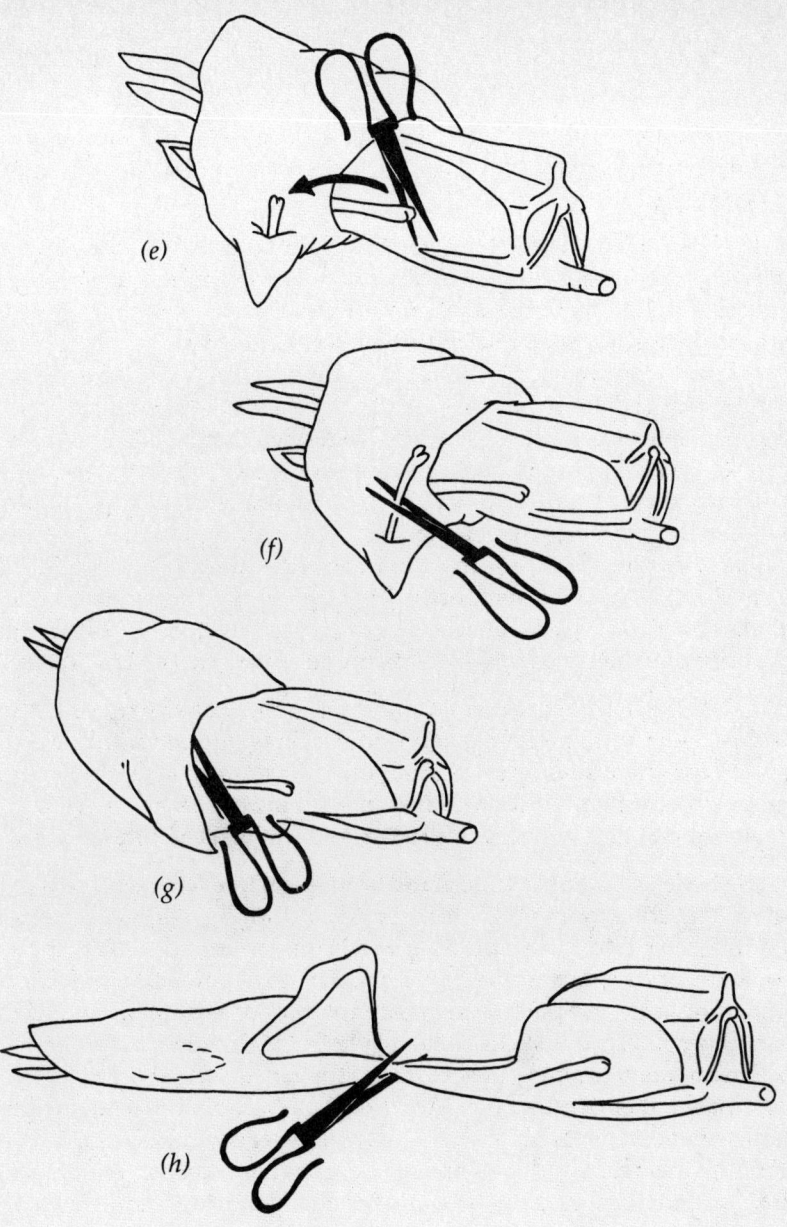

(e)

(f)

(g)

(h)

should be boiled in water for about 10 minutes, or 5 minutes if a softer yolk is preferred.

Eggs (salted):   to cook the ready-bought type covered with sooty earth, gently remove the earth, rinse and boil for 10 minutes or till thoroughly cooked. The non-sooty type is boiled for the same time. To salt your own eggs, *see page 84.*

Fermented glutinous rice: cook 450 g (1 lb) of glutinous rice as you would ordinary rice. Let it cool completely. Pound a ball of Chinese wine yeast (called 'yeast cake' or 'wine cake') to powder. Sprinkle cooled, boiled water on the cold rice and mix in the powdered wine yeast. Put the rice and yeast mixture into a carefully washed, large-mouthed jar big enough to hold the rice and a third over; it should have a plastic or cork stopper, not a metal one. Leave it in a warm place, about 25°C (80°F). If the temperature is too hot the alcoholic content will be too high, if too cool the rice will turn sour. After two days the fermentation is visible, with little bubbles moving between the rice grains. After a couple more days of fermentation in the warmth it may be removed to a dark, cool and dry place to store. It keeps for months. The storage life depends on the cleanliness of the jar, which must be free of grease or salt. As little as 130 g (8 oz) of rice may be used, in which case reduce the yeast to half a ball.

Fish balls: make fish paste (*see below*), and shape into balls by squeezing a handful of paste in the left hand so that it comes out between the left thumb and the left index finger. Pick out the ball with a spoon. Drop them into fast-boiling water and cook till they float to the top of the water. Pick them out with a brass wire mesh strainer and put in a colander.

Fish paste: use 450 g (1 lb) skinless and boneless white fish meat, 10 g (⅓ oz) salt, 1 egg white (optional), 1 tbsp ginger and spring onion juice, 2 tsp melted lard or oil, and 1 tbsp cornflour with a little water. Make sure there are no bones or dark bits in the fish meat. Rinse off any flecks of blood. Cut into thin slices, and pound them with the back of a chopper until well broken. Chop finely; if it sticks to the blade, sprinkle some water on the knife. Discard any stringy bits as they appear. When it is a sticky, cohesive paste, transfer to a bowl. Add the egg white (lightly beaten) and mix with a wooden spoon in one direction till the egg white is completely absorbed by the fish. Gradually mix in the ginger and spring onion juice mixture, and increasing the speed and vigour of stirring. Add the salt, continuing to mix in the same direction, till the paste is thick. At this stage add the melted lard, and when it is absorbed add the cornflour mixture. The important point to watch is that the fish paste should absorb the egg white, ginger and onion juice and salt before the addition of the lard and the cornflour mixture. Keep on mixing till well blended. To test if it is ready, drop a pea-size piece into some cold water; if it floats it is ready for use as directed in the recipe, or to be made into fish balls. The mincing and mixing may be done in a food processor; add the ingredients in the same order. The time taken is much shorter. When the paste gathers into a ball, test in the water. If not required immediately, keep the fish paste sealed in cling film in the refrigerator. Otherwise cook immediately, or the resilient texture will be soon lost in the warmth.

This fish paste is the basic ingredient for fish balls, fish cakes and stuffing. It is sometimes combined with meat, crab meat or prawns. Success depends a great deal on the freshness of the fish, which must still retain its resilient texture. The meat of oily or fatty fish does not have a resilient texture and is therefore not suitable. Suitable white fish are cod, haddock, whiting and shark. Too much salt will lower the resilience in the texture, but the fish paste will not bind if under-salted. A proportion of about 2 to 3% of salt, by weight, to the total amount of fish is correct. During mixing, it should be kept as cool as possible, or the texture and cohesiveness will be affected. It helps to chill or freeze the fish before mixing.

Five-spice salt: set a thick frying pan or wok on a medium heat, and dry-fry (without oil) 2 tbsp salt until it crackles. Add 1 tsp five-spice powder. Turn off the heat and stir-fry till fragrant. Cool and keep in an airtight bottle. It is best to make only a small amount, as the spices lose their strength.

Garlic: crush whole garlic with the back of a chopper, and slip the skin off before slicing, mincing or shredding.

Ginger: always peel it, then slice thinly, or shred into fine threads, or bruise and mince finely; or leave it whole and bruise it for the stockpot and other slow-cooked dishes. A slice in recipes is about 2.5 cm (1 in) square and 2 mm (1/10 in) thick.

Ginger juice or spring onion juice: pound or mince ginger or spring onion, add the equal amount of water, and squeeze. Discard the ginger or spring onion.

Ginger wine or spring onion wine: as above, but use wine instead.

Ginger, young, to pickle: use 230 g (8 oz) creamy, thin-skinned, tender young ginger. Scrape, rinse and slice thinly. Rub it with 1 tbsp salt, and let stand for 15 minutes. Place in a piece of muslin and squeeze dry. Stone 2 pickled plums (optional) and add to the ginger. Boil together 280 ml (1/2 pt) white wine vinegar with 170 g (6 oz) sugar and 1 tsp salt. Leave to cool completely, and pour over the ginger and plums. The pickle will be ready in 3 hours. It keeps for months in an airtight container in a cool, dry place.

Guoba (dried cooked rice): the term literally means cooked rice that has stuck to the bottom of the pot. It is dried, then deep-fried and served as an accompaniment to hot soup or fish or meat dishes with a sauce. One way of making this is to leave a circle of rice about 2 cm (¾ in) thick at the bottom of the rice pot when dishing up cooked rice. Add a little water to moisten, and press it down with a potato masher. Put the pot back on a low heat and cook till the rice circle is hardened into one piece and a pale golden underneath. Take out. If not completely dry, put it in a hot oven, turn off the heat and leave to dry further.

Hairweed (facai): pour boiling water over to cover and leave for about 10 minutes. Drain, discard any dry leaves or grass, and rinse in several changes of water till there is no trace of earth or sand. Simmer it in water to cover with 1 slice bruised ginger and 1 tbsp rice wine for about 20 minutes. Drain, discard the ginger, cool and squeeze out excess water. Mix in 1 tbsp of oil and squeeze again.

Hongqu (dried fermented red rice) water: tie 1 tbsp *hongqu* in a piece of muslin and boil in 20 ml (7 fl oz) of water. For a smaller quantity, soak 1 or 2 tsp in a little hot water, mash well and strain.

Jellyfish (salted): rinse in several changes of cold water. Halve or quarter and pile neatly, roll up tightly and shred finely. Pour hot water (not boiling) on to the shredded jellyfish for 30 seconds. Rinse thoroughly in cold water, squeezing out the water each time. Soak in fresh cold water for at least 30 minutes or overnight, till required. On contact with hot water they shrink dramatically, but revive after re-soaking in cold water. If not prepared in this way the jellyfish will be very salty and rubbery.

Lotus seeds: blanched lotus seeds imported recently are rather tough, owing to a change in the blanching process in China. For this reason they have to be soaked for several hours or overnight, and the water changed to remove the lye water which hardens the nuts. Unblanched lotus seeds should be boiled in water to which lye water (*see page* 223) has been added, 1 tsp to 550 ml (1 pt). Simmer on a low heat or till the skin can be rubbed off easily. Rinse well in cold water. Push a cocktail stick through the seed from one end to remove the bitter green heart.

Lotus seed paste: boil pre-soaked, blanched lotus seeds till they break up. Drain and sieve. Stir-fry the paste in a little oil in the wok till it is dry. Add sugar to taste, stirring well till it dissolves. Cook on a low heat for about 30 minutes, stirring all the time. Take out, cook and use as required. For filling moon cakes, the paste should be firm so that it does not make the pastry soggy; use lard rather than vegetable oil. In the West, where lotus seeds are difficult to come by, ready-prepared lotus seed paste is available, which is cheaper than making it yourself, and quite good. The paste freezes well.

Mung bean paste: use 450 g (1 lb) mung beans, 340 g (12 oz) sugar, and 110 ml (4 fl oz) groundnut or other vegetable oil, or lard. This is cooked in the same way as red bean paste (*see below*) except where ready-husked, split mung beans are used, when the washing and pressing stages are eliminated. Simmer the split mung beans in water to cover till they disintegrate and almost dry up, about 15 minutes, stirring regularly, as without the husks they stick and burn easily. Mash well and stir-fry in the oil and sugar in the same way as for red bean paste. This amount makes about 1.4 kg (3 lb) paste. It may be frozen.

Mung bean vermicelli: use a pair of sharp kitchen scissors to cut it into 15 cm (6 in) lengths. Cook in boiling water for about 5 minutes or till softened. Drain and rinse in cold water. Soak in cold water till required, but only for a few minutes otherwise they will swell a great deal. Drain and use as directed in the recipe. For deep-fried vermicelli, put the dry vermicelli (without rinsing) straight into hot oil for 30 seconds, take out with a brass wire mesh strainer and drain well.

Mustard, prepared: this is a dip for meat, dumplings and seafood at the table. The flavour is better if made in a larger quantity in advance and kept in an airtight jar. Gradually mix a little cooled, boiled water with 4 tbsp mustard powder to make a thin paste. Cover and leave to stand for at least 30 minutes for the flavour to develop. Stir in ½ tsp salt and 1 tsp vinegar, both of which if added earlier would inhibit the development of the flavour.

Persimmons (dried):   cover with boiling water, and leave to soak for about 10 to 15 minutes. Remove the seeds, and slice or dice before cooking.

Pickles: cucumber, radish, carrot, Chinese white radish (mouli), sweet red pepper, hot red pepper, white salad cabbage and underripe papaya are among the usual ingredients. Peel or deseed the vegetables as appropriate. Cut them into julienne strips, wedges or slices. Then rub them with some salt (about 1 tbsp to 450 g, 1 lb vegetables) and marinate for about 20 minutes. When the water begins to run out, rinse under the cold tap to remove excess salt and gently squeeze dry. Cover with a mixture of white wine vinegar, sugar and salt to taste for at least 6 hours or overnight. In an airtight jar and refrigerated, it will keep for at least a week.

Pig's intestines: if frozen, defrost thoroughly. Trim off all the fat and rinse well. Turn them inside out; they will be slightly slimy. Rub them with a handful of fine salt. Rinse thoroughly in cold water. Repeat till they are not slimy, about 5 to 6 times. Bring them to the boil in water with a slice of ginger and a stalk of spring onion and simmer till just cooked or tender, about 30 minutes. Drain and use as required. If used for sausage casing do not boil after cleaning.

Pig's tripe: if frozen, defrost thoroughly. Trim off any fat. Turn it inside out; it is slightly sticky. Rub it with a handful of fine salt. Rinse thoroughly in cold water. Repeat till it is no longer sticky. Boil in plenty of water for about 5 minutes on a high heat, and drain. Scrape off the white skin at the thick end. Rinse well. Cook as instructed in the recipe.

Pig's trotters: do not wash. Burn off the hair over a naked flame (candle or gas stove). Scrub under the cold tap. The skin may be slightly blackened, but no matter. Boil in plenty of water to cover with 1 tbsp salt for about 10 to 15 minutes on a high heat. Drain, and scrub under the hot tap or in a bowl of hot water. Rinse thoroughly in cold water. They are now ready for further cooking. This process of boiling and scrubbing removes the odour.

Plum sauce: You will need 850 ml–1.1 l (1½–2 pt) cooked plum purée, 280–400 ml (½–¾ pt) malt vinegar, 900 g–1.1 kg (2–2½ lb) demerara sugar, 2 tsp chilli powder (or to taste), 4 cloves garlic (minced), 1 tsp ground ginger or 2 tsp ginger juice. Measure all the ingredients except the sugar into a stainless steel or enamelled pot, mix well and simmer till completely blended and slightly reduced, about 30 to 40 minutes. Add the sugar, and stir till dissolved. Simmer for another 20 to 30 minutes. Cool completely and bottle in cooled, sterilized, wide-mouthed bottles or jars. To sterilize bottles in an oven: wash the bottles and leave upside down to dry up any moisture completely – do not wipe. Put them in a tray, spaced out well to avoid cracking. Place the tray in a cold oven and set it at 110°C (225°F, gas 4). Heat for about 25 to 30 minutes. This plum sauce will keep almost indefinitely if stored in a cool, dry place.

Prawn crackers: before deep-frying, lay them out on a baking tray and leave them in a warm place, such as a cool oven, to warm through and dry. This helps them to expand better when put into hot oil. Deep-fry in hot oil, but not too hot or they will colour, which would affect the taste. Drop a few at a time into the oil, move them around with a pair of long chopsticks, and when they expand and puff up, pick them out with a brass wire mesh strainer. Drain well on kitchen paper. Stored in an airtight container, they will keep for weeks.

Red bean paste: for about 1.5 kg (3 lb) paste, use 450 g (1 lb) red aduki beans, 340–450 g (12 oz–1 lb) granulated sugar, 110 g (4 oz) rose sugar or 1 tbsp rose water (both optional), 140 ml (5 fl oz) peanut oil and 1 tsp lye water (optional). Pick over the beans and discard any bad, shrivelled ones or grit. Rinse thoroughly, and bring to the boil in plenty of water. Simmer till the beans disintegrate, about 45 minutes to 1 hour. Put them in a fine sieve and wash in clean cold water in a large bowl, rubbing the beans to release the husks. Discard the husks. Let the water in the bowl settle and pour away the clear water. Line a fine sieve with a square of muslin, and ladle some purée into it. Pick up the four corners of the muslin and gather the edges together in your left hand. With the other hand, gently squeeze out the excess water. The resultant paste has a consistency rather like that of curd cheese. Continue in the same way with the rest of the cooked beans. You should have rather more than 1 kg (2½ lb) of firm purée. Set the wok on a medium heat till hot, and put in the oil, paste and sugar. Reduce the heat to low, and stir-fry for about 20 minutes. Add the rose sugar, if used, and continue stir-frying for about 20 minutes. Stir in the lye water (if used) and mix well. This gives the paste a dark, rich sheen. To test, take out a teaspoonful and leave to cool before shaping it into a ball between your fingers. If it does not stick, it is ready. The proportion of beans to sugar should not be more than 1:1¼, or the paste will be 'sandy' and crumbly. It should be spreadable or malleable, depending on its use. For a stuffing it should be cooked to a slightly firmer consistency. Commercially tinned paste is watery and sickly-sweet, and bears no resemblance to the real thing. This paste freezes well.

Red dates: rinse, and cover with boiling water for about 10 minutes or till well swollen. Cut open and discard the stones. Use as required.

Rice, to boil: put the amount of rice required in a thick-based metal pot or a Chinese *saguo* (not an enamelled pot, which will crack) with a tight-fitting lid. Rinse the rice well to remove any loose starch. Drain well. Fill it with fresh cold water. Level the rice off with your hand. Measure the level of water with your middle finger; the water should come up to about 2.5 cm (1 in) above the level of the rice. Old rice (about 2 years and over) needs slightly more water, and new rice or sticky varieties slightly less. This can only be found out by cooking the rice once, unless you are certain. Place the pot on a high heat, and when it comes to the boil immediately reduce the heat to low. If the cover lifts and rattles, put a weight on it to keep the steam in. Leave it for about 10 to 12 minutes. The timing and the heat depend very much on your stove, your pot and the rice. With gas ring it is important not to let it go out if there is a strong draught; a simmering pad may be useful here. Glutinous rice is cooked in the same way, but as it is sticky and tender, only half the amount of water is needed.

Rose petal sugar: mix white granulated sugar with some dried rose petals. The petals may be used together with the sugar. Dried rose petals are available from apothecaries specializing in herbs and spices.

Scallops (dried): rinse, and soak, in just enough cold water to cover, for about 1 hour or till softened. Add a little rice wine, and steam with the soaking liquor till tender, about 30 minutes. Set aside in the liquor till required. Before cooking, use your fingers to break the scallops into fine shreds in the juice. Use the steaming juice and the scallops together in the cooking.

Sea cucumbers (dried): cover with boiling water and leave to soak overnight. Change the water, and slit the softened ones on the underside with a pair of sharp kitchen scissors. Remove the sand and innards. (Simmer hard ones for a few minutes, and leave soaking in the hot water till they are soft enough to be opened.) Scrape the inside till spotlessly clean or they will not expand well. Soak them in cold water; the longer they are soaked, the larger they become. When they are all softened and clean, and if a softer texture is preferred, simmer them all together to soften further. Let them stand in the hot water till it cools. Drain, cover in fresh water and refrigerate till required, but change the water daily. They keep well for about a week. Just before use, boil them with a slice of ginger and a stalk of spring onion for about 20 minutes. Drain and use as required. Usually they are soaked several days in advance.

Shrimps (dried): discard any loose shells and grit. Cover in hot water and leave for about 2 minutes. Drain, and remove any shell still on the shrimps. Rinse in cold water. Cover in some hot water and leave to soak for about 5 minutes. Drain, and reserve the soaking liquor. Pound, mince or leave the shrimps whole as required in the recipe. Always add the reserved soaking liquor to the same dish as the shrimps.

Sichuan chilli paste: You will need 10–15 dried chilli peppers, 280 ml (10 fl oz) salted soya bean paste, 4 cloves garlic and 170 g (6 fl oz) groundnut or vegetable oil. Rinse the chilli peppers in hot water and soak in cold water to cover till softened. Drain and reserve the soaking liquor. Chop the chillies into 1 cm (½ in) rounds. Set the wok on a low heat, and put in the oil. When it is hot, stir-fry the garlic and chillies for about 2 minutes. Stir in the bean paste and soaking liquor. Bring to the boil and cook uncovered, stirring occasionally, till the liquid has evaporated. Cool completely before storing in an airtight jar in a cool, dry place. This keeps well for a couple of months and indefinitely in the refrigerator. A less hot and simpler version is made by mixing salted soya bean paste with chilli powder to taste.

Sichuan pepper salt: dry-fry (without oil) 6 tbsp salt together with 4 tbsp Sichuan peppercorns till fragrant. Remove from the heat, cool and grind into powder. Keep in an airtight bottle.

Sichuan pepper water: bring to the boil 30 g (1 oz) of Sichuan peppercorns in 550 ml (1 pt) of water, and add 30 g (1 oz) of peeled and bruised ginger. Reduce to half by boiling. Strain off the spices. Cool and keep in a bottle. For a smaller amount, soak some crushed Sichuan peppercorns in hot water for 10 minutes. Strain and use as required.

Sichuan pepper wine: soak some crushed Sichuan peppercorns in some wine, strain and use as required.

Silver wood ears (dried):   cover in cold water till well swollen. Snip off any yellow-stained or woody bits with a sharp pair of kitchen scissors. Rinse well, cover in cold water and bring to the boil on a high heat. Turn off the heat and let stand, covered, for about 1 hour. (If time is short, the second soaking may be left out.) Drain and use as required, or soak in cold water till needed. (*See also* 'Wood ears', *below*.)

Spinach juice: to make a green colouring, mince some spinach leaves and squeeze out the juice; there is no need to add water. Make only as much as you need; it does not keep.

Spring onions:
   Shredded: cut into 5 cm (2 in) lengths, and slice lengthwise into strands. Use as a garnish and in steamed dishes.
   Sliced: cut into 4 cm (1½ in) lengths; for stir-fried dishes.
   Diagonally cut: cut diagonally into 4 cm (1½ in) lengths; for stir-fried dishes.
   Chopped: cut into 0.5 cm (¼ in) rounds; for seasoning cooking oil, as in stir-frying, or as a garnish in soup and other dishes.
   Whole: discard any soiled leaves, cut off the roots and trim the ends.
   Knotted: bruise lightly and tie in a knot; for easy removal in slow-cooked dishes.
   Brushes: cut spring onion whites into 8 cm (3 in) lengths, and make slashes in both ends with a sharp paring knife. Place in a bowl of cold water in the refrigerator so that both ends open out like a brush. These are decorative as a garnish and useful as a brush for dipping in sauces and brushing the pancakes, as in the eating of *chunbing* and *bobing*, the spring pancakes.

Squid (dried):   see Cuttlefish.

Stocks:

Ordinary stock: bring the following to the boil in 2.8 l (5 pt) water: 1 chicken carcass (with the breast and leg meat removed), giblets and neck; 450 g (1 lb) of pork bones or pork spare ribs, chopped up, 1 slice peeled and bruised ginger, 2 stalks spring onion and 1 tsp salt. Skim well, reduce the heat, and simmer, with the lid slightly ajar for a clear stock, for about 1 hour. Strain.

Strong clear chicken stock: bring to the boil one 1.4 kg (3 lb) chicken in 2.8 l (5 pt) water with a slice of peeled and bruised ginger, 2 stalks spring onion and 1 tsp salt. Skim and simmer over a low heat for 1 hour, with the lid slightly ajar, so that the stock is crystal clear.

Vegetable (or vegetarian) stock: put some sliced bamboo shoots, some winter mushrooms or stalks and soya bean sprouts in a pot. Cover with twice the volume of water. Bring to the boil on a high heat, reduce to low, cover and simmer for 30 minutes or more; the longer it is simmered the better.

Sweet and sour sauce: for a large quantity, use 550 ml (1 pt) white wine vinegar, 230 g (8 oz) granulated sugar, 1 tsp salt, 2 tbsp Worcester sauce and 1 tbsp tomato sauce (*see below*). Dissolve the sugar in the vinegar. Simmer all the ingredients together for a few minutes. Cool and bottle. Keeps well.

Sweet salted soya bean paste: grind 450 g (1 lb) of salted soya beans (commercially ground paste is too salty) and mix with 450 g (1 lb) sugar. Stir well and steam for about 2 hours. Take out, and stir in 80 ml (3 fl oz) of sesame oil. This keeps well in an airtight bottle in a cool dry place. Use a clean, dry spoon to take out every time.

Tomato sauce (hot and spicy):   use 900 g (2 lb) ripe red tomatoes, 1 tbsp salt, 2 cloves minced garlic, 1 small chopped onion, 1–2 finely chopped hot chilli peppers or 2 tsp chilli powder, and 2 tbsp cooking oil. Rinse and chop the tomatoes. Boil in a pot on a medium heat till reduced to a purée, stirring continuously to prevent sticking. Sieve and set aside. Set the wok on a medium heat, and when hot put in the oil. Fry the onion and garlic till pale gold. Pour in the tomato purée. Add the salt. Continue to cook, stirring, while more moisture evaporates. When it reaches the consistency of a thick sauce, take off the heat and bottle in sterilized jars. (For sterilizing jars *see page* 236.)

Walnuts, to skin: pour boiling water over to cover and leave to stand for about 10 minutes. Skin with a cocktail stick, starting from the flat side.

Wheat gluten: to obtain about 170 g (6 oz) of wheat gluten, you will need

450–680 g (1–1½ lb) strong plain white flour with 1 tbsp of salt. Add enough cold water to mix into a soft dough and knead till very smooth. Continue kneading till the dough is elastic. Cover with a tea cloth, and leave to rest for at least 1 hour in a warm place. Put the rested dough in a fine sieve over a large bowl with some cold water and wash the dough, squeezing gently as you would a sponge. When the water is white with flour, pour it away (or save the wheat starch for dumplings). Wash the dough again in clear water. Continue till the water is clear, when all the starch is washed out. (If during the washing, the dough should separate, add some salt to the dough and knead till sticky, then continue washing.) What is left is raw gluten. Leave it to rest for 30 minutes before cooking. To cook, spread out in a sandwich cake tin, in a layer about 1 cm (½ in) thick, and steam on a high heat for about 1 hour. Cool, and cut into slices ready for cooking. If fried gluten is required, first steam, cool and slice, then deep-fry in hot oil till golden. A recipe may also call for the use of raw gluten. Raw gluten may be boiled, steamed or deep-fried. It may be made into small balls and boiled for about 5 minutes. They float to the top of the water when cooked. To deep-fry raw gluten balls, cook on a low heat till golden, then raise the heat briefly to colour before taking them out. Press down with the brass wire mesh strainer to submerge in the oil so that they cook through. When cooked, they puff up to three times their original size. Gluten tastes quite similar to a soya product, but is slightly sweet and has a tender, resilient texture. Oil-fried gluten tastes slightly like meat.

White peppercorns: dry-fry (without oil) on a low heat till fragrant and crackling. Cool and pulverize finely. Store in an airtight jar. Used for cooking and seasoning.

Winter mushrooms (dried): rinse in cold water and pour on just enough boiling water to cover. Weigh them down with a little saucer, and let stand for 5 minutes. Drain, and reserve the liquor. Cut off and discard the stalks, or put them in the stockpot. Strain the soaking liquor through a piece of muslin and cook with the mushrooms. Usually, the amount of water used for the soaking is very small, about 60–80 ml (2–3 fl oz) for several mushroom caps.

Wood ears (dried black): cover with water and let stand for 30 minutes. Drain, and rinse well. Pinch off any woody bits. Rub them with some salt. Repeat till there is no trace of sand or earth and no 'woody' odour. Soak in cold water till required. If you are in a hurry, use hot water and soak for only 5 minutes – but they will not swell so much.

Guide to Pinyin

Pinyin	Wade system
bao	pao
cai	ts'ai
chang	ch'ang
dan	tan
fang	fang
fen	fên
guo	kuo
hong	hung
ji	chi
jiu	chiu
kong	k'ung
lian	lien
long	lung
mian	mien
pai	p'ai
pei	p'ei
ping	p'ing
qi	chi
qian	chíen
qing	ch'ing
ran	jan
re	je
ruan	juan
se	sê
shi	shih
si	sǔ, szû, ssǔ
song	sung
ta	t'a
tang	t'ang

wén	wên
xi	hsi
xian	sian
xiao	hsiao
xue	hsueh, hsuo
yong	yung
you	yu
yuan	yuen
za	tsa
zai	tsai
zha	cha
zhong	chung
zong	tsung
zui	tsui

Index